The View from Chapultepec

The View from Chapultepec

MEXICAN WRITERS ON THE MEXICAN-AMERICAN WAR

TRANSLATED AND EDITED BY

Cecil Robinson

THE UNIVERSITY OF ARIZONA PRESS   TUCSON

The University of Arizona Press
Copyright © 1989
The Arizona Board of Regents
All Rights Reserved

This book was set in 10/13 Linotron 202 Ehrhardt.
♾ This book is printed on acid-free, archival-quality paper.
Manufactured in the United States of America.

93 92 91 90 89   5 4 3 2 1

Library of Congress Cataloging-in-Publication Data

The View from Chapultepec.

Translated from Spanish.
Bibliography: p.
Includes index.
1. United States—History—War with Mexico, 1845–1848
—Public opinion. 2. Public opinion—Mexico. 3. Authors,
Mexican—Attitudes. 4. Mexico—History—1821–1861.
I. Robinson, Cecil.
E415.2.P82V54 1989   973.6′21   88-36260
ISBN 0-8165-1083-0 (alk. paper)

British Library Cataloguing in Publication data are available.

For Madeleine

CONTENTS

PREFACE

The war between the United States and Mexico, fought in the mid-nineteenth century, was to Mexico a national trauma comparable to what the Civil War was to the United States. But there were significant differences. Whereas the Civil War resolved a festering problem, the Mexican-American War caused one, particularly for Mexico. And the wound to the Mexican psyche seems to have grown in the course of time. One of the surprising revelations gained, to an American reader at least, from reading Mexican authors writing at the time of the war was that large segments of the Mexican population viewed the war with indifference. It was only as Mexico gained a strong sense of national identity that the anguish caused by defeat and by loss of immense territories grew. Those Mexican authors who were contemporary to the war and who expressed their feelings on the subject were not, of course, among those who were indifferent to the conflict. But they represented an intellectual minority, and some of them, most notably Mariano Otero, wrestled with the problem of the lack of popular support for the war effort.

As time distanced the events of the war, writing about it in Mexico

became of necessity retrospective and colored by the particular concerns of succeeding Mexican generations. But as more nationalistic and
broadly based governments came into power and as education was more
widely disseminated, the war emerged, in the Mexican consciousness,
as a central event in Mexico's history and destiny.

In contrast, as Robert W. Johannsen has ably documented in *To the
Halls of the Montezumas* (1985), the Mexican-American War brought on
a tremendous outpouring of nationalistic fervor in the United States in
support of the war and of "manifest destiny"—during the period of the
war itself. In time, and especially because of the eclipsing experience of
the Civil War, the memory of the Mexican-American War receded in
the United States. The blotting out of this event from the popular mind
has now become so pervasive that the American man or woman in the
street would be hard put to give the approximate dates of the war or to
name the major events or personalities connected with it.

So we are faced with the situation of two contiguous nations that
have shared an experience which to one of them is still a burning issue
and for the other is almost forgotten. Such a state of consciousness
cannot be healthy for relations between the neighboring nations. This
volume presents the Mexican view of a conflict, the memory of which
still rankles, and in so doing attempts to help rekindle an awareness on
the part of North Americans of a historical past that impinges on the
present and affects basic attitudes with which Mexicans approach their
relations with the United States.

The selections from Mexican authors presented here have been
translated from the Spanish by myself. They range from pieces written
during the time of the war to writings by Mexican authors of our time.
The writers themselves are historians, journalists, statesmen, philosophers, literary people, or, as is so often the case in Latin America, a
combination of several of these.

ACKNOWLEDGMENTS

I should like to give thanks for valuable assistance and advice to Carlos Bosch García, Raquel Rubio Goldsmith, Lewis Hanke, Miguel León-Portilla, Michael Meyer, Elizabeth Shaw, and Josefina Zoraida Vázquez.

I should also like to express my appreciation to the American Philosophical Society for the grant which enabled me to do research in Mexico City.

INTRODUCTION

The Mexican-American War, fought between 1846 and 1848, occurred in the period of Mexican history known as the *criollo* era. The *criollos* were people born in Mexico but considered to be of pure Spanish blood. Before Mexico's war of independence against Spain, between 1810 and 1821, most positions of public office were held by native Spaniards, the hated *gachupines*, as these Spanish officials were pejoratively called. Upon the achievement of independence, Mexico promptly expelled all the *gachupines*, and into their places of office stepped the *criollos*. At the time of the war with the United States, almost all positions of high authority in government, army, and church were held by the *criollos* to the exclusion of the *mestizos* (people of mixed Spanish and Indian blood) and the Indians. Since Spain had autocratically governed Mexico for three hundred years and had insisted that all important governing officials be people brought over from Spain, most native Mexicans lacked the experience of exercising governmental authority on their own soil, although some had been members of the Spanish Cortes. The newness to self rule and the lack of experience in government among the *criollos* have been cited as factors in the outcome of the Mexican-American War. After the war of independence, Mexican governments replaced each other in bewildering succession. It was rare for a Mexican president to complete his alloted term of office. In most cases he was thrown out of office by a *cuartelazo,* a revolt which had its origins in the army officers' quarters. While chaos ruled in Mexico City, the vast reaches of territory in the northern regions of Mexico were greatly underpopulated and almost completely neglected. Large desert areas were in reality ruled by the Apaches. The situation was such that the northern areas, as noted by several Mexican writers, positively seemed to invite foreign intrusion.

Such was the state of affairs in Mexico leading up to the Mexican-American War. Apart from the larger political and continental considerations, the specific events contributing to the outbreak of war were the Texas Revolution in 1835–36 by which the American colonists in Texas won their independence from Mexico, and the annexation of Texas to the United States in 1845, a move that Mexico had declared to the United States would be considered an act of war. These local events were seized upon by the United States as justifications for pursuing large designs upon Mexican territory.

During the periods of the Texas Revolution and of the Mexican-American War, the dominant figure in Mexico was Antonio López de Santa Anna. This showy man was the personification as well as a caricature of the *criollo* era in Mexico. Not only because of his position of leadership—he was at times both president and supreme general of the Republic—but because of his personality in an era of *personalismo,* he set the tone of his times and must be reckoned with in any effort to understand the period.

Mexican writers from his own period to the present have studied him. The austere and highly intelligent historian and statesman, Lucas Alamán, avoided the usual hyperbole in describing the man he knew well: "a conjuncture of good and bad qualities; a natural and sprightly talent, without moral or literary cultivation; an enterprising spirit, but lacking in fixed purpose or determined objectives; energy and disposition for governing, obscured by great defects; clarity of perception in forming general plans for a revolution or a campaign, yet great ineptitude in the directing of a battle."[1] This spare description, characteristic

of its author, declined to go into detail about "great defects." A modern
North American writer has been more specific:[2]

Santa Anna was a typical *caudillo* of his times, come too far, too fast. . . . Again,
that vanity stimulated by a clinging, colonial sense of inferiority knew no
bounds. Santa Anna as president began to design incredible uniforms for
himself; he rode in gaudy coaches; he demanded near-regal honors and displayed complete irresponsibility. His private life became vulgar and corrupt. He
had once been a good soldier, and could still conduct an energetic campaign.
But with his fantastic uniforms, callous cruelty, crates of fighting cocks and
hordes of passing whores, and his incredible blindness to anything but the
superficial, he was a disastrous ruler.

One might well expect that Mexican writers, in view of the fact that
Santa Anna presided over the twin catastrophes of the Texas Revolution and the Mexican-American War, would also view him as having
been a disaster, but this is not universally so. The complexity of his
personality was to make of him a fascinating subject of study. Different
periods of history would, quite naturally, invest him with their own
concerns. The 1930s, for example, which comprised in Mexico a decade that was pronouncedly antimilitaristic, denounced Santa Anna as a
militarist.

The episodes in Santa Anna's career that have provoked the most
interest and denunciation in the United States have been his conduct at
the Alamo and at Goliad, both actions having taken place during the
Texas Revolution. Tradition has it that Santa Anna ordered the military
band accompanying the Mexican troops that had invested the Alamo to
play the chilling Degüello, literally the throat-cutting, to indicate that
no quarter was to be given to the American colonists defending the
Alamo. José C. Valadez, a modern Mexican historian, insists that there
is no proof that Santa Anna gave orders that the defenders were to be
slaughtered without mercy (*sin piedad*). This idea, Valadez maintains,
was promulgated by Mexican politicians who were enemies of Santa
Anna and by American patriots. In fact, he says, the defenders of the
Alamo chose to fight to the last man.[3]

At Goliad, more than three hundred Texans under the command of
Capt. James Fannin were surrounded by a superior Mexican force. The

Texans surrendered "at discretion" on March 27, 1836. When they had
given up their weapons, they were taken out and shot—at Santa Anna's
express orders. The commander of the Mexican force, General Urrea,
was appalled at these orders and sent a message to Santa Anna asking
for clarification. Santa Anna confirmed the orders. The massacre at
Goliad, more than anything else, blackened Santa Anna's international
reputation, but it has been a subject of dispute among Mexican historians. At issue was a decree promulgated by interim president Barragán
on December 30, 1835. This decree, no doubt with the recently rebelling Texans as a consideration, declared that foreigners caught on national soil with arms and hostile intent would be tried and punished as
pirates, that is, put to death. In his own account of the Texas Revolution
and the Mexican-American War, Santa Anna maintained that most of
the rebels in Texas were outsiders, and it is a fact that most of the
Texans in arms were newcomers to Texas, many of whom had not
obtained Mexican citizenship, in contrast to the earlier settlers who had
come to Texas with Stephen Austin and the other American *empresarios.*
As for the situation at Goliad, Santa Anna claimed that he had not
known at the time that a capitulation had been negotiated. In giving the
orders he did, he was acting so as not to place himself in violation of the
law. Had he been apprised of the capitulation, even though General
Urrea had no authority to grant it, he would have petitioned Congress,
in the name of humanity, to grant Fannin and his men immunity from
the law.[4]

Luis G. Zorilla, modern Mexican historian, defends Santa Anna, in
effect, by paraphrasing the general's own arguments. Citing the decree
of 1835 declaring that foreigners caught with arms would be considered
pirates, Zorilla asserts that most of the Texas armies consisted of
filibusterers brought recently from the States who were not, as were the
Texan colonists, Mexican citizens. He says that of the 183 men who
defended the Alamo only 32 were colonists and that almost all of
Fannin's men were American citizens from Georgia, Kentucky, and
Alabama. Thus, "the so called Texas war was in fact the first war that
Mexico sustained with the United States."[5]

Other Mexican historians of our times have not agreed with Zorilla.
Rafael F. Muñoz writes that no matter how one might make excuses by

citing the law declaring the "adventurers" to be pirates or by noting that Santa Anna had pardoned eighty-three prisoners captured in Copano, "El Alamo and Presidio [Goliad] have marked him with the sobriquet 'the villain'."[6] Back at his hacienda "Manga de Clavos," continues Muñoz, Santa Anna wrote his attempted justifications, "repeating his rationalizations to the point of boredom. . . . Nothing convinces. All the waters of the oceans will not wash off the stains which he brought with him from the swamps of Texas."[7] José Fuentes Mares compares Santa Anna's conduct at Goliad with that at the battle of San Jacinto. There Sam Houston's army surprised the Mexican army under Santa Anna while the general himself was taking a siesta. With the rude awakening, Santa Anna fled his tent and, by changing into common garb, tried to melt into the general mass of Mexican soldiers and avoid capture. "There [Goliad], as a little bit later at San Jacinto," writes Fuentes Mares, "Santa Anna proved the state of his soul. As a petty pirate, he ordered no quarter for the unfortunate prisoners, and, showing another but not unrelated face, he abandoned his uniform as General and President to cover his escape that day in which the Texans surprised him in his sleep. Blind to all values, physically resolute in the face of risks, he almost always, at the critical moment, lost his moral bearings. A hybrid-like specimen, he roared like a lion and fled like a gazelle. Such, in short, was the expression of his interior drama."[8]

Despite the argumentation, it would seem that Santa Anna's defects were plain enough, but so also were his remarkable talents. He clearly had a genius for organization. In spite of the depleted state of the Mexican treasury, he could raise a new army—after the loss of previous ones—with the speed of Cadmus sowing the dragon's teeth. In January 1847, after earlier defeats in the north of Mexico, Santa Anna saw his opportunity. General Zachary Taylor, after having been victorious at Palo Alto, Resaca de la Palma, and Monterrey, moved farther south. At this point, President Polk commanded him to withdraw his forces to the protected position of Monterrey. Meanwhile the great expedition under General Winfield Scott, which was to land at Veracruz and fight its way to Mexico City, was outfitted and sent to sea. Many of Scott's men had formerly been in Taylor's army, which was now depleted. Taylor had no taste for seeing the glory pass on to Winfield Scott; so he disobeyed orders. Instead of withdrawing his forces, he stayed, with his reduced army, in the highly exposed position of Saltillo in the northern state of Coahuila. Santa Anna quickly raised a numerically superior army and set out from San Luis Potosí. In bitterly cold weather in the open plateau region, he accomplished the remarkable forced march of forty-five miles in less than twenty-four hours. Taylor, given short notice of Santa Anna's approach, was forced to burn his stores and to retreat rapidly northward to a narrow defile near the hacienda of Buena Vista, where he could set up a position. There on February 23, 1846, the Battle of Buena Vista (known in Mexico as La Angostura, the narrows) was fought. The carnage was tremendous, and by nightfall the out-flanked American army "hung by a thread." But the next morning this army, to its amazement and immense relief, woke up to find that the Mexican army had disappeared. Several military analysts have con-cluded that Santa Anna had won the day but did not realize it. Taylor won by default. This combination of brilliant organization and tactics crowned by a miscalculation seemed characteristic of Santa Anna.

As Santa Anna dashed to Mexico City to claim victory, his army of the north dispersed along the plains of Coahuila. He was to raise another army to again meet defeat, this time at the hands of General Scott at Cerro Gordo, north of Veracruz. Another army was lost. The final desperate battles were fought outside of Mexico City with yet another army. T. R. Fehrenbach has this to say about the military situation in this last phase.

Santa Anna's generalship was good. The conventional Mexican wisdom that blamed him for the disasters of this campaign is not based on military evidence. He knew that if he could deal Scott a single, stunning setback, he could probably bring the invaders to disaster. Scott was fighting in the valley of Mexico with less than a modern division, supported by a tenuous and difficult supply line, surrounded in hostile territory.[9]

It was not Santa Anna's fault that he was not able to make use of the opportunity that he knew was there. At a critical point in the defense of Mexico City, he recognized that he must consolidate his forces. He ordered General Valencia at Contreras to fall back and join forces with General Anaya at Churubusco. Valencia, jealous of Santa Anna and thirsting for personal glory, refused to move, and his forces were defeated by Scott, whose army then drove forward and defeated Anaya. Thus the Mexican army was destroyed piecemeal, despite the sound tactical plans that Santa Anna had developed. Through misjudgment in one instance and bad fortune (and treachery) in another, Santa Anna's brilliant military leadership foundered.

The general's political abilities were clearly not on a par with his military acumen. There was no doubt that he had considerable political cunning. He could make conservatives think that he was conservative and liberals that he was a liberal. But toward the larger issues he was blinded. In his lack of concern for anything but his own fortunes, he was characteristic of the *criollo* class that he represented. When after a brief period of disgrace he was recalled to the presidency of Mexico, he further burdened an almost bankrupt nation with megalomaniac public displays staged in his honor. The story of his first meeting with Benito Juárez and its aftermath seem emblematic.

In 1829, during the early period of the *criollo* general's rise to power, Santa Anna was feted at a supper given in his honor by a professor of an educational institute for young men in Oaxaca. Students of the institute were waiting on table, one of these being Benito Juárez, an impoverished Indian boy in white smock and bare feet. Lacking the gift of prophecy, Santa Anna had no inkling that in the person of Juárez he had looked upon the face of that redoubtable Mexico that was to assert itself upon the passing of his own ephemeral and betasseled era. But with the politician's flair for remembering faces, he did not forget the encounter. Years later when Scott's army had entered Mexico City, Santa Anna, fleeing southward, sought asylum in the state of Oaxaca. The governor of that state, who had always thought that Santa Anna was bad news for Mexico, refused him entrance. The governor was Benito Juárez. In assessing the situation later in his Cuban exile, Santa Anna wrote: "He could not forgive me because he had waited on me at table in Oaxaca, in December 1829, with his bare feet on the floor and in his linen smock and trousers. . . . It is amazing that an Indian of such low degree should have figured in Mexico."[10] Characteristic of himself and of his age, Santa Anna missed the point entirely and thought only in terms of caste.

Though as politician Santa Anna had been nimble enough to move from one political constituency to another, there was in fact a growing ideological split in Mexico which the war with the United States served to point up. According to American historian Charles A. Hale, "it was the war that gave focus to a well-articulated and self-conscious 'conservativism' [the term had not been used earlier]. The war pointed up an ideological cleavage which was to characterize Mexican political life until 1867" (the date of the downfall of Maximilian's French-supported empire in Mexico).[11]

The impetus that the war gave to Mexican conservatives was the opportunity that it presented for blaming the liberals for Mexico's defeat. The liberals, according to these conservatives, were a group of deracinated Mexicans whose misguided admiration for alien principles, particularly those of the mongrelized democracy to the north, resulted in chaos in Mexico and a general unpreparedness to face the invasion by that very country so much admired by the liberals. These liberals were a highly educated group of *criollos* who represented a vanguard of the enlightenment in a Mexico whose social, cultural, and political norms still bore the stamp of the heavily medieval imprint of Spanish colonial rule. French political theory and North American political practice attracted them greatly. They wanted newly independent Mexico to become a democratic republic along the lines of the advanced political thinking of their times. They were clearly out of step with the opinions and institutions of *criollo* Mexico at large.

The liberals were divided between the moderates (*moderados*) and the pures (*puros*). Of these, the *puros* were the more highly intellectualized and the more uncompromising. Their principal representatives were Valentín Gómez Farías, José María Luis Mora, and Lorenzo de Zavala. Gómez Farías was an honorable man of complete integrity, but he tended toward the abstract and never quite comprehended the weaknesses of the general run of humanity. He served Mexico in a number of offices, however, and once held the unlikely position of vice president under Santa Anna. Mora was the *puro* who most clearly understood Mexico's dilemmas and who contributed importantly to Mexico's liberal tradition. Zavala, from faraway Yucatán, ended up in Texas. He so passionately defended the federalist position against Santa Anna's centralism, that he sided with the Texans in their revolt and ended up as the first vice president of an independent Texas. Generally considered a traitor in Mexico, he has been called by the historian José Fuentes Mares a "tragic man of opposites." The *moderados* were the more practical men of affairs such as José Joaquín Herrera, Mariano Arista, and Ramos Arizpe. Charles A. Hale has summarized the position of the liberals of this period within the larger Mexican society.

In conclusion, we have seen that in the main liberals of the pre-Reforma era were mesmerized by the ideal society to the north, and by the spectacular material progress of the United States under republican federal institutions. They talked openly of imitating the United States in reforming Mexico. The more penetrating thinkers, such as Zavala and Mora, came to distinguish between the goals of liberal reform and the methods for achieving those goals. For them the United States could serve as a model for goals but not for methods. The two societies and their respective histories were too different. Zavala's liberalism went bankrupt in Texas, whereas Mora's provided the roots of a continuing tradition. An important aspect of Mora's significance is the fact that he was less drawn to the United States than were many of his colleagues. Still, the nagging question of the North American model persisted to become a permanent feature of the liberal tradition in Mexico. Mora's problem was how to modernize a traditional Hispanic society without Americanizing it and thereby sacrificing its national identity. The problem is yet to be solved.[12]

Charles A. Hale has pointed out another dilemma which beset the *criollo* liberal. The source of his liberalism was the European enlightenment, but he still remained, in many of his ingrained responses, a Mexican *criollo*. He feared revolt from the Indians as much as did any conservative, and his sense of their racial inferiority was bred into him. All of this was hard to accommodate with his theoretical belief in human equality. Added to this was another conflict. Mexican Indian society was communal, but the liberal intellectuals of this period held the bourgeois concept of individualism based upon private property.

The conservatives had no such intellectual problems. They staunchly believed in law and order—Spanish colonial style—and placed much emphasis upon religion and paternalism. Mexico's defeat in the war with the United States gave the conservatives the dubious honor of being able to say in effect to the liberals: "We told you so"—though the issues in fact were far from being that clear. Nevertheless, the liberals felt betrayed by their model, which had turned against them, and their credibility lay in ruins. The defeat in war strengthened the right in Mexico and in all probability was a factor in leading to the later intervention of the French and the imposing upon Mexico of a European emperor.[13]

A central question among Mexican writers during the war—and later—was the role or lack thereof of the Roman Catholic Church in the war effort. Even after independence, the Church in Mexico retained most of its ancient privileges. Citizens had to be Roman Catholics, and despite the formal disappearance of the Inquisition, the Church maintained its control over the intellectual life of the nation. Education was almost totally in its hands. It was in possession of great wealth and was by far the greatest landowner in Mexico.

The role of the Church was a central point of dispute between conservatives and liberals. To the conservatives, the Church was the very focal point of Hispanic culture. To the liberals, the cultural, economic, and political power of the Church was the greatest single factor in maintaining Mexico's status as a backward nation. A complicating factor for Mexican liberals was that all of them were at least nominally Catholic, and most of them had pious wives who deplored their anticlericalism.

It would seem that the Catholic Church in Mexico should have been anxious about maintaining its unique position of power in the face of the invading heretics from the north. But to all appearances, its greatest concern during this period was fending off its enemies at home. The most celebrated case of this was the revolt of the "Polcos." When, in January 1847, Santa Anna was in the process of raising an army in San Luis Potosí in order to march northward to encounter Zachary Taylor at Saltillo, he pressed Vice President Gómez Farías to raise money for this venture. The Church, despite its wealth, had refused to lend money to the Mexican government to fight the American invaders. Now Gómez Farías, the *puro,* known for his anticlericalism, responded to the pressure from Santa Anna by getting congress to authorize the seizure and sale of several millions in Church properties. The response of the clerical faction was to gain the allegiance of the National Guard in

Mexico City, known popularly as the "Polcos" because its dandified *criollo* officers had chosen an airy polka as the anthem of the Guard. The "Polcos" rose in revolt and, though the Mexican government now knew that Scott's army was off the shore of Veracruz, they refused to march southward to defend the nation.

The manner in which Mexican writers of the various periods have handled the revolt of the "Polcos" has been in accordance with the prevailing concerns of the times. The liberals of the Juárez period, and after, accounted for Santa Anna's retreat from Buena Vista by maintaining that he had to get back to Mexico City to face the Polco revolt. Through this avenue they attacked the Church.[14] On the other hand, Justo Sierra, writing in the positivist era of the early twentieth century—a time which stressed objectivity in the writing of history—claimed that Santa Anna took his army north where it met disaster at Buena Vista in order to escape the great political pressures in the capital on the issue of church loans. Gómez Farías was left to face the problem, and his solution, in turn, led to the revolt of the "Polcos."[15] Mexican historians during the era of the great Revolution, 1910 to 1921, returned to the theme of the Mexican-American War primarily to attack or defend the Church. The anticlericals accused Santa Anna of being in league with the clerical faction to bring on war with the United States so that a defeated and humiliated Mexico would call upon a European monarch to restore status and stability. Defenders of the Church blamed Gómez Farías for having sold out Mexico to Protestant interests in the United States and for generally having aligned himself with the United States against Mexico.[16] The most searching discussion of the role of the Church written during the period of the war itself was written by Mariano Otero, whose essay on this and other subjects appears in this book.

Suspicions such as those directed against Gómez Farías by Mexican writers were not uncommon. The admiration that the *puros* had for the United States made them suspect in the eyes of the conservatives, and American diplomacy in Mexico in the years before the war seemed designed, in the opinion of Mexican writers, to further alienate Mexicans from each other. Luis G. Zorilla felt that the American diplomatic offensive was more brilliant, in a sinister way, than was the American war effort in achieving the destruction of Mexico.[17] The first United States representative in Mexico was Joel Poinsett, sent by John Quincy Adams as Charge d'Affairs in 1825. Poinsett set about cultivating the Mexican liberals. One of his instruments was the York Rite of the Masonic Order. The York lodges were just being formed in 1825, and, according to American historian Gene M. Brack: "Many of Poinsett's liberal friends belonged to these new lodges and the American minister, himself a York Rite Mason, helped them to obtain a charter from the grand lodge in New York. And as the new lodges proliferated Poinsett sought to employ them on behalf of Mexican liberalism. For to promote liberalism, of course, would be to promote, indirectly, the American interest in Mexico."[18] Though Poinsett was in many ways a subtle man, he was ingenuous enough to mention in as open a forum as the Mexican Congress that the United States was interested in buying Texas, thus causing something of an uproar. He did not understand Mexican sensitivities about the national territory. In this matter, his liberal friends were as intransigent as the conservatives. The degree to which Poinsett deliberately tried to further divide the factions in Mexico in order to soften that country for a later American invasion has been much argued, but he was undoubtedly a meddler and finally became persona non grata in Mexico and was brought home by Andrew Jackson. But rather than sending a qualified replacement, Jackson sent down as minister to Mexico an old crony, Anthony Butler, with orders to make every effort to purchase Texas. Butler was a crude man and a racist. His personal offensiveness made failure a foregone conclusion in such a sensitive matter as acquiring from Mexico part of its national territory. A combination of factors exhausted whatever measure of goodwill toward the United States existed in Mexico at this time. Among these were the maneuvers concerning Texas, the American policy of pushing the Indians westward—thus giving Mexico the sense that it might be in for similar treatment—slavery in the United States, and the United States support for claims against Mexico by U.S. citizens, many of which were thought to be fraudulent. Thus "the ambivalence with which Mexicans had previously viewed the United States gave way almost totally during the 1830s to disenchantment and hostility."[19]

It was in such an atmosphere that the revolt of the North American colonists in Texas took place, setting in motion the events that were to lead to the Mexican-American War. Since both Joel Poinsett and Anthony Butler had pressed the Mexican government to sell Texas to the United States, that government readily came to the conclusion that the United States was abetting that revolt. Zorilla maintains that Anthony Butler violated his role as a diplomatic emissary by appearing at Texas meetings that were agitating for rebellion and, while in Mexico City, by maintaining a correspondence with the pro-independence faction in Texas. Furthermore, according to Zorilla, Mexican enemies of Santa Anna's centralist policy, now exiles in New Orleans, formed a committee in support of revolt in Texas. Among these were Valentín Gómez Farías, although he still nominally held the title of Vice President of Mexico, General José Antonio Mejía, and Lorenzo de Zavala. In company with various North Americans, these Mexicans, through the committee, raised seven thousand dollars and two companies of volunteers to help the Texan rebels. Many more American volunteers were to follow.[20] In writing of the Texas revolt, historian José María Carreño has made the point that Texas had no more right to secede from Mexico than the southern American states had to secede from the Union.[21]

When the American colonists in Texas first began to agitate against the Mexican government, their protestations took a different form from their later demands for independence. The moderates under Stephen F. Austin, who at first were the prevailing faction, joined their voices to others in Mexico who were protesting the trammeling of the constitution of 1824, which provided for a federal republic. When Santa Anna chose to ignore this constitution, he did so in favor of a centrist policy which deprived the states of the rights which they had formerly enjoyed. The Texans at this stage still proclaimed their loyalty to Mexico, but they made common cause with the federalists. When Santa Anna sent an army under General Cos into Texas to bring that province into line, that army was chased out of Texas. The radical faction in Texas was now in control, and independence was its goal. Whatever Gómez Farías's purported activities in New Orleans, it seems unlikely that, given his lifelong service to his country, he would have participated in any activities designed to separate a large area of territory from the Republic. To the degree that he might have given support to the Texas rebels, this would in all likelihood have been given in terms of their earlier stated aims as reformers within the Republic rather than in their later role as secessionists.

Once having achieved its independence, Texas remained an independent nation for ten years. However, almost from the outset of its national existence, Texas petitioned the United States to accept it as a state in the Union. A complicating factor was the opposition of the northern states to the accepting into the Union of another slave state. But there were also much wider forces at work. The British and the French objected to the annexation of Texas. These European powers talked of establishing a "balance of power," a phrase ascribed to the French minister Guizot, on the American continent similar to that which was continually being sought in Europe. James K. Polk, a presidential candidate, and his fellow expansionists reacted angrily against foreign efforts to limit the growth of the United States and turned European declarations on this subject to good use in drumming up support for their position in favor of annexation. But the British persisted. They finally persuaded the Mexican government to write a treaty in which Mexico recognized the independence of Texas on condition that Texas pledge to remain an independent country. But Mexico was too late. In April 1844, under President Tyler, with John C. Calhoun as secretary of state, a treaty of annexation was signed between the United States and Texas. The treaty was defeated in the United States Senate, largely due to northern Whigs and abolitionists. But in the presidential election in the fall of 1844, Polk, the democrat and avowed expansionist, was elected. With the public mood made clear, outgoing President Tyler brought the annexation measure before a joint session of the two houses. Thus by a joint resolution, rather than a treaty, the measure was passed and signed by Tyler on March 1, 1845. Mexico had officially notified the United States that it would consider the annexation of Texas to be an act of war. Therefore, with annexation having become a reality, the Mexican minister to Washington, Juan N. Almonte, asked for his credentials and went home. Mexico then broke off relations with the United States.

However, the Mexican president at that time, José J. Herrera, was a man who felt that Mexico could ill afford to face a full-scale war with the

United States. He recognized that the United States could use Texas as a pretext to pursue its larger territorial aims against Mexico. But Herrera faced a highly inflamed public opinion which had become a force in itself. As to the attitude of the Mexican public, the American minister to Mexico, William Shannon, wrote to his government that while there were indeed intelligent individuals among the Mexican citizenry who felt that Mexico should accept the annexation of Texas as inevitable rather than face war, none of these people would be "bold" enough to express such opinions in public. Therefore, they were "compelled to join the public clamor, in order to maintain their positions."[22]

Despite this tremendous pressure, Herrera was "prepared to accept the inevitable annexation, provided national pride could be salved. The final loss of Texas must be made to appear not a Mexican defeat. To hold power, and to save Mexico, as he saw things, he desperately needed to preserve appearances."[23] Accordingly, in August 1845, Herrera dispatched a confidential note to the United States government to the effect that Mexico was willing to negotiate. He was ready to meet with a U.S. "commissioner" authorized to discuss the Texas boundary issue. In response, President James K. Polk appointed John Slidell to undertake a secret mission to Mexico. However, Slidell's instructions considerably exceeded the parameters indicated by Herrera. Slidell was authorized to purchase New Mexico, which included most of the present-day Southwest, for five million dollars and California for twenty-five million. In return, Mexico was to approve the Rio Grande as the Texas boundary. In addition, the United States would assume the claims of its nationals against Mexico.

The episodes that surround the Slidell mission are a classic example of cultural blundering on the part of the United States in its dealings with Mexico. As T. R Fehrenbach has noted, if the United States had sent down a person of the type of Stephen F. Austin, who understood the nuances of Mexican culture, a mission of this extreme delicacy might have been pulled off. Instead, the American president and his emissary pursued a heavy-handed course. The need for maintaining appearances was never understood nor was the difficulty of Herrera's position. Herrera had every intention of carrying on negotiations outside of formal channels. Against Herrera's protestations, Slidell insisted

upon being granted full diplomatic recognition as envoy extraordinary
and minister plenipotentiary, all in the glare of the public eye. Herrera
could do nothing but refuse to receive him, but already Slidell's mission
was the undoing of Herrera's government. Word of Slidell's proposals
were gaining currency. Herrera was excoriated for any connection he
might have had with Slidell's visit. The conservatives behind Lucas
Alamán believed that Mexico's legitimacy could only be restored by
placing a European prince upon a Mexican throne. Thus Mexico would
regain respect among the other nations of the world. They therefore led
an attack on Herrera, accusing him of "selling out the national soil and
honor." Mariano Paredes, who was seen as an interim figure, was
persuaded to pronounce against the government. Thus the monarchy
issue was thrust into the Slidell crisis. General Paredes, grandly proclaiming that he would defend all Mexican territory, was swept into
office through the usual coup. It did not take him long to discover that
his position was in all respects as unenviable as had been that of
Herrera.

When Slidell's report on the failure of his mission reached Washington on January 12, 1846, Polk ordered General Zachary Taylor to
proceed to the Rio Grande. The president did this in the full knowledge
that the Nueces River, about a hundred and twenty-five miles to the
north, had been accepted since Spanish times as the southern boundary
of Texas. As a province of Spain, Texas had a southern boundary,
drawn in 1816, which separated Texas from Tamaulipas by the Nueces
River and from Coahuila by the Medina River. At the time of the Battle
of San Jacinto, by which the Texans won their independence from
Mexico, this line was still in effect. But the Texas legislature established
a new boundary which ran from the mouth of the Rio Grande to its
source. "By the new line, major parts of four Mexican provinces,
including the capital of one of them, Santa Fe, were embraced in Texas.
The validity of the line rested on a vague agreement extorted from
Santa Anna when he was a prisoner of war, an agreement repudiated at
once by the only treaty-making authority in Mexico—the Congress."[24]
Thus Texas gratuitously extended its borders. The American government accepted the claims of Texas as to its southern border and rejected
the Mexican offer to have the matter submitted to European mediation.

To have accepted such mediation would have been, in Polk's conception, a violation of the Monroe Doctrine since, in his expanded interpretation of that doctrine, even advice from Europe was to be considered an intrusion upon the affairs of the American continent. Therefore, when Taylor's army marched into Point Isabel nine miles north of the mouth of the Rio Grande, he entered what in reality was foreign territory. President Polk undoubtedly anticipated a clash, and before long he got one. On April 25, 1846, a small force of American dragoons under Captain Seth Thornton was attacked and surrounded by a larger cavalry force under Gen. Anastasio Torrejón. Eleven Americans were killed, five wounded, and the rest captured. Taylor reported to Washington that hostilities had begun. On May 11, Polk delivered his war message to Congress saying that "American blood had been shed upon American soil." Congress then, on May 12, declared that a state of war existed between Mexico and the United States.

Though Mexican writers do not exculpate the United States for what they universally call "the North America Invasion," some of them have come to terms with geopolitical realities that inevitably influenced the play of forces on the North American continent. The great desert areas of the northern reaches of the Republic had never attracted Mexican settlers. People much preferred to stay in the fertile, cultivated, and civilized area of the central valley of Mexico, traditionally the populated area of the country. Even the Aztecs, who once ruled that valley, referred to the north as the great Chichimeca, a term which contemptuously included the various nomadic Indian tribes of the north, considered barbarians by the peoples of the highly civilized Aztec federation. While the Mexican Republic laid claim to these vast areas, it managed to establish its presence only in isolated, widely separated military presidios. Even these were barely maintained and were generally neglected by governments in Mexico City absorbed by their coups and counter coups. A contemporary account of the presidio of San Antonio in Texas gives a vivid picture of the dangers and neglect inherent in the garrison life in one of these presidios:

Although the land is most fertile, the inhabitants do not cultivate it because of the danger of Indians which they face as soon as they separate themselves any distance from their houses, to which these barbarians come often in the silence of the night to do damage without fear of the garrison, for when it becomes aware of this damage, which is irreparable, it is unable to apply any other remedy than the mounting of a continual watch, because of the sad fact of a total lack of equipment, especially military, that leaves no other recourse. These unfortunate troops have often gone for months, even for years, without pay, without clothes, and continually engaged in desert campaigning against the savages, maintaining themselves with the meat of buffalo, deer, etc., exhausting themselves in the hunt, with no alleviation from these hardships forthcoming from the government, in spite of continuous appeals.[25]

This account of struggles with nomadic Indians adds another reason for which life in the desert frontiers was unattractive to potential settlers. Luis Zorilla indicates that the policy of the United States toward its Indians aggravated, though perhaps inadvertently, the problems of the Mexican north. When the United States forced Indians from east of the Mississippi to settle in the West, they added to the Indian population already there. To manage this more crowded situation and to contain the nomadic western Indians, the United States government set up reservations along the Mexican frontier. Many of these nomads found more liberty in crossing the border into Mexico where they were able to continue their depredations free of U.S. supervision.[26] Although Zorilla is not in complete possession of his facts here, especially in terms of dates and locations of reservations, he is right in the main point of his argument. Andrew Jackson, during his two terms of office, pressured eastern Indians into signing ninety-four "treaties of evacuation" by which they were moved onto lands west of the Mississippi, thus increasing the general pressure in the borderlands.

The scarcity of Mexican settlers in the north had a direct bearing on developments in Texas. When the American colonists were first admitted into Texas, there were only approximately three thousand Mexicans living there, and almost all of them settled southwest of the Colorado, far from contact with the new immigrants. Therefore, there was no intermixture, intermarriage, or absorption. The new Texans had no reason to learn Spanish, even though they were nominally Mexican citizens. They were almost totally neglected, in the first years, by the Mexican government, and this proved acceptable to them. They developed their farms, often rich ones, built their own schools, and maintained contacts with their kinsmen to the north of them. Within ten years, the North American colonists outnumbered the original Mexican settlers ten to one.

In time, the Mexican government recognized the potential danger of that situation. In 1828, stirred by rumors of restiveness among the Texan colonists, the government sent General Manuel Mier y Terán on an investigatory mission to Texas. Mier y Terán, a man of strong character and ideals, could be counted on to make a thorough study of the situation. In his report to the Mexican president, he expressed his dismay at the isolation of the colonists and the low esteem they had for Mexicans:

It would cause you the same chagrin that it has caused me to see the opinion that is held of our nation by these foreign colonists, since, with the exception of some few who have journeyed to the capital, they know no other Mexicans than the inhabitants about here, and excepting the authorities necessary to any form of society, the said inhabitants are the most ignorant of Negroes and Indians. . . . Thus I tell myself that it could not be otherwise than that from such a state of affairs should arise an antagonism between the Mexicans and foreigners, which is not the least of the smoldering fires which I have discovered.[27]

A few discerning Mexican writers during the period of the war itself recognized the shortsightedness of Mexican policy in Texas. One of those to acknowledge this failed policy was the distinguished historian and literary man José M. Roa Bárcena:

Now came the palpable recognition of the serious difficulties which the nation faced. Its territory was both greatly overextended and very underpopulated. The rich endowment of natural resources was no better than sterility where there were no willing hands to exploit them. . . . The loss of Texas was now a fact. Through inexperience and lack of foresight, that state was permitted to harbor a nest of vipers under the guise of honorable colonists, who soon revealed themselves to be land speculators. When attempts were made to curtail their activities, so prejudicial to and dangerous for our country, they rose up with the rest of the colonists and, under the pretext of siding with those Mexicans who opposed the change from the federal system of government, ended by separating themselves entirely from Mexico and seeking the protection of the United States.[28]

When John Slidell arrived in Mexico with his menu, which contained considerably more than the item of Texas (the only matter that Herrera had agreed to discuss), both his government and the incoming government of Paredes were put on notice that Texas was just to be the initial wedge by which to pry open much larger areas of the national patrimony. As for the American president, James Polk, the connection between Texas and other areas of northwestern Mexico was constantly in the forefront of his mind. In fact, he hardly took pains to conceal his sense that Texas was the road to California, the area that was really the land of his heart's desire, as it was for other ardent expansionists of the era. George Bancroft, who was Secretary of the Navy in Polk's cabinet and a prominent historian, recorded later that soon after Polk took the oath of office he listed the items in his program in a conversation in the White House office. " 'There are four great measures,' said he, with emphasis, striking his thigh forcibly as he spoke, 'which are to be the measures of my administration: one, a reduction of the tariff; another, the independent treasury; a third, the settlement of the Oregon boundary question; and, lastly, the acquisition of California.' "[29]

Both Texas and California had for Polk a common shadow hanging over them—British watchfulness and designing. And there is little doubt that an important component in Polk's urge toward expansion on the American continent was his constant dread that the British would get there first and coopt American possibilities, becoming in the process a general threat to American growth, stability, and well being. There was in Polk's aggressiveness a generous mix of defensiveness.

Polk's fears regarding California were not completely groundless. There was precedent dating back to the sixteenth century. Francis Drake, in 1579, in a voyage around the world "symbolically seized the province from Spain and renamed it 'Nova Albion.' " When he finally returned to England, he was pointedly honored by Queen Elizabeth.[30] From then on, Britain never lost its interest in California, but the real extent of its designs remained obscured in the thickets of diplomatic verbiage. However, Polk was very adroit at raising the specter of alleged English maneuvers in California in order to give a further spurt to the expansionist spirit in the United States. He would cite reports to the effect that Britain planned to make a move toward the absorption of California under the pretext that Mexico had failed to satisfy British monetary claims and must therefore forfeit California in payment, or he would repeat the rumor that Britain would succeed in getting land grants in California for British citizens and would use these grants, as had the Texans, to wrest territory away from Mexico.

In his constant public references to the British threat in California, Polk would cite the Monroe Doctrine, that declaration made in 1823 by which it was stated that any intrusion into the Western Hemisphere, such as military action or the establishment of colonies, by European countries would be considered an act of hostility toward the United States. Though undoubtedly there was an element of genuineness in Polk's apprehension of British competition in the hemisphere, he was able to turn his anxiety to good effect by exaggerating, through skillful propaganda, the magnitude of the British menace. In the course of his declamations, he distorted the real intent of the Monroe Doctrine by using it as a cover for his aggressive designs in the West. As Frederick Merk put it, referring to the Monroe Doctrine: "That declaration had been intended to give protection to Latin American states against a prospective oppression by a European league of monarchs. It was being used by the Polk administration to oppress and despoil a neighboring Latin American state, the Republic of Mexico."[31]

If the British presence was spectral in California, it was very real in Oregon. There a joint habitation by British and Americans became a flash point for Polk's administration. American inhabitants demanded the expulsion of the British and all of Oregon for themselves. Expansionists joined them in the battle cry of "Fifty-four forty, or fight!" with Polk at the head of the pack. But various considerations caused him to tone down his stridency, and he ended by signing an agreement with Britain on June 15, 1846, in which the forty-ninth parallel was agreed upon as the northern boundary of Oregon. There were howls of treason and sellout directed at Polk, but at least he was spared from having to fight two wars simultaneously, much to the disappointment of the Mexicans. A number of historians have claimed that Mexico maintained a stiff front in the face of American territorial demands because it

counted on America's becoming weakened as a result of being em-
broiled in a war with England over Oregon.

Mexican historians had generally understood that the episodes of the
Texas Revolution and the Mexican-American War were related to
western expansionism in the United States. However, Homer Campbell Chaney maintains that it was not until the 1930s, the era of
Cárdenas, that Mexican historians appreciated the full extent of the
power of the concept of Manifest Destiny.[32] Writing in 1948 in an
article entitled "Lo Que Perdimos y Lo Que Nos Queda" ("What We
Lost and What We Have Left"), Jorge L. Tamayo traces the history of
North American pressure on and depredations against the Spanish
borderlands dating from Spanish colonial times. He notes various
American publications on the subject of Manifest Destiny and quotes
Senator Stephen A. Douglas as having said: "You can make as many
treaties as you want to contain . . . this great Republic and it will shrug
them off and its path will be directed toward a limit that I will not dare
describe."[33] Tamayo ends this section of his article by saying: "These
ideas, thoroughly propagated and accepted by an important majority of
Americans in the mid-nineteenth century, explain, without justifying,
the North American attitude toward Mexico a hundred years ago."[34]
Tamayo then goes on to examine the neglect of the northern areas of
Mexico by both Spain and the Mexican Republic. He admits that this
neglect is not easy to explain and proffers his own ventured solutions to
this historical problem. Perhaps the Spanish colonizers when they
encountered in their explorations northward only barren plains and arid
deserts lost interest in this region. In addition, they did not find the
mineral riches which now are being exploited in the area. Finally, they
faced the serious impediment of dangerous tribes of "barbarous and
aggressive" Indians who could not be brought under control until the
middle of the last century when "our neighbors applied the cruel
apothegm that 'the only good Indian is a dead Indian.' "[35] Tamayo also
noted that even as late as the mid-nineteenth century there existed in
Mexico only sketchy accounts and inferior maps of the northern region.
Such absence of information indicated a lack of interest, even a disdain
for this area. Tamayo draws the conclusion that concessions made by

Spain and Mexico to the North Americans in the frontier region were done in geographical ignorance. By the 1970s, a Mexican historian could put the vulnerability of Mexico in its northern areas in clear perspective, as in this succinct statement by Luis González: "Apart from a population shortage, the people, as in colonial days, were compressed into the central part of the country; nobody wanted to go to the vast zone of the north which, lacking people, was a danger, an invitation to pillage, an open arc."[36]

In discussing Mexico's defeat at the hands of the American army, Mexican authors adduced reasons other than the lack of development in the north. The liberal senator Mariano Otero, in an essay which appears in this volume, systematically examines each sector of Mexican society and finds almost all to be grievously lacking. A country in such a state could not possibly defeat a vigorous invading army. Another author, also contemporary with the war period, came to similar conclusions from a conservative point of view. José Fernando Ramírez in *Mexico During the War with the United States (Mexico Durante Su Guerra Con Los Estados Unidos)* gives a fascinating behind-the-scenes account of life in Mexican society during the war. He also makes a number of pronouncements on the state of people and things. As a distinguished archaeologist and a man who had held prominent political positions, he was a man who did not suffer fools gladly. The fact that many entries in his book came in the form of letters written to a friend in his native Chihuahua probably accounts for the freedom with which he condemned whole orders of people. True to his conservative convictions, he was not inclined to put much trust in the masses. For example, he was very exasperated at the coup by which Paredes displaced Herrera during the Slidell crisis and has this to say about popular reaction: "At the same time people who had gone up into the towers of the cathedral and of all the other churches started to ring the bells furiously by way of celebrating. Now try to believe in the sovereignty of the people! Strain your mental powers to the bursting point to find anything that can justify their actions! These citizens of ours are nothing but a flock of sheep that need the lash. They are good for nothing except to maintain a few ambitious and ignorant demagogues in power."[37] In a more sober analysis, he states that democratic government is the end product of long development under specific conditions. "The system can thrive only if it is nourished by customs which themselves are the products of toil and industry, stimulated by institutions that have attained the power to develop as they have in the United States. We lack both these elements. . . ."[38] Ramírez then proceeds to a sweeping condemnation of wartime Mexico which is unable to unite in the face of a common enemy.

Beginning with the men who run our affairs, we find that we have a Congress without prestige, without power and without ability. What is worse, it is undermined and disrupted by partisan hatreds which prevent it from seeing anything clearly, except when it wishes to wound its opponents. You have probably noticed that history records innumerable cases substantiating the oft repeated saying that 'a war with a foreign foe preserves a feeling of nationality and strengthens institutions.' In our privileged country quite the contrary has happened on the only two occasions there have been to prove the truth of the maxim: namely, the Spanish conquest under Cortes, and the Yankee conquest under Scott. And to make the terrible comparison complete, both set foot upon the shores of Veracruz during Holy Week. The reason for the difference is clear. A sensible, patriotic people unites and offers a solid front at the first hint of the common peril. A people that is neither sensible nor patriotic grows weak, thus smoothing out difficulties for the invader, who wins without opposition.[39]

Ramírez concludes his censorious remarks by referring again to Congress. "I have no doubt that every one of those individuals who on the rostrum or in the public press have so furiously been preaching war to the death, branding as 'traitor' anyone who even says one word about a truce, is at heart convinced of our absolute helplessness not only to carry on the war successfully but even to continue fighting in the face of defeat."[40] For Ramírez there remains only the bitter hope that through the mutilation of the country will come an overthrow of the military and finally a democracy.[41] Justo Sierra, the positivist historian writing in 1902, sees Mexico's inability to wage war against a foreign invader in economic terms. He recites a circular series of events that occurred in Mexico since independence. A revolution occurs. The followers of the victor demand increased rank and salary. There is insufficient money in the treasury to meet these demands. Recourse is made to the infamous *agiogistas*, the money lenders whom Sierra refers to as "merchants of

Venice." The government struggles to meet at least the interest on the loan until the next revolt occurs, causing the repeat of the process and putting the nation still further in debt. Meanwhile, the economy is incapable of replenishing the treasury. The masses of peasants in the countryside are unproductive because, being tied to the estates by inherited debt, they lack incentive. Furthermore, they are often systematically brutalized by alcoholism to keep them docile. The commercial class has been ruined by the demands and forced loans made upon it by government to the point that commerce has fallen into the hands of foreigners, the returned Spanish and the French. "Under these conditions," writes Justo Sierra, "we were conquered in advance."[42]

Certainly the economic chaos in Mexico underlay a great deal of her difficulties and had a bearing on the origins and the outcome of the Mexican-American War. Fehrenbach states that "the new men running Mexico [after the independence] had absolutely no grasp of that elusive European concept, money. In the long run, economic naivete was to do more damage to the republican Mexico than the landowners, Church, or army. The financial problems exacerbated all the others and caused the government to be organized as a permanent revolution."[43] Early in the years after independence, Mexican governments developed the habit of making loans from other nations, particularly England and France. But Mexico discovered that it could not put off foreign governments in the way that it could its own citizens. France, after its loans and the claims of its citizens against the Mexican government had been ignored, seized the island fortress of San Juan de Ulua and blockaded the harbor of Veracruz in 1838, in what came to be known as the Pastry War, named after a French pastry shop in Mexico City that had been sacked by drunken Mexican army officers. Santa Anna lost a leg in that war and gained considerable glory, which he was to capitalize on later. But the unfortunate Mexican president, Bustamante, had to buy off the French by a guarantee of 600,000 pesos from the customs. The question of foreign claims against Mexico dogged Mexican governments continually. In 1843, Mexico halted payment of more than two million dollars in damages to United States nationals that had been authorized by an international claims commission in 1840. James Polk placed unpaid claims by American citizens high on his list of complaints against Mexico and cited them as part of the justification for war. Mexican historian Alberto María Carreño takes up the matter of claims by American citizens against Mexico. In *The Special Diplomacy Between Mexico and the United States, 1789–1947*, he reprints sections of correspondence between President Andrew Jackson's representative in Mexico, Powhatan Ellis, and the Mexican Secretary of Foreign Relations, José Ortiz Monasterio, on the subject of American claims. The tone of Ellis's letter is abrupt, impolitic, and demanding. He accuses the Mexican government of indifference to flagrant violations in terms of law, life, and property against American citizens. Monasterio replies suavely. He reprimands Ellis for language unsuitable for the correspondence between two friendly nations and maintains that many of the claims are totally unsubstantiated and that many of the claimants are known adventurers dealing in contraband and engaging in other illegal activities. He also reminds Ellis that while Mexico is accused of not answering correspondence relating to claims, the United States government has left unanswered the most urgent notes from the Mexican government on matters of the greatest import dealing with the annexation of Texas. Carreño concludes that the claims uproar was a cover-up for the power politics of annexation.[44]

Though American aggression against Mexico has been a pervasive theme among American historians, there have been some American historians who have looked at a reverse side of the fabric and have claimed that Mexico shared in the blame for having started a war. Justin H. Smith, true to his general thesis, even depicted Mexico as being the prime instigator:

[Mexico's] treatment of Texans and Americans violated the laws of justice and humanity, and—since there was no tribunal to punish it—laid upon the United States, both as her nearest neighbor and as an injured community, the duty of retribution. In almost every way possible, indeed, she forced us to take a stand. She would neither reason nor hearken to reason, would not understand, would not negotiate. Compensation for the loss of territory, in excess of its value to her, she knew she could have. Peace and harmony with this country she knew might be hers. But prejudice, vanity, passion and wretched politics inclined her toward war; her overrated military advantages, her expectations of European aid, the unpreparedness of the United States, and in particular the supposed inferiority of Taylor and his army encouraged her; and she deliberately launched the attack so long threatened.[45]

T. R. Fehrenbach, who on the issue of Mexican culpability is more akin to Smith than are most modern American historians, sees the Mexicans as having been recalcitrant in not having been willing to surrender their territories. Mexico, in its bitter pride, would not sell to the United States land that it could not develop and "apparently could not use." Fehrenbach conceded that "the Mexican governments had legality completely on their side, because Washington had recognized Spanish sovereignty over Texas in the 1819 treaty fixing boundaries at the Sabine." "But," continued Fehrenbach, "the Mexican governments set too much store in the permanence of this treaty."[46] In imputing blame to Mexico, writers have cited the legitimacy of the cause of Texan independence and thus of the right of annexation, and they have also cited the Mexican refusal to deal with the American emissary, John Slidell.

As the danger posed by Texas and, by extension, the United States became more apparent to the Mexican government, Mexico began to search for ways to protect itself. Luis Zorilla notes that in February, 1830, Lucas Alamán, secretary of foreign relations, proposed to all the Latin American countries that they form a close union for the purpose of countering United States expansion and aggression at their expense. Though the proposal was greeted with general approval, nothing concrete was done about it "because of the instability of all those countries and their narrow and egotistic vision (from which Mexico herself did not escape)."[47]

Some of the proposed measures, coming at the eleventh hour, had an aspect of the frantic about them. Lucas Alamán proposed that convicts be pardoned and that they and their families be induced to settle in Texas. One of the proposals that appeared in the report on Texas that Mier y Terán delivered to the Mexican president was that European families be brought over to develop European types of farms in the Texas region. Nothing came of these plans because the capital, as usual, was preoccupied with its own immediate alarums and excursions and would not put up the money for these ventures.

Later historians in their evaluations of the Mexican leadership of the war period have given their prescriptions for what should have been done. Justo Sierra, making the point that Santa Anna had alienated not only the Texans and the Americans but the world at large, said that the idea of the reconquest of Texas should have been dropped. The secession of Texas was inevitable, and Mexico should have recognized this fact and thus have avoided two wars and much loss of territory.[48] According to Daniel Cosío Villegas, Mexico should have recognized the fatality of the push westward by the United States and should have negotiated, thereby perhaps saving some of the territory that was lost.[49]

Other Mexican writers have viewed the war within the wider framework of different and often irreconcilable cultural attitudes. Puritan America was seen as looking upon inefficient and sinful Mexico with condescension if not disdain. In his biography of Joel R. Poinsett, first U.S. minister to Mexico and a man accused by many Mexicans of having been a prime agent of North American subversion in Mexico, José Fuentes Mares characterizes his subject as a man who "sought the indulgence of a healthy nation for a depraved one, of an enlightened people for an ignorant, of a Protestant toward a Catholic nation, of the Anglo Saxon toward the Spanish. Poinsett was, in Mexico, the advance guard of the Army of Salvation."[50] Luis Zorilla saw the American decision to open a second front in its war against Mexico as a demonstration of the Puritan spirit of legalism: "The North American High Command decided, in November of 1846, to change the general plan of combat, once the United States had assured the boundary line which it had claimed for Texas and had taken possession of New Mexico and California, the other two territories which it coveted. Now it attempted to oblige Mexico to accept these conquests; the Anglo Saxon Puritan spirit wanted to obtain a document through which it could legalize the spoils already consummated, although, in order to secure them, it had resorted to violence."[51] Thus the invasion of Veracruz and the march upon Mexico City. In contrast, Daniel Cosío Villegas maintained that it was Mexico, as the weaker nation, that resorted to the shield of legality, the juridical approach, while the United States operated from the stance of "realpolitik." Sometimes, according to Cosío Villegas, this approach was successful for Mexico, for example, Mexico's success in regaining the Chamizal area from Texas. At other times the insistence on legalism was quite unrealistic. As an example of this, Cosío Villegas cited the attempts by the United States to gain the cooperation of Mexico in the problem of the devastating forays carried out by the Apaches on both sides of the border. Lafragua, minister of foreign relations under President Lerdo de Tejada, answered the American appeal for cooperation by informing the United States government that Mexico could do nothing about the incursion of the Apaches for re-grouping in Mexico because Mexican law allowed all persons to enter Mexico. Lafragua's response was, according to Cosío Villegas, a "beau-tifully written paper but absolutely unrealistic" because Mexico was suffering as much as the United States from the Apache raids. Cosío Villegas used this example to illuminate Mexico's decisions relating to the annexation of Texas by the United States. From a purely legal standpoint, Mexico was thoroughly justified in insisting upon the re-conquest of Texas, a mutinous part of the national territory. But as a matter of "realpolitik" such a posture was doomed to failure and to bring along with it disastrous consequences.[52]

The modern Mexican philosopher, Antonio Caso, sees the historical events, including the war, which occurred between the United States and Mexico as resulting from contrasting national personalities. To Caso, the United States is a prosperous, infantile, and monotonously contented country, while Mexico is unalterably romantic and tragic.[53] The contemporary Mexican poet and essayist Octavio Paz develops the same line of argument in considerably greater detail. To be sure, the North Americans are realists of a sort, and this realism accounts for their success in external things. They have the Puritan habits of "asceti-cism" and the Puritan "cult of work for work's sake," but their realism is abstract and superficial. They are "devastated by the arid victory of principles over instincts." In fact, in the deeper sense the American seeks to avoid reality:

Would it not be more accurate to say that the North American wants to use reality rather than to know it? In some matters—death for example—he not only has no desire to understand it, he obviously avoids the very idea. . . . In contrast, one of the most notable traits of the Mexican's character is his willingness to contemplate horror: He is even familiar and complacent in his dealings with it. The bloody Christs in our village churches, the macabre humor in some of our newspaper headlines, our wakes, the custom of eating skull-shaped cakes and candies on the Day of the Dead, are habits inherited from the Indians and the Spaniards and are now an inseparable part of our being. Our cult of death is also a cult of life, in the same way that love is a hunger for life and a longing for death. Our fondness for self-destruction derives not only from our masochistic tendencies but also from a certain variety of religious emotion. . . . We are sorrowful and sarcastic and they are happy and full of jokes. North Americans want to understand and we want to contemplate. They are activists and we are quietists; we enjoy our wounds and they enjoy their inventions.[54]

Clearly Octavio Paz admires the deeper quietism of Mexico over what he conceives to be the superficial activism of the United States, even if this activism results in military triumph over Mexico. But despite his distaste for a number of the personal traits of North Americans, he is forthright in his admiration for the political system of the United States and its origins. The North Americans created a new society, whereas the Latin Americans, despite their wars of independence from the mother country, did not. Herein lies the greater efficacy of the United States as a body politic.

It is true that the programs and language of the Independence leaders [in Latin America] resembled those of the revolutionaries of the epoch, and no doubt they were sincere. That language was "modern" and an echo of the French Revolution and above all, of the ideas of the North American War of Independence. But in North America those ideas were expressed by groups who proposed a basic transformation of the country in accordance with a new political philosophy. What is more, they did not intend to exchange one style of affairs for another, but instead—and the difference is radical—to create a new nation. In effect, the United States is a novelty in the history of the nineteenth century, a society that grew and expanded naturally. Among ourselves, on the other hand, the ruling classes consolidated themselves, once Independence was achieved, as heirs of the old Spanish order. They broke with Spain but they proved incapable of creating a modern society. It could not have been otherwise, because the groups that headed the Independence movement did not represent new social forces, merely a prolongation of the feudal system. The newness of the Spanish American nations is deceptive: in reality they were decadent or static societies, fragments and survivals of a shattered whole.[55]

Thus the vulnerability of Latin America in the face of a modern and activist United States.

There was one specific aspect of American culture, particularly strong in the nineteenth century, which Mexicans early came to recognize and which they not only deplored but eventually came to fear. North American racism was seen to be a definite factor in the aggressiveness of the United States. Americans did not reserve their contempt for the darker under classes of Mexico only. The most refined and Europeanized Mexican gentleman could become the object of a North American racial snub. The Mexican minister to the United States during the Texas Revolution was Manuel Eduardo de Gorostiza. He was a distinguished playwright and man of letters and a seasoned diplomat. During his stay in Washington he not only heard a number of statements expressing dislike and disdain for Mexico, he himself was treated rudely and contemptuously by high American officials. According to Gene M. Brack, "Gorostiza, who would subsequently hold a number of high places in the Mexican government, never forgave the Americans for their insolent treatment of him and his country."[56] He hardened his attitude toward the United States and strongly urged upon his countrymen that the American advance be stopped at its starting point, in Texas. To Gorostiza, the essence of the contemptuous and aggressive American was the frontiersman, whom he described unflatteringly but yet with a certain grudging admiration:

Let us consider the character of those who have populated the lands adjoining our border. Who is not familiar with that race of migratory adventurers that exist in the United States, composed of the most reckless, profligate and robust of its sons, who always live in the unpopulated regions, taking land away from the Indians and then assassinating them? Far removed from civilization, as they condescendingly call it, they are precursors of immorality and pillage. . . . [They] take possession of a new land and remain there for one or two years, building a log cabin for shelter, and when they grow tired of the place they sell it to others, less daring than they. Then once more, with hatchet in hand and rifle on shoulder, they go in search of new lands.[57]

Another Mexican official, José María Tornel, who was secretary of war during the Texas campaign, traced North American aggressiveness to the old Anglo Saxon tribes of northern Europe:

It has been neither an Alexander nor a Napoleon . . . who has inspired the proud Anglo-Saxon race in its desire, its frenzy to take control of that which rightly belongs to its neighbors; rather it has been the nation itself which, possessed of that roving spirit that moved the barbarous hordes of a former age in a far remote north, had swept away whatever had stood in the way of its aggrandizement.[58]

Brack sums up the reasons for which Mexicans in the period before the war became more and more apprehensive of American racism:

Over the years Mexicans had become increasingly aware that many Americans, especially those who most vociferously advocated Southwestern expansion, looked upon Mexicans as inferior beings. This had frightening implications. For Americans had respect for neither the rights nor the culture of those whom they considered inferior. They had been merciless in their treatment of the Indian and had reduced blacks to a brutal form of servitude. Mexicans were perceptive enough to recognize that a similar fate threatened them should they fall under American domination.[59]

Such fears seem thoroughly justified by the evidence of the rash of popular histories of the Mexican-American War written during and after the war, many written by ex-servicemen. According to Robert W. Johannsen, these books, with few exceptions, took Anglo-Saxon racial superiority as a matter of course. The Mexicans were portrayed as a decayed race as the result of mongrelization and because of Spanish oppression. Another contributor to their moribund condition was the twin oppression exercised by the church and the military. Thus American victory was a foregone conclusion because of America's superiority in race and in republican institutions.[60] Quite beyond these popular histories, the record of North American racism directed against Mexico is amply documented in the literature of the American Southwest written during the nineteenth century.

The American historian who has written the most thoroughly documented history of the war with Mexico, Justin H. Smith, was not beyond sweepingly racist assessments, such as in the following observations about Mexicans: "Though generally amiable, and often brilliant or charming, they lacked common sense, principle, steadiness, and knowledge of the world. They were passionate, suspicious, over-subtle, self-confident and fond of gambler's risks." Smith even ascribed Mexico's financial problems to racial defects: "Of all the fields of Mexican misgovernment the worst had been the treasury, for it not only required a care and a good judgement that were peculiarly foreign to the national temperament, but provided opportunities for illegitimate gains that were most congenial."[61] In discussing the rude and insulting aspect of the diplomatic correspondence of the United States with Mexico, Glenn Price states that this offensiveness cannot be understood without a comprehension of the racial contempt for Mexico which underlay this correspondence:

It is quite impossible to make sense of United States—Mexican relations in the period through the war and later without an understanding of this psychological factor, and it was in no way complex or subtle. One has always to keep in mind that United States actions issued from American conceptions of Mexico and of Mexicans; America was, and it has always been, a racist society. Thus President Adams could sit in the capital of his country on the Atlantic shelf and instruct his minister to Mexico to persuade the Mexicans that they should take advantage of the opportunity of getting their capital city nearer to the center of their territories by transferring Texas to the United States. If that is not understood, much else will not be understood.[62]

The forebodings that Mexico entertained as it watched the United States pushing westward, breaking, in the process, earlier treaties made with the Indians, proved amply justified. War descended upon Mexico and with it the bitter dregs of defeat. There remained the question of the peace treaty. Despite defeat in all the set battles, there had been continual guerrilla action on the part of Mexican partisan fighters throughout the war, and the raids of these irregulars had proven increasingly effective against Scott's attenuated supply lines. It is quite possible that had these guerrilla actions continued they might have eventually forced the evacuation of the American forces. Santa Anna urged this type of warfare, and in this he had the support of the *puros,* but by now Santa Anna was thoroughly discredited. Congress was at this time dominated by the moderates who, together with the conservatives, feared the anarchy that might result from continued guerrilla war. Yucatán in the south, with a long history of separatism, was faced with a civil war in which armed Mayan Indians had risen against their *criollo* masters and were causing them to flee for their lives into the cities of that state. The states in the north were threatening to secede. Under these fears and pressures, the *moderados* were determined to make peace. A provisional government was established in Querétaro with the chief justice of the supreme court, Manuel de la Peña y Peña as interim president. This government, negotiating with General Scott and with Nicolas Trist, the U.S. state department representative, worked out the Treaty of Guadalupe Hidalgo. The terms of the treaty were the cession of Texas, the New Mexico territory (which included all the area of what is now considered the Southwest), and California to the United States. On its part, the United States agreed to cancel the Mexican debt and pay an additional fifteen million dollars. This treaty was not arrived at without considerable debate, much of it acrimonious, within Mexico. Two strong essays, representing opposite sides of this question, are included in this book.

Also debated have been the legacy of the war and the lessons that can be derived from it. Most Mexican writers have found little salutary in the events of 1846–47. Whatever lessons have been learned have been bitter ones. The intrepid statesman and historian, Ignacio M. Altamirano, true to the ideals of the reformist era of Juárez, declared that though the war was a disaster it at least showed up the ineptitude of the generals of the old order, who had already—before the war—exhausted the country with their revolutions. As for the ruling class, it showed its true stripe when it refused to make sacrifices in the face of foreign invasion.[63] The debate goes on into the modern era, and the bitterness of tone lingers. To Daniel Cosío Villegas, the war was only the first of painful episodes yet to come in the relations between Mexico and the United States:

So Mexico and the United States are different countries, and their paths differ also. Nevertheless, they have not been able to go their different ways; they are neighbors, whether their interests coincide or clash. There is a conflict between them, latent at times, at other times acute; a conflict that perhaps will not again lead to war, but which is not any less real or less painful because of that fact. It is now exactly a century since the first stage of the conflict began. Mexico crossed the path of the "manifest destiny" of the United States; its territory was in the way. The avalanche came and demolished it. This was the first adjustment Mexico had to make in the crushing process to which it has been subjected, to which it still is subjected because of its "good-neighborhood" with the United States.[64]

Octavio Paz shares with Cosío Villegas a stinging sense of injustice. Yet for Paz, the war, however unjust, provided an opportunity for the formerly beleaguered liberals to reshape the nation:

The liberals not only had to fight the conservatives but also take into account the military, which changed allegiance according to its own interests. While these factions struggled, the country disintegrated. The United States took advantage of the situation, and in one of the most unjust wars in the history of imperialist expansion, deprived us of over half of our territory. In the long run this defeat produced a salutary reaction, because it gave the death blow to the military bossism as exemplified by the dictator Santa Anna. . . . A new generation— heirs of José María Mora and Valentín Gómez Farías, leader of the liberal intelligentsia—undertook the task of building new foundations for the nation.[65]

The works of such writers as Cosío Villegas and Octavio Paz demonstrate that the Mexican-American War continues to provide a potent theme for Mexican writers. From the period of the conflict itself to our own times, writing about the war has had its constant theme as well as its interesting variables. The constant has been an expression of a sense of the injustice perpetrated against Mexico by an unprovoked invasion, one which gained for the invader enormous spoils of war. The variables have occurred as succeeding eras have considered the war in different lights. Though there have been interesting crosscurrents throughout the history of this war literature, one can make some generalizations. During and immediately after the war itself, Mexican writing on the subject reflected the division between liberals and conservatives. The period of *La Reforma*, dominated by the figure of Benito Juárez, emphasized the class and caste aspect of the war. The dominant and race-proud *criollos*, who had denied the *mestizos* and Indians—as well as the poor and lower middle class in general—any real access to nationhood, paid for their anachronistic attitudes and their overall ineptitude by a crushing defeat in the war. Of course, not only the *criollos* but the country as a whole had to pay the price. But the war cost the *criollos* their commanding position in Mexican society. The last decades of the nineteenth century and the early twentieth century saw the dominance of positivism in Mexican thought. The Mexican writers of this period, while hardly condoning the Americans, sought to apply the positivist ideal of scientific objectivity to the writing of history. Modern Mexican historians such as Daniel Cosío Villegas, Jorge L. Tamayo and Josefina Zoraida Vázquez have followed contemporary practices in the writing of history by drawing upon the techniques of the social sciences.

American historiography on the Mexican-American War, as well, can be related to the concerns of different periods of the national history. Also, as Mexican historian Josefina Zoraida Vázquez has observed, there is a discernible leitmotiv of an expression of guilt running throughout North American historical writing about a war in which the United States profited enormously at the expense of a defeated neighbor. But, as a countering force, some American historians have set themselves in opposition to this pervasive sense of guilt, taking pains to justify the role of the United States in that conflict.

Hubert Howe Bancroft, whose massive works on Mexico and the American West were actually the products of many hands, but under the master's guidance, set the prevailing tone in such books as *History of Mexico, V, 1824–1861* (San Francisco, 1885) and *North Mexican States and Texas, II* (San Francisco, 1889) of blaming the United States generally and the Polk administration particularly for instigating a despoiling war of aggression. Polk's rapport with southern ideas and feelings particularly brought on Bancroft's ire. Southern slave interests, according to Bancroft, were the real instigators of the Texas rebellion and by extension the Mexican-American War. In his lack of sympathy for the Texas rebels, Bancroft takes issue with many American historians. "The Texas rebellion and secession," wrote Bancroft, "were the result of a preconcerted plan . . . to establish a market for African slaves in contempt of the Mexican laws and afterwards to annex the new country to the United States."[66] As for the Texans' declared reasons for taking up arms, Bancroft wrote that "an insignificant minority as the Texans then were, had no right to arrange the whole country's administration to its own liking. If that minority disliked the changes it was at liberty to leave the country."[67] Bancroft claimed that the leaders of the Texan war party were determined on revolution and contemptuously disregarded efforts by such Mexican generals as Cos and Ugartechea to calm down the situation by declaring that a general military occupation and rule of Texas was not contemplated by Mexican authorities.[68] Bancroft's lack of sympathy for the cause of the Texans set the basis for his argument against Polk, who so strongly supported the annexation of Texas, and against the American position in the war which was waged during Polk's administration.

Two historical works written in the early 1900s also place the blame on Polk for forcing war upon Mexico. Jesse S. Reeves in *American Diplomacy Under Tyler and Polk* declared that "if Polk had had no ulterior designs upon Mexico, the Mexican War would not have taken place."[69] The point is strongly made by George Lockhart Rives in *The United States and Mexico, 1821–1848* that Polk used the Taylor invasion as a lever to force Mexico to make territorial concessions at the very outset. Rives accuses Polk of ethnocentricity but concedes that Polk possessed a powerful will and that he directed that force toward gaining possession of that most coveted land, California.[70] However, another work written in the early twentieth century, *Texas, a Contest of Civilizations* by George P. Garrison, takes a different view. Influenced by F. J. Turner's thesis of the powerful role of the frontier in America's history, Garrison sees the Texas Revolution and the Mexican-American War as inevitable results of the ongoing expansion of the American frontier.[71]

Though Garrison's was a dissenting voice in his time, the real revisionist work, a book which was the product of exhaustive research, was Justin H. Smith's *The War with Mexico.* Because of the amount of scholarship that went into it, the book remains a monument, but it is now generally recognized to have serious flaws. From the outset, Smith was an advocate of the American cause, which he felt had been seriously betrayed by the historians who had preceded him. A characteristic statement from *The War with Mexico* is the following: "Of all the conquerors we were perhaps the most excusable, the most reasonable, the most beneficent. The Mexicans had come far short of their duty to the world. Being what they were, they had forfeited a large share of their national rights."[72] As to Smith's method of work, Glenn Price says—in specific reference to Smith's treatment of the Texas border question:

"Smith was unable to convince himself by his own argumentation; so he compromised by taking the 'American position' in the narrative and running away from it in his notes."[73] Elsewhere in *Origins of the War with Mexico,* Price says that "Smith's history of the war of the United States with Mexico is one of the most flagrantly biased works in American history." Some pages earlier he wrote that "Smith's work, in all its arguments that pertain to the origins of the war, was simply preposterous as history; it was an extraordinary case of special pleading."[74] The contemporary Mexican historian, Josefina Z. Vázquez, adopts a less strenuous tone but makes much the same point in writing that "the historians of the neighboring country . . . have produced a work which continues to be a classic for its exhaustive use of the documental sources of the two countries. *The War with Mexico* by Justin Smith, published in 1919, is, nevertheless, an antiquated work which is partisan in the extreme."[75]

The attitudes expressed by Smith in his study of the Mexican War were to some extent influenced by the nationalistic fervor which was generated in the United States by the First World War. The early 1940s, with the United States again facing war, saw another rise in nationalistic feeling. *The Year of Decision 1846* by Bernard DeVoto (1943) looked back upon the major era of American expansion with a strong sense that the country was fulfilling its destiny. DeVoto, though far from being a simplistic nationalist, took no issue with the major decisions that the United States made in the crucial year of 1846, including the decision to go to war with Mexico. However, unlike Justin Smith, he faced squarely the fact that James Polk sought a war of conquest. In dealing with the episode in which Polk dispatched General Taylor into the Rio Grande area claimed by Mexico, he noted that Polk had been preparing a war message before having given his orders to Taylor. In this message Polk was to ask Congress for a declaration of war on the grounds of unpaid war claims, the failure of Mexico to acknowledge the true boundaries of Texas, Mexico's refusal to receive Slidell, and Mexico's warlike rhetoric. As to this message in draft, DeVoto wryly noted that "it would have needed a strong bellows to blow that up to war size, but Polk seems to have been confident of its acceptance [by Congress]."[76] Nevertheless, DeVoto added, Polk was relieved to receive the dispatch from

Taylor informing him of the military clash in the Rio Grande area. DeVoto duly noted, without giving his approval, the dissent of such New England intellectuals as Sumner, Greely, Parker, Lowell, Emerson, and Thoreau against the involvement of the United States in war with Mexico, quoting Emerson as saying "Mexico will poison us."[77] But DeVoto also stated that even Brook Farmers reluctantly recognized Manifest Destiny.[78]

American historians in the 1960s, an era which was not inclined to take official pronouncements of the United States government at face value, mounted a revision of the earlier position established by Justin Smith. This later revision was in fact in the direction of the attitudes expressed by the historians of the very early twentieth century, who had blamed Polk for starting an unjustifiable war. Frederick Merk in *The Monroe Doctrine and American Expansion, 1843–1849* (1966) maintained that expansionists like Calhoun, Tyler, and Polk extended the conception of security beyond the prevailing understanding as it had existed when the Monroe Doctrine was formulated. Being eager to consummate the annexation of Texas, these men defined the security of the United States so as to include the necessity of protecting slavery in Texas. The rumor that Britain planned to grant a substantial loan to an independent Texas on condition that it get rid of slavery alarmed these men, who would have considered such an action to be an unwarranted intrusion. In the same category was thought to be the advice given to Texas by Britain and France that it remain an independent country, as well as the pressure which Britain brought to bear upon Mexico to recognize the independence of Texas with the proviso that Texas remain an independent nation. Thus the act of advising in itself, when done by a European nation to a nation in the Western Hemisphere, was considered by the new interpreters to be a violation of the Monroe Doctrine. Such logic made mandatory the immediate annexation of Texas. Merk sums up the reinterpretation of the Monroe Doctrine as it was done in the age of Polk:

In Polk's mind the twin concepts of defense and advance never were separated sharply. On the contrary they were fused, as often happens with expansionists. The language of Monroe, interpreted to fit the new situation, appeared, therefore, repeatedly in the messages and instructions of the administration. The chief defense problem was the British, whose ambition seemed to be to hem the nation in. On the periphery of the United States, they were the dangerous potential aggressors. The best way to hold them off was to acquire the periphery. This was the meaning of the Monroe Doctrine in the age of Manifest Destiny.[79]

Polk's operations in the borderlands were also the object of analysis in Glenn Price's *Origins of the War with Mexico: The Polk-Stockton Intrigue*. Though this book focuses on specific events, it examines, in the process, the various strands that came together to produce a war situation. The subject of examination in Price's book was Polk's efforts, through his agent Commodore Stockton, to persuade President Anson Jones of Texas to launch a Texan attack against Mexico at Matamoros. The advantage for Polk of having an independent Texas move on Matamoros was that after annexation he could be seen to be merely defending Texas in an action already begun. Thus the "responsibility for the war would not appear to rest with the United States. That war would enable Polk to accomplish one of the 'great measures' of his administration, the acquisition of California."[80] Price's source for the account of this intrigue was Anson Jones' *Memoranda and Official Correspondence Relating to the Republic of Texas*. This account by the last president of Texas was published posthumously in 1859. Price says of the general neglect in historical writing of Jones' *Memoranda:*

This account of President Polk's attempt to "annex a war," as told by the President of Texas, has been available to historians for over a century. If it had been accepted as an authentic and valid account, the interpretations in American histories of the origins of the war with Mexico would have been significantly different; to portray Polk as being basically intent upon a peaceable solution of the financial claims and the boundary question would have been impossible. But the report on these events by President Jones has either been ignored or denied and rejected in its essential points by all but a few American historians.[81]

As to the question of the southern border claimed by Texas, Price writes that "the difficulty which historians have had in treating the Rio Grande border claim is very easily explained: it is impossible to make Polk's military and diplomatic moves in relation to Mexico appear to have a just and reasonable and 'peaceable' character unless some case can be made for the American claim to the Rio Grande border; and it is impossible to make even a shadow of a case."[82]

The positions taken by Merk and Price, namely that it was not Mexico that provoked war—despite the assertions of Justin Smith— are given basic support by a book written in the seventies that made use of sources which had hitherto been untapped. Gene M. Brack's *Mexico Views Manifest Destiny, 1821–1846* examines Mexican newspapers and the private correspondence of prominent Mexicans to trace attitudes in Mexico toward the United States from the beginning of independence to the outbreak of the war with the United States. The reader can follow the change of attitudes in Mexico toward its neighbor to the north through sources that give a remarkable sense of immediacy. News-papers and letters, which at one point reflect a friendly or at least neutral attitude, become increasingly critical as Mexico becomes more and more aware of racist and expansionist attitudes and policies in the United States. Finally, one hears the voice of despair as Mexicans recognize that they must either give up great amounts of territory or face a war that they are not prepared to fight.

Parallel to Brack's presentation of the Mexican view from the street as the Mexican nation was hurried toward war is Robert W. Johannsen's *To the Halls of the Montezumas,* which gives the American popular response to the war. One discovers that Manifest Destiny was not just a phrase used by expansionist statesmen such as Polk. It was a national mystique, a positive delirium. The reader of this book discovers that a war, now dim in the popular memory, was once greeted by outbursts of ecstasy by the American people. Johannsen, following a technique similar to that of Brack's, had recourse to newspaper accounts and to private correspondence as he analyzed the passionate response to a war which now is looked upon sourly by most of the Americans who think about it at all. The 1840s in the United States, it appears, constituted a period of an almost touching naiveté. Belief in the republican form of government was intense and evangelistic. There was a missionary as-pect to the ardor that Americans brought to their belief in democracy. Such ardor, of course, can be not only affecting, but also be danger-ous—as it proved to be to the southern neighbor. "By identifying the conflict with republican principles," Johannsen notes, "the war's supporters gave it an idealistic thrust."[83] As against America's self idealization in this period was its thorough denigration of Mexico as a sham democracy, a stronghold of Roman Catholic superstition, and the dwelling place of a racially inferior people, thus a nation deserving to be conquered by a superior country which could serve as a model. *To the Halls of the Montezumas* is highly readable and is a significant study of American nationalism.

The summary above of the American historiography of the Mexican-American War is designed to provide another perspective against which the Mexican reaction to that war can be measured. That reaction is gauged in this volume by selections from Mexican writers who have dealt with the war. The selections range from the work of writers who were contemporary with the war, including essays for and against the Treaty of Guadalupe Hidalgo, to an essay by a representative of the Mexican positivists, and the writings of contemporary Mexicans dealing with the war. All of the selections that have been chosen and translated for this volume are the work of important Mexican writers who have demonstrated keenness of perception and power of expression in dealing with the great Mexican trauma.

NOTES

1. Epigraph to Rafael Muñoz, *Antonio López de Santa Anna.*
2. Fehrenbach, *Fire and Blood,* 373.
3. Valades, *Santa Anna y la Guerra de Texas,* 202.
4. Santa Anna, *Las Guerras de Mexico con Tejas y Los Estados Unidos* 29:26–29.
5. Zorilla, *Historia de las Relaciones Entre Mexico y Los Estados Unidos,* 108.
6. Muñoz, *Antonio López de Santa Anna,* 118.
7. Ibid., 129.
8. Fuentes Mares, *Santa Anna,* 156.
9. Fehrenbach, *Fire and Blood,* 400.
10. Quoted in Ralph Roeder, *Juarez and His Mexico* (New York, 1947) 1:74.
11. Hale, *Mexican Liberalism in the Age of Mora,* 15.
12. Ibid., 214.

13. Interview with Miguel León Portilla, Mexican historian and anthropologist, June 5, 1969.

14. Chaney, Jr., "The Mexican-United States War," 91.

15. Sierra, *Evolución Política del Pueblo Mexicano*, 270–73.

16. Chaney, "The Mexican-United States War," 92.

17. Ibid., 186–210.

18. Brack, *Mexico Views Manifest Destiny*, 31.

19. Ibid., 57.

20. Ibid., 104–5.

21. Carreño, *Mexico y Los Estados Unidos de America*, 101.

22. Brack, *Mexico Views Manifest Destiny*, 135. Brack quotes Shannon.

23. Fehrenbach, *Fire and Blood*, 392.

24. Merk, *The Monroe Doctrine and American Expansion*, 27.

25. Sanchez, *Viaje a Tejas*, 29.

26. Zorilla, *Historia de las Relaciones entre Mexico y los Estados Unidos*, 96–97.

27. Howren, "Causes and Origin," 395.

28. Roa Bárcena, *Biografía de D. José Joaquín Pesado*, 32–33.

29. Price, *Origins of the War With Mexico*, 36.

30. Merk, *The Monroe Doctrine and American Expansion*, 105.

31. Ibid., 288.

32. Chaney, "The Mexican-United States War," 182–84.

33. Tamayo, "Lo Que Perdimos," 36.

34. Ibid., 37.

35. Ibid.

36. Luis González, "El Parentesis de Santa Anna," 93.

37. Ramírez, *Mexico During the War*, 34.

38. Ibid., 42.

39. Ibid., 121.

40. Ibid.

41. Ibid., 140–41.

42. Sierra, *Evolución Política*, 239–40.

43. Ibid., 364.

44. Carreño, *La Diplomacia Extraordinaria*, vol. 1, 227–41.

45. Smith, *The War With Mexico*, vol. 2, 311.

46. Fehrenbach, *Fire and Blood*, 377.

47. Zorilla, *Historia de las Relaciones*, 98.

48. Sierra, *Political Evolution of the Mexican People*, 231–32.

49. Interview with Daniel Cosío Villegas, June 6, 1969.

50. Fuentes Mares, *Poinsett*, 88.

51. Zorilla, *Historia de las Relaciones,* 183.
52. Interview with Daniel Cosío Villegas, June 6, 1969.
53. Caso, *El Problema de Mexico,* 86–87.
54. Paz, *The Labyrinth of Solitude,* 22–24.
55. Ibid., 121.
56. Brack, *Mexico Views Manifest Destiny,* 76.
57. Quoted in Brack, *Mexico Views Manifest Destiny,* 96.
58. Tornel, "Tejas y Los Estados-Unidos de America." In Castañeda, *Mexican Side of the Texas Revolution,* 296.
59. Brack, *Mexico Views Manifest Destiny,* 181.
60. Johannsen, *To the Halls of the Montezumas,* chap. 9.
61. Smith, *The War with Mexico,* vol. 2, 310.
62. Price, *Origins of the War with Mexico,* 18.
63. Altamirano, *Historia y Política de Mexico,* 53–55.
64. Cosío Villegas, *American Extremes,* 38.
65. Paz, *The Labyrinth of Solitude,* 124–25.
66. Bancroft, *History of Mexico V,* 167.
67. Ibid., 166.
68. Bancroft, *North Mexican States and Texas,* vol. 2, 159–60.
69. Reeves, *American Diplomacy,* 189.
70. Rives, *The United States and Mexico,* 2 vols.
71. Garrison, *Texas: A Contest of Civilizations.*
72. Smith, *The War with Mexico,* vol. 2, 322.
73. Price, *Origins of the War with Mexico,* 156.
74. Ibid., 117, 103.
75. Vázquez, *Mexicanos y Norteamericanos,* 10.
76. DeVoto, *The Year of Decision 1846,* 189.
77. Ibid., 208–14.
78. Ibid., 9–10.
79. Merk, *The Monroe Doctrine,* 289.
80. Price, *Origins of the War with Mexico,* 47.
81. Ibid., 115.
82. Ibid., 156–57.
83. Johannsen, *To the Halls of the Montezumas,* 21.

MARIANO OTERO

One of the most clearly formulated and at the same time most devastating reactions to the war was recorded in a pamphlet written by the young intellectual and statesman, Mariano Otero. The authorship of *Considerations Relating to the Political and Social Situation of the Mexican Republic in the Year 1847* was officially attributed to "Various Mexicans," but internal and external evidence has established Mariano Otero as the true author. At the time the pamphlet was written, Otero was minister of external and internal relations, and it would have been highly impolitic for him to have put his name to the document, considering the pessimistic analysis he gave of conditions prevailing in Mexico. *Considerations* was published not only in pamphlet form, but appeared serially in the widely read newspaper *El Monitor Republicano.*

A meteoric figure in Mexican politics and letters, Mariano Otero, born in Guadalajara in 1817, lived a short but productive life. When he died at the age of thirty-three, he had already achieved a prominent position in the public and intellectual life of his country. Otero shared with his fellow Mexican liberals of the period the dilemmas that stemmed from being at cross purposes with a nation which, though nominally independent, was still responding with the conditioned reflexes of Spanish colonial rule. As a product of the enlightenment as it made itself felt in Mexico, Otero was a moderate liberal whose rationalism derived from the French, British, and North American political and social thinkers whose books were much disapproved of by the powerful Mexican Catholic Church, which still dominated education in the country. As was true for most of the Mexican liberals, there was for Otero a natural alliance between romantic literature and liberal politics. He read Chateaubriand, Lord Byron, and Victor Hugo, as well as the Swiss political theorists Benjamin Constant, for antimonarchist views,

and Sismonde de Sismondi for federalist ideas. Alexis de Tocqueville
warned him about the continuance of feudalism into the age of the
industrial revolution and gave him his first ideas about the United
States. Later he would read the Americans themselves: Franklin,
Adams, Jefferson, and Hamilton. It was Jefferson who encouraged him
in his belief that it was the small property owner who would be the
bulwark of democracy. The contemporary Mexicans who were most
influential upon Otero were Mora and Zavala.

The field of most of Otero's political activity was in the Mexican
Congress, although he served for a time in the cabinet of President
Herrera as secretary of the interior and of foreign relations. He was to
be granted only eight active years, 1842 to 1850. When, with the
occupation of Mexico City by American forces, Congress reconvened
in Queretaro in 1848, Otero was one of the four deputies who voted for
a continuation of the war. He felt that once territory was ceded, the
United States would become insatiable and demand from Mexico more
and more of her land. Otero was aware of the Whig and New England
opposition to the war, and he hoped that if the Mexican forces could
manage to remain in the field the country could eventually get better
terms. He favored guerrilla operations.

For many years, the writings of Mariano Otero lay scattered about as
individual articles, essays, and pamphlets. They were collected and
published in 1967 by Jesus Reyes Heroles in the two-volume *Mariano
Otero Obras* (Mexico, D.F., Editorial Porrua). After Otero was elected
as a deputy to Congress in 1842, he wrote a series of articles on
legislation and on political economics for *El Siglo XIX*. During this
period he also published his *Essay on the Real State of the Social and
Political Issues Which are Confronting the Mexican Republic*. This work
presents an analysis of Mexican society, of the nature of property in
Mexico, of the social classes, and of their relations to each other and to
the state. In view of the fact that Otero was living in the very midst of all
the matters that he was dealing with, one is the more impressed that he
had been able to produce such a detached and farsighted analysis. He
saw the approach of war with the United States and urged national unity
upon his country.

How far the country failed to achieve this unity is treated with a restrained bitterness in Otero's *Considerations Relating to the Political and Social Situation of the Mexican Republic in the Year 1847,* which has become a classic analysis of this divided country at war. Otero was the voice of Mexican liberalism of his time. Despite his undeniable patriotism, his continuing admiration for the United States was barely suppressed in this pamphlet. He noted that, unlike the Mexican armies engaged in endless civil wars, the American army of occupation paid for everything that it used and strove hard to preserve discipline and limit outrages, much to the relief and appreciation of the populace affected. When discussing the Mexican clergy, he could not forbear drawing a contrast between its absolute authoritarianism and its vast landholdings and, on the other hand, the toleration and pluralism that characterized religion in the United States. In his assessment of the Indians of Mexico, Otero, like other liberal *criollo* gentlemen, was characteristically ambivalent. He deeply sympathized with the much exploited Indians, but he used such words as "semi-savage" and "brutalized" to describe them and thought that the only solution to their depressed condition lay in their absorption into general Mexican life.

In his pamphlet, Otero set for himself the task of explaining how it could be that a small foreign army should succeed in conquering a highly populated nation while encountering at the same time relatively little resistance. He was clearly exasperated at foreign commentary that attributed Mexico's defeat to weakness and decadence in the Mexican people themselves. How then to explain the disaster? The answer for Otero lay in the disarray which afflicted Mexican society and institutions. A nation so at odds with itself lacked the will or even the capacity to form a united front against a common enemy. To develop his argument, he analyzed "with brutal clarity"—as one American historian put it—the various social and racial groups that made up Mexican society. He also characterized, in the same vein, the administration of justice, the workings of industry and the mines, and the state of the skills and trades. The second part of the essay consists of an exploration of the attitudes and procedures of the only groups in Mexico that would seem to have had a real stake in the system: the army, the church, and the bureaucracy. In the course of this section, Otero gave his explanation as to why even these groups could not unite to repel the invasion.

The tone in this work and the uses of emphasis and de-emphasis are, to some extent, those of a polemicist. For example, in the first sentence Otero wished to establish the point that Mexican armies had offered little resistance and stated that "with the exception of the bombarding [of Veracruz], the action at Cerrogordo, and the minor encounters that it had with the Mexican troops in the immediate environs of the capital, the [American] army has not found enemies with whom to fight." To be sure, the battle of Cerrogordo was something of a rout for the Mexican army, but the battles "in the immediate environs of the capital," those of Churubusco, Molino del Rey, Chapultepec, Belen Gate, and San Cosme Gate were fiercely contested engagements with substantial casualties on both sides. The northern battle of Buena Vista was, according to several military analysts, an American victory only because Santa Anna had not realized that he had won the day and withdrew his troops under the cover of night. In the interest of his thesis, Otero apparently wished to minimize the severity of those engagements. A principal point of his conclusion was that Mexico could not resist as a nation because it was not in fact a nation, lacking, as it did, "all the elements that make for its happiness and well being" as well as lacking respect from abroad. One might wonder whether there are many countries that are commonly assumed to be nations which do in fact have "all the elements that make for . . . happiness and well being." In the main, however, Otero's pamphlet is quite convincingly argued.

Though the analysis which Otero gives us of conditions prevailing in Mexico during the Mexican-American War is certainly a pessimistic one, the voice of the reformer can be heard throughout. Had he lived, he would no doubt have played a significant role in the vitalizing of Mexican law, government, and society known as La Reforma, the era presided over by the redoubtable Benito Juárez. As it was, Otero fittingly characterized the closing of his own era. T. R. Fehrenbach aptly sums up this twilight in two sentences: "Soon after the publication of his pamphlet the brilliant young statesman died of cholera. His death marked the end of an era, a custodianship of the *criollos* that had failed."

Considerations Relating to the Political and Social Situation of the Mexican Republic in the Year 1847

AUTHOR'S PREFACE

The fact that a foreign army of ten or twelve thousand men should have penetrated from Veracruz to the very capital of the republic; the fact that, with the exception of the bombarding of that port, the action at Cerrogordo, and the minor encounters that it had with Mexican troops in the immediate environs of the capital, this army has not found enemies with whom to fight—while it has swept across three of the most important and populous states of the Mexican federation, states with more than two million inhabitants—these facts assume such proportions that they cannot but give rise to the most serious reflections.

Petty-minded men, those who judge events solely on the occurrences themselves, usually fall into serious error. For this reason it is not strange that, as we have already seen in some foreign journals, the Mexican people have been characterized *as an effeminate people, a degenerate race that does not know how to govern or to defend itself.*

Translated from Mariano Otero, "Consideraciones Sobre la Situación Política y Social de la República Mexicana en el Año 1847 (Diciembre de 1847)," *Obras*, Vol. I, ed. Jesus Reyes Heroles, Mexico, D.F.: Editorial Porrua, S.A., 1967, pp. 95–137.

But the man of thought, the man who is not content to accept the superficial appearance of things but searches for their underlying causes, will readily find in Mexico the real reasons for which these people, far from taking an active part in the campaign, have remained cold spectators of the fray. Once these reasons are perceived, only the blindest prejudice would contend that the situation is due to special defects in the Mexican race rather than to the inevitable results of definite and determined causes. The object that we propose in this exposition is to analyze with the greatest possible clarity those heterogeneous elements with their characteristic defects that make up the society of the Mexican republic. Beyond a doubt, this method is the best way to demonstrate the true and only causes that have led to the decadence and prostration in which the republic now finds itself. In the course of such a demonstration, we hope to rectify those errors that we hear from the mouths of even enlightened people, errors that attribute as special to the Mexican people defects which are in fact common to the entire human race.

If, on the one hand, ordinary people throughout the world are not given to thought and therefore are not inclined to be generous to the unfortunate, on the other hand, people who consider themselves to be above the commonality and thus presume to have their own opinions must recognize that true judgment can only be arrived at through analysis and impartial thought. Such men cannot consider the Mexican republic in its present sad situation to be composed of a people who suffer from defective origins through the effeminacy or degradation of their race but rather of a people who have been the victims of a defective education and a worse organization. From this point of view, we believe that Mexico, far from deserving the deprecation and mockery of the other nations, merits, if not the assistance which as a nation it might hope for from the other nations of the world in the name of universal justice, at least the sympathy which any good heart should feel toward a nation that sustains a just cause and which, after great sacrifices, not so much succumbs to the greater material force levied against it as falls victim to the immobility which results from a society that is divided by the most contrary and opposing interests.

We will not exhaust ourselves in useless protestations. Such is not our style, and in any case a great outpouring of words would do nothing toward vindicating the Mexican republic. Instead, let a simple account of the component parts that make up the nation suffice to explain its present situation.

PART ONE

I. Population

Although the data that we have for the population of the republic are very inexact, with some writers putting the figure at only a little more than six million inhabitants and others maintaining that there are more than nine, we might calculate the population as reaching seven million, of whom, according to the least exaggerated reports, four million are Indians and three million Europeans, mixed, for the most part, with the indigenous strain.

II. Indians

The Indians are spread throughout the entire territory of the republic, grouped in small communities and forming really a family apart from the white and mixed races. The miserable way of life of the Indians today differs little or not at all from what it was when they were subjects of the great emperor Montezuma. The only difference that can be noticed between the Indians of that time and those of today is the abolishment of idolatry with its barbarous sacrifices of human blood, for today's Indians have been taught to worship God *in their own manner,* and to hope for blessings in the life hereafter, something which, we might well suppose, they believe in firmly, being completely persuaded that there is nothing good to be hoped for in this vale of tears. Neither in the time of the viceroys nor later of the independence has there been adopted an adequate system of education for this race, an education which would on the one hand improve the condition of the individual, raising him from the brutalized state in which he exists, and on the other hand make him useful to society. Neither early nor late have these people been taught anything more than to fear God, the priest, and the mayor, and the ignorance in which they live is such that perhaps three-quarters of the Indians have not yet received the news of the attainment of national independence. That they remain in this error is all the more credible in view of the fact that in many places they are still charged tribute for the king of Spain in the same spirit in which they are asked for donations for the ransoming of captives and for the holy places of Jerusalem.

The work that they are generally put to is cultivating the earth for a small daily stipend, and since this pay is not always sufficient to cover the costs of their sad existence, they often ask the owner of the hacienda on which they work for wages in advance to be paid back by their labor, thus obliging them to stay put until they have paid their debt. In this way, and since the stipend they earn hardly suffices to maintain life, one can be sure that from the moment in which an Indian makes this kind of contract the owner is due to lose the sum which he has lent, but the Indian will remain sold to the owner of the hacienda and in effect will belong to him. The result of this situation is that, although contrary to express laws, there exists in many places in the republic Indian slavery.

In addition, there is a system which *so happily* prevails among the Mexican clergy by which, while the so-called higher clergy and bishops live opulently in the capital, the parish priests find that their very survival depends upon the income from their parish *rights*. For this reason, these representatives of the God of goodness and mercy make it a point not to allow any Indian to be born, to marry, or to die with impunity, that is, without paying the *established rights*. In this way, the parish priests take their cut from the scant resources that the Indians count on for their livelihood.

Those Indians who live close to the great population centers go to them to sell vegetables, poultry, firewood, coal, and other such goods which fetch them a small price, but even this paltry sum is further reduced by the cut taken at the city gate by collectors who, in the name of the nation, commit against these people the most infamous and repugnant extortions.

To put the finishing touch on this canvas, which faithfully portrays the sadness of Indian life, we need but add that the only active part that the Indians take in the public life of the country is to serve as soldiers in the army, a role which is forced upon them. And in this capacity, rather than serving their country, they act as instruments for the aggrandizement of their officers, who in times of peace give them little bread but a big stick (*poco pan y mucho palo*) and in war often abandon them at the moment of danger. For all these reasons, it is easy to understand why this important sector of the population has no interest in preserving an order of things of which it is the victim. Certainly the Indians have watched the entrance of the North American army with the same indifference with which they watched in the past the Spanish armies taking dominion of the country, and with the same calm with which, after the independence, they have watched the comings and goings of our troops engaged in our continual revolutions. Without any further necessities than those demanded by their semi-savage level of existence, without relationships or pleasures of any kind which might arise out of a contact with society, with neither interests nor affections that tie them to it, and with the confidence that their abject condition could not be worsened, they look upon all that might happen with the most apathetic indifference.

III. The White and Mixed Races

We shall now proceed to examine the 3 million inhabitants of European or mixed descent who comprise the populations of the capitals and other cities and towns of importance in the republic. Of this number, we can deduct 1.8 million as women, children, and old people, a figure which is in no way exaggerated. This leaves us over 1.2 million useful men, or, more precisely, men capable of being so, because in fact they are not, as we shall proceed to demonstrate.

With the exception of about three hundred thousand men, the top figure for those employed in agriculture, industry, mining, business, and certain trades and offices, the nine hundred thousand remaining account for the unproductive classes, such as the clergy with all of its subordinates and dependents, the military, the bureaucracy, lawyers, doctors, and finally that multitude of loafers and vagabonds that abounds in the main cities of the republic.

From this unexaggerated estimate, we might judge of the sad situation that afflicts that quarter of the population which works and produces and therefore must necessarily support the other three quarters. What an enormous disproportion! Here is the origin of the backwardness and discouragement encumbering all sources of the national wealth. Here is sufficient cause for the destruction of not only the nascent Mexican republic. It would suffice to destroy the most flourishing nation on earth!

IV. Commerce
[Editor's Summary]*

Because of a traditional prejudice against commerce, Mexico has allowed its import business to fall into the hands of foreigners. And because of the country's "monastic education," Mexicans themselves have no interest whatever in business except to spend whatever money they can get their hands on. Since Mexico has no goods to exchange for European imports, it has to purchase them with hard money. The fiscal system is thoroughly antiquated. For example, foreign merchants are harassed with all kinds of petty requirements. This being the case, they either refrain from doing business with Mexico, with a consequent loss of customs duties, or they bribe customs officials not to exact these duties—with the same result. Despite a clamor for a reform of the system, nothing in fact is being done.

V. Agriculture
[Editor's Summary]

Because three quarters of the country's lands belong to religious corporations, those who manage and work these lands feel no incentive to improve methods, feeling themselves to be, in fact, only renters. Farmers with only a small capital—therefore most of them—are victimized by the unpredictable variations of good and bad harvests. They do not have enough money to hold out in a good year, thus flooding the market and lowering prices. Because the soil is so rich, farmers feel that with little effort they can produce a bumper crop—more than is needed to

---

*The editor's summaries here and in the following pages indicate sections where the editor has chosen to summarize rather than to translate verbatim.

support a stabilized state of underpopulation. They are therefore content to produce the minimum and feel no need for advanced methods. Farmers are also at the mercy of the antiquated state fiscal system and can sometimes lose the value of an entire crop through failure to comply with some petty government regulation having to do with transporting foods to market. On top of other impositions, farmers have the added burden of the church tithe which, though not compulsory, is expected from men of "conscience." If they do not pay, they may be labeled in public as heretics. There are cases in which a priest has denied the last rites to a dying man until he has paid up the arrears of his tithes.

VI. Administration of Justice
[*Editor's Summary*]

The maladministration of justice particularly affects the commercial and agricultural sectors, those elements which provide the very cement for an orderly society. Instead of a clear code of laws, Mexican legislation is a chaos from which even the honorable litigant, out of the multiple diversity of laws, can string out legal procedures eternally and can prevent judgment even on a simple point. These lengthy procedures are, of course, very costly. Sometimes they go for three generations.

New criminal offenders are thrown indiscriminately into jail with vicious, hardened criminals, and thus the prisons become schools for crime. Criminals are turned out on the public all too easily to repeat their crimes.

Because of the maladministration and costliness of judicial procedures, people seek settlements outside of court even if this means dealing with scoundrels or with the very criminals or assassins who caused the trouble in the first place.

VII. Manufacturing
[*Editor's Summary*]

In order to avoid dependency upon foreign investment, a Credit Bank (Banco de Avio) was established to aid Mexicans who wanted to build factories and to set up industries. However, this enterprise was greatly mismanaged, with large sums being withdrawn as loans but put to other than the stated uses. There was a consequent defaulting on loans with the government treasury being the loser. Industrialists have frequently used their influence to have protectionist legislation passed. When later, in 1840 and after, efforts were made by the government to ease trade restrictions so as to let in some foreign goods—the object being to use customs revenues to support the army of the north—pressures on the part of industrialists brought about changes in government and reinstated protectionist policies.

VIII. Mines

The mining industry is the only one which, in the midst of the oppression and disarray of all the classes of society, shows up brilliantly, presenting an aspect of progressive prosperity. It would appear that in this country, except for the people themselves, all nature conspires to contribute to the welfare and happiness of its inhabitants. In the mines of the republic, production in minted silver and gold and in mining paste is increasing to more than eighteen million pesos, an amount which could be doubled or perhaps tripled if it were not for the high price of mercury. Nevertheless, since the profits of this kind of industry go only to the mine owners themselves or to others engaged in mining production, the rest of society does not gain from the prosperity of this enterprise other than by receiving the benefit of the greater amount of coin in circulation. But this benefit is always a transitory one because the annual export of this coinage amounts more or less to what the mines produce, and, as we have said elsewhere, gold and silver are the only products that we have to offer in exchange for foreign goods.

IX. Skills and Trades

There is little good to be said about the standing of those Mexicans who dedicate themselves to the skills and trades. Unfortunately, there still persists among us the error inherited from the Spaniards who, with their lofty notions of chivalry and nobility, taught us to look down upon any man who follows a trade. To be a man of respectability it was necessary to be a military man, a government official, a clergyman, a lawyer, or at least a doctor. All others in society were considered to be the inferior classes, and even businessmen were looked upon with contempt, being referred to as rag dealers. As a result of such ridiculous, not to say pernicious ideas, no father of any means, however moderate, wanted, nor still does want, his sons to learn a trade. He would even be ashamed to apprentice them to a commercial house or to any other business, because the idea of *serving a master*, as the saying goes, whether in a workshop or in a store, would seem to him to be a very denigrating thing.

This concern about status reaches such a proportion that many artisans who have lived decent and honorable lives in their trades, far from teaching them to their sons, put them in a college to learn law or medicine, or, as soon as they get out of school knowing something of reading, writing, and arithmetic, try to get some influential person to prevail upon the government to bestow upon these sons a civil or military post. Such a course of action does not, in fact, entail a great deal of effort, and the good artisan, if he has succeeded in it, can feel satisfied and proud in the knowledge that his sons have gone higher than he. There are many fathers also who, before apprenticing their sons to any trade, would prefer that they had no profession at all and would abandon them to the fate of searching out their livelihood in any way that *God might give them to understand,* but without, of course, giving up their status as gentlemen—*hombres decentes*—that is to say, without working at any job that might dishonor them, because for this class of men working itself is dishonorable, and they do not think that this is true of spending their entire lives as vagabonds and swindlers.

And so it has come about that, while the republic is plagued by hundreds of generals, thousands of superintendents and officials, bureaucrats, clergymen, and doctors, one cannot find a single distinguished Mexican in any art, skill, or trade: and it is certain that, in any of the important population centers, the best architect, the most able painter, the best sculptor, the best carriage maker, the most intelligent upholsterer, the most painstaking cabinet maker, and even the best cobbler will turn out not to be a Mexican but a foreigner. This is a truth all the more sad when one considers that there is no lack of ability among the Mexicans and that they are even famous for their skills in making fine reproductions.

As a consequence, the class of artisans, which in other more fortunate countries constitutes the real core of the nation, because of its intelligence and energy is in Mexico insignificant and despicable both in terms of its numbers and of the ignorance and contempt that surround it.

X. General Observations

In view of this simple and true account of the state in which the productive classes—the smallest part of the Mexican republic—find themselves, it is easy to understand the sense of permanent malaise in which they live. And this, in turn, sufficiently explains the detachment and indifference with which these classes, on the whole, have looked upon the present war through which the republic is suffering. Say what one might, patriotism, that noble and chivalrous sentiment which in other countries moves the people and raises them to such a pitch of fervor that they would a thousand times prefer death to permitting the slightest offense against their country, this sentiment cannot exist in a country without education and in one which has been lacerated by thirty-seven years of travail and misery.

In the first place, the eleven years duration of the battle for independence amounted, for the productive classes of the country, to eleven years of blood, devastation, and ruin. It can be asserted without exaggeration that the damages sustained by these classes mounted to hundreds of millions of pesos. Once independence had been won, the proprietors, the farmers, the merchants, and, in fact, all those men who desire order because it is the only state in which they can prosper and provide for themselves a future, were pleased to think that a new era of peace was about to begin, one in whose protecting shade they would succeed in indemnifying themselves for the terrible damages which they had suffered. In this they were deceived. In the twenty-six years which have transpired since the gaining of independence, all forms of government have been tried. But because these attempts have not been real but merely verbal and because the great reforms demanded by civilization today have not been undertaken, the country has been precipitated, day by day, toward its destruction and annihilation. This state of affairs has been brought about by the combined action of the social vices that have carried over from the colonial system and those which have mounted up throughout twenty-six years of disorder.

The men who have figured in the directing of our public affairs have shown neither the proper science nor the consciousness of the great duties imposed upon them by the high posts that their ambitions have elevated them to. None of them have shown the least concern for the removal of those strong obstacles to the welfare and happiness of the nation. All of this is very natural in a country where men never ascend to power through the free vote of the citizenry but are always placed there either through intrigues on the part of one or another faction or, as is often the case, by revolutionary action on the part of the armed forces.

This system, certainly original in a republic, of presenting the people with their rulers without first consulting them and obtaining their consent, has necessarily resulted in the emergence of picked officials whose least concern is with the welfare of the people. It could not be otherwise in view of the fact that the parties, which represent this or that special interest, do not seek in their candidates independent men devoted to the general interest of the country but rather men who will adhere strictly to the special interests of the party. Accordingly, these same men in taking power feel obligated to honor their commitment to serve faithfully the party that elevated them to office.

For these reasons we have seen that some governments have decidedly protected the army, others the clergy, others the bureaucrats, and some others all three classes at once. However, there has never been a government which has put a brake on the pretensions of the privileged classes while reforming or destroying their abuses. None has dedicated itself to the protection of the industrious classes which most merit the attention of any government that would be enlightened or patriotic. For these classes there has been nothing but pompous promises which have never been fulfilled. In order to discredit the government which they have wanted to overthrow, factions in revolt have hurled charges to the effect that this government has not protected industry or commerce. Furthermore, all new governments, in the beginning, have not neglected to put forward as their first and principal concern the development of agriculture, commerce, the arts, and so forth. These offers, however, have remained strictly on paper and, far from being fulfilled, are usually superseded by some quite different contribution paid out in order to satisfy pledges made in return for support for the new revolution.

One would have to concede that such a system, practiced for twenty-six years, could only bring about the most profound disgust between the industrious classes and their governments. What bonds or sympathies could possibly exist between these classes and the various governments, considering that the latter, instead of lending them some support, have burdened them daily with more taxes of all kinds in order to satisfy the ambitions of thousands of men of the privileged classes who, with no decent title to it, have proposed to live at the expense of the nation? None, certainly. On the contrary, the industrious classes, vexed and ridiculed in so many ways, have become accustomed, and with reason, to considering their governments as nothing but the most declared enemies of their tranquility and well being. From the sad experiences of the past and present, these classes have, in fact, lost any remote hope for the future.

As the inevitable result of so many cruel and repeated deceptions, they are now in a state of mortal discouragement. This being the case, could anyone maintain that they should now go on to sacrifice what remains of their fortunes as well as their very lives for their country? And in defense of what? To insist upon this would be to assume that Mexicans are a people possessed of different feelings from those which characterize the peoples of the rest of the world. The time has passed, and passed forever, in which people will destroy one another as a result of the force of one man's will. It can no longer be demanded of any people, and much less of classes that have some degree of enlightenment, that they sacrifice their well-being and their lives in the defense of words that are empty of meaning, and without doubt *the national honor* is one of those vain phrases in a country where the productive man has had to live isolated from the rest of society, without being able to quietly enjoy the fruits of his labor because of the maladministration of justice.

To these definite considerations, which should certainly suffice to explain, at least to enlightened men, the apathy which has characterized most members of the industrious classes during the present war, should be added the observation that the United States army has not entered the republic in the same spirit in which armies in the past have marched through conquered countries, spreading terror and death everywhere, robbing or destroying property, violating the women, and, in short, perpetrating all kinds of crimes against the conquered populace. On the contrary, with the inevitable exceptions that occur when a foreign army surges across a country in wartime, the American army, sustaining itself on its own resources and paying good prices for whatever it needed for its subsistence, has respected private property. No peaceful Mexican has been persecuted. Everyone has been allowed to continue working freely in his trade or occupation. And finally, far from oppressing the people with heavy taxes, the American army has considerably reduced import duties in the occupied ports, and in the cities and towns of the interior, it has abolished the customs houses and tax-collecting stations which had formerly vexed and harassed all who sought their livelihoods in the mercantile trades.

In view of all this, it is clear that the property-owning and industrious classes of Mexico have not had any material interests to defend in the present war. And furthermore, in all frankness, it can be said that the sympathies of those classes must naturally have gone to whatever has brought about the destruction of that reign of disorder and pillage of which they have been the victims for so many years. Therefore, to characterize as the special crime of the Mexican race the indifference which those classes have shown in the present conflict, attributing it to cowardice, effeminacy, and the complete lack of dignity seems to us the extreme of ignorance and levity. If, for example, the industrious classes in some other country had felt themselves to be as overburdened, as longsuffering as they have been here, those foreigners would not have contented themselves with a mere show of indifference. Without doubt they would have joined the invading army in order to avenge themselves for the many wrongs received and to better their individual condition as well.

Can it be demanded of the property-owning and of the industrious Mexicans that they bring about their own ruin or even death in defense of those same abuses of which they are the victims? This would be, in our opinion, an absurdity. On the contrary, we are persuaded that if the industrious Mexicans had sacrificed themselves, with all the attendant bloodshed, in defense of the same order of things that has gone on to this day and from which they have nothing to hope but ruin and misery, they would, with complete justice, have merited the invective which has been directed at them, because they would have proved that they lack even that common sense which distinguishes men from animals.

And yet, despite all these reasons cited, the industrious classes of Mexico have, in fact, given no little proof of the extent to which they esteem the honor and good name of their country. Without mentioning here the enormous sums which, over a period of twelve years, they put forth for the war in Texas, for it is well known that during this time the various governments have used this war as their grand pretext for asking for money from everyone and paying back no one, we will limit ourselves to the present year of 1847. One can see in the periodicals for this year notices of the millions of pesos which the government has received in the form of donations, loans, extraordinary contributions, and so forth. These sacrifices are all the more meritorious when it is considered that most of those who made them did so in the knowledge that their efforts would be sterile. They had no illusions that their money would be used for the purposes for which it was given. It is a matter of public knowledge that, while the army of the enemy advances without opposition toward the capital, some of the generals, colonels, and men in high office, not to mention other infamous favorites of the government, dispute for the few resources that still come into the treasury, and, acting as though each peso would be the last that they could snatch from the government, they have rushed in to seize it with the same greed with which a gang of bandits would grab for the watch or any other object of value which the dying traveler, left stretched on the highway, had on his person.

In addition, we have witnessed the youth of Veracruz—a united band of only three or four thousand soldiers—roused to a pitch of fervor by no other considerations than their devotion to the honor of the region which gave them birth. From within the decrepit walls that surround their city, they have defied an army of twelve or thirteen thousand men and, with honor and equanimity, they have withstood a horrible bombardment, which in eighty or ninety hours of firing dropped into the plaza more than six thousand shells, causing tremendous havoc and ruin. And when these young men realized that their military leaders were engaged in talks with the enemy aimed at the surrender of the city, they angrily threw their weapons into the sea rather than allow them to fall into the hands of the conqueror.

In Mexico City, also, many families are still mourning the loss of a father, a husband, a son, or a brother who, in the engagements at Churubusco and Molina del Rey, paid with their lives for their desire to contribute personally to the defense and honor of their country—this being their only motive, because they were not attached to the regular army, nor had they received any salary for military service. To be sure, these examples have not been, throughout the republic, numerous; because here, as everywhere else, there has not been an abundant harvest of men endowed with sentiments so noble and generous that they are willing to sacrifice themselves voluntarily for the honor of all the others and with no thought of reward but that of posthumous fame.

PART TWO

In the first part of this exposition, we have undertaken to demonstrate that the Indians as well as the classes that make up the industrious and productive sectors of the republic could not have taken any more interest than in fact they have taken in the present war, and that they have even done more for the war effort than could have been expected of them, considering that the enemy has not damaged them directly in either their persons or their property.

It now remains for us to consider the three classes which are the true masters of the country: the army, the clergy, and the government bureaucracy. Since these are the only groups that have enjoyed its privileges and have decreed, according to their whims, its fate, it would seem that they should have taken on the present battle as a personal cause, being well persuaded that in any new and enlightened order of things all those abuses by which they have lived up until now would, undoubtedly, be swept away. However, in examining the particular modus of these classes among themselves, we shall see that—although they have been very potent in imposing upon the country a static condition, heading it in the direction of total ruin—they have been utterly without force when it has come to uniting against a foreign invasion, convinced though they must be that that thrust will be more fatal to them than to the rest of the country.

I. The Army

We will start with the army because this class is the most immediately responsible for the loss of national honor, for whose defense this same army has been continually maintained at a cost to the country of millions of pesos in the twenty-six years that have elapsed from the independence to the present.

We have said elsewhere that the soldiers, in general, are Indians, forcibly made to serve, and we have also observed that these Indians have little or no conception of nationality, and no interest whatever in maintaining an order of things in which they figure only as beasts of burden. Nevertheless, it must be truthfully said that as soldiers they are really quite good, because—aside from not being cowards—they have great endurance in the campaign. They have shown that they can cross hundreds of leagues over bad roads, barefoot, badly clothed and worse fed, and this without complaining or committing any notable act of insubordination. Without doubt, if these same Indians were led by officers with good training and some sensibility, they would be as good as the soldiers of any other country. The trouble, therefore, with the Mexican army is not with the soldiers but with the officers, who, with a few and honorable exceptions, are assuredly the most ignorant and demoralized on earth. Nor could it be otherwise, when the attainment of military rank among us has nothing to do with competence or valor but rather with appointments based on the most contemptible favoritism.

From the time in which we gained our independence, a multitude of obscure and ignorant men have been presenting themselves to the new government, alleging the important services and immense sacrifices that they are supposed to have made in defense of the national cause, and asking to be given, in recompense for these services, high military posts—many of them expecting to be made generals, while the more modest among them would settle for the rank of colonel. It is true that many of these absurd claims were thrown out, but there were many that were acted upon, and in this way men were brought into the army who had had no previous experience of military service and were absolutely ignorant of the art of war and therefore worthless in terms of the careers they were presumed to be following. Later, the abuse of handing out military posts reached such a point of scandal that any Mexican who would consent to remain a peasant would seem to be positively admirable, so easy had it become for anyone who wanted a military post to get one.

Above all, during twenty years of this kind of thing, the favorite occupation of the army has been, with but a few intervals, the making of revolution. Consequently, the disorder within the military has reached its culmination. Every new government, elevated to power through a military revolt—as they all have been—has felt obliged to immediately reward that part of the army which installed it, and thus preferments are awarded to all the leaders and officers of that faction. On the other hand, the government that was about to fall had given new posts to the other part of the army that had remained faithful to it before its fall. These last-minute promotions have always been recognized by the new government in order to keep everybody happy. In this way, each revolution has resulted in a swelling of the officer corps and at the same time in a new wave of promotions for those officers already in grade. In the light of this, it should not appear at all strange that those farces known as *pronunciamientos* should recur so frequently, because it is clear that by this route a former second lieutenant, for example, who has taken part in six consecutive revolutions, will undoubtedly have made it to the rank of general.

And so it has come to pass, as we have said before, that military rank has not been the reward for intelligence, for valor, or for honorable and decent deportment, but rather the prize for vices expressly condemned in the military code as well as in all human laws. Here we find, in effect, that military posts are awarded to the base flatterer, the vile informer, and to many types of men who have rendered services even more repugnant and contemptible. There have been many cases in which men who are simply peasants have been given the rank of colonel. Officers have been promoted who, contrary to their oath of obedience to their government, have deserted their flag to support the other one of revolution, with the object, perhaps, of concealing the disappearance of the payroll for their troops, and whose crime, with the triumph of the revolution, not only will be forgotten but will be rewarded. Thus the very ideas of morality, subordination, and discipline have disappeared. And without these, any army is nothing but a fearful uproar.

As a consequence of so much disorder and also of the facile appointments and promotion of officers, it is not surprising that one can hardly find, although there are hundreds of generals, thousands of colonels, lieutenant colonels, commanders, and so forth, a single general in whom one would confide the command of a small division, because many of them do not even know the rudiments of the art of war, and they would be in a dilemma should they be put in charge of a company on patrol. Also, one could count on the fingers of the hand the number of colonels in whom one could trust the command of a single regiment in combat, and finally, as for junior officers, there are very few good ones because, along with their other defects, they are given to insubordination, which makes them useless for any sort of service.

One is forced to conclude that such an army, when faced with its first national war against a foreign army that is at least tolerably well organized, is bound to play the same ridiculous role that was played by the Pope's soldiers before the armies of Napoleon.

It is not in the least difficult to count the number of defeats which our army has suffered in the present war. One has only to know beforehand how many engagements it has had with the enemy, because it has so happened that each battle has been a defeat, with some of the skirmishes lasting only a few minutes. But, however disgraced our military has been at arms, it has not been sparing in giving out proclamations, manifestos, and explanations to the public, because, on the "literary" side, our army surely has no equal in the world. There are generals who have felt called upon to issue a proclamation upon taking charge of their troops. This has been followed by another proclamation each time they have passed through a city or town en route. They even make proclamations, upon getting out of bed in the morning, to their valiant comrades in arms. Colonels who have abandoned their troops on the field of battle have not, on that account, lost their positions, because, once having delivered a manifesto to the public in defense of their conduct, all is then set to rights for them. And finally, even junior officers who have been accused by their commanders of having deserted their standards at the moment of action have also directed themselves to the public, denying the charges or begging the people to suspend judgment until all the facts are in, facts which they themselves will publish to prove that their honor stands pure and without blemish. All these suspended judgments have remained, of course, in just such a state for many years and will probably remain so until the end of time.

In the midst of all this uproar and disorder, there still can be found men of the Mexican army who have all the training and integrity that is indispensable to the noble profession of arms. But some of these have retired, disgusted by this very disorder which has been introduced into the army, or because they could not tolerate seeing themselves out-ranked by men with no more right to their positions than their having obtained, without merit, the favor of the government. The others who have continued in the service have daily found new reasons for being disgusted with their profession and have only stayed on because they have had no other means of supporting themselves.

In effect, if one examines it, there is no real motivation for the intelligent and honorable officer who wants faithfully to fulfill his duties. In the first place, positions of command are never given to the officer who is more knowledgeable or honorable but rather to the one who best knows the art of adulating the government in order to gain its confidence. For this reason, the officer who is not a flatterer or revolutionary, even though he has been in a hundred battles and conducted himself well, cannot advance in his career. The officer who does not flatter forfeits both favor and his current pay and is obliged to sell his property at four or five percent of what he paid for it, as a result of the discredit in which, because of all this disorder, the total national debt has fallen. Furthermore, in the report which each general forwards concerning a military action, the officer who stood firm in the face of danger, fulfilling his duty, fares no better, in terms of recommendations, than does the coward who fled during the action to hide behind the military equipment several leagues away from the field of battle.

This total lack of truth and justice naturally discourages all good officers, or perhaps converts them into bad ones because in the present scheme of things even the basic motives for human action are missing: the hope of reward and the fear of punishment.

Furthermore, in all well-organized societies an officer knows that should he die in battle his family, at least, will be taken care of by the government, and if he should be incapacitated he can count on a soldier's home where he can pass the rest of his life comfortably and decently. In Mexico these things do not obtain. Though a veterans' institution and a pension fund for military widows exist in name, any incapacitated veteran can be sure that he will perish, at the end, in utter poverty, after having begged for his subsistence from public charity. If, on the other hand, he is killed in action, his family will without doubt be the victims of misery or of the prostitution which is its consequence, and his cadaver will serve as meat for the birds and animals because frequently, if not always, it is allowed to remain stretched out on the field of battle without anyone taking the trouble to bury it.

In view of all this, it is easy to understand that an army, the majority of whose officers are ignorant and corrupt, an army which gives no stimulus to the well-trained and honorable officer to fulfill his duty, will gather unto itself all those elements that will ruin the country which tolerates them and none of the elements that will empower it to defend the country from a foreign invasion. We believe, therefore, that the shame with which the army has covered itself in the present conflict cannot justly be attributed to special defects in the Mexican race, because it is certain that any army in the world, mounted upon the same base of disorder and demoralization, would have shown the same results. A proof of this truth can be seen in the pains that are taken everywhere to maintain the morality and discipline of armies and also in the insistence upon rigorous punishment for the slightest infraction, because it is axiomatic that "without discipline there is no army."

In spite of all this, we have been able to distinguish, in the various encounters that our troops have had with the invader, the few good leaders and officers whom we have had in the army, because some have been left behind, dead on the field of battle, others have been wounded, and others have been taken prisoner because they stood firm where their duty bade them stand, and they have, therefore, received from the very enemy himself all the considerations that are due to the honorable and valiant officer who succumbs after having loyally fulfilled his duties.

II. The Clergy

Let us go on now to examine the situation of the clergy, in whose hands resides the largest portion of the property of the republic—a fact which accounts for the great and baneful influence the clergy has exercised upon society. In view of this vast ownership, it would seem only natural that the clergy would ardently defend the nation or, more precisely, these same properties, being persuaded that any other even half-enlightened government that establishes itself in the country must necessarily despoil it of all these immense holdings and reduce it to the simple exercise of its purely spiritual mission upon earth. The clergy should be the more determined to resist with all its capacities the advance of the enemy forces because this army represents a people for which the absolute toleration of various religions forms the very basis of its social system. This being so, it is evident that should Mexico succumb in the fight the clergy here would not only have to fear the loss of its material interests but also of that sole and absolute power which it has exercised without opposition in a country in which no other religion but theirs is tolerated.

In view of all this, the blind self-centeredness which the clergy has shown in a cause that one would have thought to have been its very own would seem inexplicable were it not for two considerations. The first of these is the very ignorance of the individuals involved, by which they have shown themselves to be incapable of comprehending the difficult times in which they are living, being unable to foresee the dire consequences which lie in store for them as a result of the stupidity and egotism of their present conduct. Secondly, and more importantly, one must consider the inequality that exists within this privileged class itself, by which a small minority lives surrounded by the greatest abundance while the rest are left with hardly enough to sustain themselves in a decent manner. One has only to survey the disproportion that exists among the various groups making up the clergy in order to substantiate the exactness of these observations.

The Mexican clergy consists of bishops and canons, curates and vicars, private clerics or chaplains, and members of religious orders— of both sexes. The bishops and canons, who make up what is known as the high clergy, are supported by tithes. Although the income from this source has been reduced a good deal since the workers have been relieved of the obligation to pay them, it is still a considerable sum. It is estimated from informed sources that the income of the archbishop of Mexico has now reached the amount of fifty thousand pesos annually and that the salary of the poorest bishop in the republic is no less than ten thousand. Since that part of the income from tithes which is set apart for the archbishop and bishops amounts to less than half of the total, one can readily estimate that what remains for the canons and capitulars is no inconsiderable sum.

In the great cities such as Mexico City, Puebla, Guadalajara, Queré-taro, Orizaba, and others, there is a multitude of clergy who are quite useless, and in these same cities the bishops and canons lead comfort-able and even sumptuous lives, remote from all inconveniences and enjoying all the pleasures that riches can provide. In contrast, those who really give a service to religion, the curates and vicars, with rare excep-tions, must endure lives overburdened with work and destitute, some-times to the point of sheer misery.

[At this juncture, in order to amplify his discussion of the role of the parish priests, Otero includes a lengthy quotation, summarized below, from "Mexico and Its Revolutions" by Jose-María Luis Mora, an intellectual leader and forerunner among the liberals. Though Mora lived during the first half of the nineteenth century, the influence of his work was not really felt until the succeeding era of the Reform.]

The parish priests suffer all kinds of privations, being constantly on call and having to travel long distances to say mass and dispense the sacraments in remote places. Sunday, the day of rest for all others, is their heaviest day. Yet for all this travail they receive only the donations that might be forthcoming from the faithful for baptisms, weddings, funerals, and so forth. As observance of these sacraments is on the decline, so too is the livelihood of the poor parish priests.

The private clergy are those who are not attached to any particular ecclesiastical office. They are known as chaplains because they are supported, or are supposed to be supported, by funds established through private donations called chaplaincies. The total value of these foundations throughout the republic is very considerable, because to them goes the principal share of all religious donations, which, according to the lowest estimate, exceeded eighty million pesos in the year 1804. Nevertheless, the distribution of these funds is done in a very niggardly manner, so that each chaplaincy amounts to only three thousand pesos, the revenue from which—a scant hundred and fifty pesos a year—is not enough to decently support a clergyman in Mexico City. It would, in fact, not even provide enough for basic food. The awarding of these chaplaincies falls to the archbishop and to the bishops in their respective dioceses. This function is subject to much abuse because the awards are distributed to favorites in such a way that some clerics, and even non-clerics, enjoy the revenues from four, six, or more chaplaincies, while others get nothing at all. These last, who make up the greatest number, go through life suffering great privations, and they can only make up for what they lack through alms given privately in return for masses said toward the attaining of some pious goal. But such alms grow scarcer by the day because of the general poverty as well as for reasons that go beyond the scope of this essay.

PART THREE

Bureaucrats

As for the bureaucrats, their history is very similar to that of the military. Amidst the perpetual disorder and dissolution of our governments, nevertheless, public jobs continue to be handed out in great profusion—perhaps to truckle to this or that personage who has made a recommendation or maybe to reward the slightest service given to one of the people in government. Seldom, or very rarely, is there an effort to establish the honesty or capacity of the person being considered for a job, but what is certainly taken into account is whether the recommender has some degree of influence. Once this is established, the applicant is, of course, given a position—without further inquiry. There are also many cases of important jobs being obtained through the donation of money to those who have access to the government and enjoy its favor.

The result of this facile manner of handing out jobs is that there are many people in public employment who cannot handle the grammar of their own language or do simple arithmetic, nor can they write at even a medium level of proficiency. As for morality, the examples are as many as they are scandalous of employees who have made tremendous fortunes, abusing the confidence which the government has so ineptly reposed in them. Corruption of this kind has become so well established and generally accepted—even in society—that nobody is scandalized to see a public employee who earns an annual salary of between two or three thousand pesos buy himself haciendas, furnish his townhouse with the most exquisite and costly appointments, and generally maintain his family at an extravagant level of luxury. None of this attracts any attention because such cases are innumerable, and the public has become accustomed to seeing that all employees—with very few exceptions—who have any access to public funds spend three or four times more than they earn.

Despite this scandalous corruption and ineptitude on the part of most bureaucrats, the government, even if it wants to, is powerless to remedy the situation. According to the laws of the Republic, the employee who is given a government office acquires in the act of being hired a *property*, which nobody, not even the government itself, can deprive him of without establishing just cause. The posing of this condition, given the way justice is administered in the country, is tantamount to declaring that the bureaucrats can do anything they want, secure in the knowledge that nothing will dislodge them from their jobs.

There have been, indeed, some cases in which employees have been forcibly dismissed from office; but these dismissals have only been temporary. In a short time their jobs have been restored to them, such being the weakness which characterizes all of our governments. Moreover, a dismissed employee, no matter how justified the government might have been in discharging him, is always well received by the opposite party, whose newspapers immediately begin a clamor against the *horrible attempt* on the part of the government to attack the employee's *property* without respect for due process of law. The government accused of taking such an action is branded as arbitrary, despotic, and tyrannical, and the most gross epithets are used against it, even to the point of the most infamous calumnies—all with the object of discrediting the government and making it appear to be criminal, when it might in fact be simply attempting to rigorously enforce justice. And since the government always represents the weakest part of society and will be sure to include among its members individuals who have good reason to fear the attacks of the press, this government will decide that the only way to quiet the insufferable uproar is to restore the aggrieved employee to office and nevermore even to think of firing him, even if he later gives the same or even more compelling reasons for doing so.

From the above it would seem that the best office one could aspire to in Mexico would be that of government employee, and in effect these employees would have veritable sinecures if it were not for the fact that their very excess in number jeopardizes their situation as a group. In those countries that boast some kind of order, the number of employees hired corresponds to the number needed for specific offices; but in Mexico, where everything tends to go in reverse, the offices are created to accommodate the employees. The abuse in handing out jobs has been such that above and beyond the greater number of them needed for each office because of the complicated system of workloads, there are many job slots that cost the treasury four or five salaries, because while only one worker is actually occupying a slot there might well be three or four more who have been declared to be on leave or retired—on full pay. In this way special favorites of the government are taken care of.

The necessary result of all of this is that there are more employees than the country can afford and that only those persons who enjoy special favor are given certain positions where they receive their salaries—or even somewhat over and beyond them—punctually. Meanwhile, all the rest are given barely enough with which to eke out a miserable living, or sometimes nothing at all. This type of inequity would be unjust and odious even if it were confined to people of the same degree of worth, but is much more odious when, as often happens, the favorite employees with their special preferences are not the ones who show the greatest degree of honesty, performance, or capacity.

For all these reasons, it can be seen that in this class of government employees, as with the military and the clergy, there does not exist, nor can there exist, an *esprit de corps*. Consequently, although this group is potentially strong enough to put a great deal of pressure upon society, it does not have the incentive to promote its individual interests by resort to concerted action, not even in defense of the very abuses upon which it thrives.

PART FOUR

Conclusion

We have now brought to a conclusion this sad description of the state in which all classes of society in the republic now find themselves. It has certainly been, and especially for a Mexican, a burdensome task to have to paint a portrait of his own country without being able to present anything that might brighten it. But here in Mexico we write in the presence of thousands of witnesses; and far from being afraid of having exaggerated, we do not doubt that we have omitted a good deal of tinting that would have rendered even darker and more horrible the picture of our unhappy situation. To discover that we have been guilty of error would indeed be cause for celebration, because we are, after all, Mexicans and would like nothing better than to see our fatherland happy and respected throughout the world; but we cannot indulge in illusions, and we do not believe that, in the picture we have traced of our society, we have told anything but those truths which nobody can deny, because they are visible to all who, free of emotional bias or delusion, are willing to see the reality of things.

Therefore, it seems utterly useless for foreign writers to seek feverishly such explanations as the *feminization or degradation of the Mexican race* in order to account for the indifference which this nation has shown toward the present war. It is equally ridiculous for Mexicans to engage in mutual recrimination over what has happened. For our part, we believe that everything is to be explained in these few words: IN MEXICO THERE IS NOT, NOR IS THERE A POSSIBILITY OF DEVELOPING A NATIONAL SPIRIT, BECAUSE THERE IS NO NATION. In effect, if a nation cannot call itself such without having all the elements that make for its happiness and well being internally while being at the same time respected abroad, then Mexico cannot properly call itself a nation.

It is useless to point out that the Mexican Republic possesses an immense territory of more than 120,000 square leagues [approximately 840,000 square miles], bathed by two great oceans, with a multitude of navigable rivers, with the most varied climates in which all the fruits of the globe can be produced, with virgin territories whose astonishing fertility gives the farmer practically a 100 percent yield; where, as a culmination to the special bounty bestowed upon this land, there are great hills and mountains loaded with the most precious metals. All of this only serves to prove that this country has all the natural elements to make up a great and happy nation and that in the passage of time, on this very ground that we now tread upon, there will be a people who will without doubt occupy one of the prime positions among the most rich and powerful nations of the earth. But as long as fanaticism, ignorance, and laziness continue being the basis of our education and as long as we do not have a government which is truly enlightened and energetic, taking all the measures necessary to ensure the advancement of this society, the Mexican people, although treading on gold and silver, will be a weak and unfortunate people and will continue to present to the world the humiliating spectacle of a beggar emaciated by misery and hunger, living in a beautiful palace full of gold and all types of riches which he does not know how to make use of, not even for his own well being and happiness.

JOSÉ MARÍA ROA BÁRCENA

EDITOR'S INTRODUCTION

José María Roa Bárcena was one of the most productive and versatile Mexican writers of the nineteenth and early twentieth centuries. During a life which spanned from 1827 to 1908 he exercised his substantial literary gifts in the writing of poetry, fiction, biography, history, and geography. He was the prototype of the cultivated *criollo* gentleman, and, not surprisingly, his political orientation was conservative, Catholic, and monarchical. As a man of considerable intellectual force, he strove in his writings to preserve a classical balance and clarity. Though he could be quite satirical, he was never rabid in the expression of his opinions.

Roa Bárcena was born in the city of Jalapa in the state of Veracruz. His father was a member of the landowning gentry of the region, and the son grew up with the loyalties and pieties characteristic of that class. His Roman Catholicism was at the core of his personality and culture and was the basis from which he looked askance at the largely Protestant society to the north, which he felt was culturally inferior to Catholic latinity.

In accord with this general orientation was his political conservatism, and in the battles that raged between the conservatives and the liberals, he wrote with ardor for the conservative press. While the conservatives had their center in Mexico City, where Roa Bárcena took up his long residence, the liberal leaders were the "caciques," or bosses, of the outlying states. From this situation arose the opposing forces of the centralists and the federalists. Thus when Santa Anna took on the persona of a centralist, he led the onslaught against the state capitals, strongholds of federalism. After the state of Zacatecas was devastated, Santa Anna turned his attention to Texas, another federalist enclave, but the outcome was to be quite different there. In his account of the war with the United States, Roa Bárcena was to blame federalism, which granted a considerable amount of autonomy to the states, for the weakness of the Mexican war effort, because, he asserted, many states, proud of their "sovereignty," refused to cooperate with the capital in uniting the country's resources against an invader.

The opposing alignments of conservative versus liberal in the political life of Mexico were paralleled in that nation's literary divisions. The neoclassicists were conservatives and the romantics were liberals. Roa Bárcena was at the forefront of the neoclassical writers of his time, but his classicism did not prevent him from being adventurous, and he worked with considerable success in most of the literary genres, publishing several volumes of poetry, a number of novels, and several collections of short stories. His novels and stories were realistic and presented a faithful reflection of the manners of his age. In the stories, particularly, there was an effective rendering of local color and custom.

Sometimes his literary gifts were put to the service of his anti-American sentiments. This is true in several of the poems in the collection *Poesías Líricas*. For example, in a poem entitled "La Unión Norte Americana" he accuses the United States of the hypocrisy of preaching liberty while enslaving Negroes. In the novel *El Quinto Modelo (The Fifth Model)*, he excoriates the Mexican liberals and satirizes their efforts to imitate North American ways while downgrading Hispanic culture.

Roa Bárcena was able to give full play to his devotion to Hispanic and Catholic culture in his biography of Junípero Serra, the splendid and enterprising Franciscan priest who in the eighteenth century established the chain of missions along the coast of California, where they remain as enduring monuments to the Spanish enterprise on the North American continent. Here again, Roa Bárcena develops a contrast between Hispanic and North American culture. The missions, still breathing an air of serenity and holiness, are set against the tawdriness of the American California that was coming into being during the latter years of Roa Bárcena's life. In the last paragraph of the biography, the author dwells on the sad plight of California, now in the hands of Protestants and robber barons. The person of Mexican descent has become a stranger in his own land. For all of this, the Mexican liberals were much to blame.

The disavowal of traditional Spanish and Catholic values by the Mexican liberals was looked upon by Roa Bárcena as akin to the sacrilegious. Mexico's defeat by northern heretics, therefore, was seen to be a visitation of divine retribution upon Mexico for her ungodliness. This concept is expressed in a bitter passage in Roa Bárcena's biography of the classical poet José Joaquín Pesado:

Days fit for mourning, in which our commanders displayed more patriotism, energy, and valor than they did strategy or military discipline; in which our soldiers, inferior to the invader in physical vigor and in armaments, had to face death in the principal battles almost always without the glimmer of the prospect of victory, while watering the earth with their blood and covering almost the entire territory of the Republic with their bones, and in the process forcing the admiration of the enemy. Divine Providence pressed the cup of bitterness upon the Mexican people, inflicting them with domination by a foreign race, different in speech, religion, and customs, as punishment for their faults and errors of the past and pointing out to them, by means of this temporary foreign occupation, the dangers which lay in the future, which could only be avoided through unity, concord, and morality! (*Biografía de D. José Joaquín Pesado*, p. 72)

In his historical studies, Roa Bárcena adopts a less strenuous tone and writes with classical clarity and restraint. The historical works were: *Catechism of Mexican History*, 1863, *Attempt at a History of Mexico in Anecdotal Form*, 1883, and, that same year, *Memories of the North American Invasion, 1846–1848, by a Youth of That Period* in three volumes, the work that Roa Bárcena is most known by. The *Memories*, in fact, first appeared in publication as a series in the newspaper *El Siglo XIX*, beginning in 1879. The complete first edition appeared in 1883. The title is something of a misnomer as only chapters 19 to 22, dealing with the American army in Jalapa and Perote, are actually recollections. The rest is historical narrative. The constraint and temperance of tone in this work resulted in a remarkably impartial book, in which Roa Bárcena reined in his ardent patriotism in the interests of an objective presentation.

The first selection from the *Memories*, which follows this introduction, needs little commentary. In its vivid and poignant account of the trial and execution of two young Mexican officers, who were captured as part of a guerrilla unit by the Americans, this passage speaks for itself. The events were powerfully imprinted upon the mind of the young José

María Roa Bárcena as he witnessed them in his home town of Jalapa in
the state of Veracruz. Beyond the human drama, there is in this personal
account a confirmation of what the historians have maintained, namely,
that the American army in Mexico, fearful of a really developed guerrilla campaign against its extended lines, treated captured guerrillas
much more harshly than it did regular prisoners of war.

The second selection from the *Memories* is a historical narration and
interpretation of the events of the Texas Revolution and the Mexican-
American War. To Roa Bárcena, the steps that led to the colonization of
Texas by Americans, the revolt of that colony against Mexico, and the
later incorporation of Texas into the United States were all events that
were planned and orchestrated from the very beginning by the United
States. The extent of involvement by the U. S. government in the affairs
of Texas during that period has been much argued by historians on both
sides of the border. However, upon the weight of the evidence, it would
appear that when Moses Austin, father of the famous Stephen, applied
to the governor of the province of Texas, in 1821, for permission to
settle three hundred American families in that territory, he was acting
on his own and in the name of his followers. Other *empresarios* were to
follow with their groups of settlers. Some of them were European. It
would appear that Mexico, in the early nineteenth century, despairing
of getting Mexican settlers into that remote, vast, and inhospitable
region, permitted, even encouraged others to come in to develop that
region for Mexico.

However, American governments in the early 1800s did not attempt
to conceal their covetousness for Texas. Joel R. Poinsett, sent as emissary to Mexico by John Quincy Adams in 1825, and Anthony Butler,
sent by Andrew Jackson in 1830, both carried orders to negotiate with
the Mexican government for the purchase of Texas. As the situation in
Texas ripened toward revolution, Andrew Jackson exhibited a lively
interest in Texan affairs. Sam Houston, originally from Tennessee, may
have been an unofficial agent of Jackson. A number of American volunteers fought in the Texas Revolution. To what extent Jackson's government subsidized the revolution, if at all, is not known. Officially, the
United States kept its hands off.

Roa Bárcena says, in this second selection, that the rebellion in

Texas was "more due to the emancipation of the slaves in Mexico than to the fall of the federalist constitution of 1824." In this observation, the Mexican author calls attention to one of the finer ironies in the Texas affair. The Texas rebels spoke out in the name of freedom, and their "Declaration of Causes" for taking up arms against Mexico was modeled on the parent document, the American "Declaration of Independence." However, the American colonists in Texas, most of them from the American South, had taken with them into Texas their black slaves. When, in September 1829, President Vicente Guerrero issued his emancipation proclamation, Texas was thrown into a panic. Obviously one of the freedoms cherished by the American colonists in Texas was the freedom to maintain slavery. In this crisis, Stephen Austin appealed to the political chief of the region, Ramón Músquis, to Governor Viesca of Texas and Coahuila, and to General Mier y Terán. It was largely through their offices that Texas gained an exemption from the emancipation proclamation. This affair, incidentally, demonstrates a little understood cooperation that existed between the American colonists and the Mexican officials in Texas. Roa Bárcena, in an appended note, expresses his surprise that such an exemption should have been granted.

Also in this section, Roa Bárcena makes reference to the "initiatives" put forward by Lucas Alamán. In 1830, Alamán was Minister of Relations and the real power in the government of President Anastasio Bustamante. Alarmed by the growing aggressiveness of the Americans in Texas, he proposed a series of measures which became the substance of a bill which passed the Mexican congress on April 6, 1830. The bill provided for the prohibition of further immigration into the Mexican border states, which of course included Texas. It also set up a program, which never really got under way, by which Mexican convicts and their families were to be shipped to Texas. This last desperate effort to colonize Texas with Mexicans was later derided by the positivist Mexican historian, Francisco Bulnes.

Roa Bárcena also makes reference to "extensive and illuminating information presented by General Don Manuel de Mier y Terán." In the 1820s, the Mexican government sent General Mier y Terán to Texas to report on the doings of the American colonists. Rumors of their growing restiveness had reached the Mexican capital. In his official report, Mier y Terán warned that there were dangerous antagonisms between the foreign colonists and native Mexicans on racial and institutional grounds.

In his account of the Mexican-American War, Roa Bárcena gives a generally objective summary of the various military campaigns. Some of his asides are of interest to the modern reader. Mexican writers have, with considerable justice, accused North Americans of racism in their attitudes toward Mexicans. The reverse can also be true. At one point in his account, Roa Bárcena indulges in a favorite Mexican stereotype of North Americans. He says about the Texas Revolution that "it was the result of a plan by the United States, calculated and executed calmly and cold bloodedly in a manner truly Saxon." About his own people, he makes the curious comment that one of the disadvantages that Mexico faced in confronting the American army was "the physical inferiority of our races." Since most of the foot soldiers in the Mexican armies were Indians, this remark might be a reflection of *criollo* racial prejudices. In contrast, several American officers noted that the Mexican officers, almost all *criollos*, were generally ineffective but that the Indian foot soldiers had incredible endurance, toughness, and bravery and would, with proper leadership, have made up a formidable army. At another point, Roa Bárcena stated that the Mexican political organization was not only deficient but it was "weakened and made even more complicated by our racial heterogeneity."

Roa Bárcena completes the part of this chapter in which he deals specifically with the Mexican-American War by giving Santa Anna credit for his considerable abilities, despite his faults, and by granting a generous recognition to the good qualities of the American army in Mexico and its two principal generals, Taylor and Scott.

The second selection from Roa Bárcena's *Memories*, translated for this volume, concludes at this point, but Roa Bárcena goes on to draw some long-range conclusions about the lessons of the Mexican-American war. Unlike many Mexican writers on this subject, he was not perturbed by the loss of territories though he expressed great regret that so many Mexicans had to live as foreigners in their own land as a result of the war and the treaty. But he added that he did not regret "the loss of territory which was valueless in our hands. We would never have been able to populate our great expanses without repetitions of the Texas situation, expanses whose very extensiveness always constituted for Mexico one of its greatest administrative burdens and the greatest danger to its political order and its very nationality" (Vol. II, p. 517).

As to other results of the war, Roa Bárcena felt that Mexico had missed a great opportunity. The catastrophe should have had a cleansing effect on Mexican institutions and society, and the reparations paid by the United States offered Mexico a chance for a fresh start. But instead, Mexico returned to its old ways and bogged itself down in bitter internecine war. As the country seemed to be approaching the abyss, some in Mexico felt that what formerly had been rejected so fiercely must now be sought, not only to bring order to the country but to exert counter pressure against the United States, which sought hegemony over Mexico. The proposed solution was to turn to Europe for help. Roa Bárcena does not at this point express his personal position, but it is a fact that he was a member of the Junta de Notables, which voted for the monarchy, that is, the installment of Maximilian of Austria as Emperor of Mexico, in 1863.

Roa Bárcena ends this chapter by an expression of pessimistic foreboding about the very survival of Mexico in the face of the United States, whose new tactic will be not territorial expansion but economic imperialism. He calls upon Mexico to make an alliance with the other Hispanic American nations so that under the civilizing banner of Roman Catholicism, which once before, in Rome, had repelled the barbarians of the north, a united Latinity could make a stand before the new northern barbarians.

Memories of the North American Invasion, from Vol. I

On the 19th or 20th of November, 1847, a North American advance party in the vicinity of Jacomulco fell upon some of the guerrillas of Rebolledo and apprehended and took to Jalapa the colonel himself, Lieutenant of the Eleventh Infantry Regiment Don Ambrosio Alcalde, the lieutenant of a corps from Veracruz, Don Antonio García, the lieutenant or captain of the National Guard of Jalapa, Don Rafael Covarrubias, and one or more other officers, leaving them under guard in two rooms of the Posada Veracruzana. They were then brought before a military commission which commenced to judge them summarily and, finding that García and Alcalde, at the surrender of Veracruz, had given their word, before they were released, that they would not again take up arms, condemned these two officers to death. Rebolledo, Covarrubias, and the other prisoners, who were not in the same situation, succeeded in getting their case postponed and were taken off to the fortress of Perote, notwithstanding the fact that the

Translated from *Recuerdos de la Invasión Norteamericana, 1846–1848, Por un Joven de Entonces*, Mexico, D.F.: Imprenta de V. Agüeros, 1902, Vol. I, pp. 498–503.

judges had wanted to condemn the first of these to death because he was, to begin with, the leader of the group and also because they were ill disposed toward him because of what seemed to be a derisive smirk on his face, which was, in fact, a permanent facial tic.

Alcalde's parents, supported by Mr. Kennedy—a rich and respectable Scotchman who had resided for many years in Jalapa and to whom this city had rendered notable services during all the period of the invasion—took immediate steps to solicit the commuting of that young man's sentence as well as that of his companion in misfortune. They saw the governor and military commander (Colonel Hughes, if I remember correctly) and Major General Patterson, who was there at that time; but both of them maintained that the sentence of the court martial had already been confirmed and that they had not the power to revoke it. Hughes on his part, nevertheless, suggested that the city council should solicit the commutation, and in so saying he named a commission from that body consisting of the First Mayor, Don José María Ruiz; the councilmen Don José Ruiz Sánchez; Don Macario Ahumada; Don José Luis Rodríguez, and the trustee Don José María Rodríguez Roa, who, accompanied by Mr. Kennedy serving as interpreter, obtained a long and cordial audience with Patterson without, however, achieving their objective.

The commission put forth the following arguments: that the [Mexican] government obliged its commissioned officers to continue in the service; that these officers found themselves in a state of misery and helplessness after the capitulation of Veracruz; that Alcalde and García were not captured in the course of guerrilla action but rather in carrying out some commission of Governor Soto; and even that Alcalde's youth should be taken into account, his being only twenty or twenty-one years old. Patterson repeated his earlier reply and added that the sentence was just because perjury on the part of the defendants had been proven. In addition he maintained that pardon under those circumstances would be prejudicial to the Mexicans themselves because in future combat situations no quarter would be given to the [Mexican] prisoners in the knowledge that they could break their word with impunity. If he were to yield in this matter he would lose among his subordinates that essential prestige by which he was able to keep them within bounds.

That very morning, he said, he had had two Negroes from a corps of volunteers hanged for the crime of homicide without yielding to the entreaties of their officers. If, therefore, he were now to accede to the desires of the city council he would lose the necessary power to guarantee, as he intended, the lives and property of those living in the vicinity. Nor were the ecclesiastic authorities successful in their supplication, nor the ladies who presented themselves en masse at the house of Governor Hughes and in whose name Don José Ignacio Esteva spoke out eloquently. Not even the spectacle of a lovely little girl of a few months old, Alcalde's daughter, held before the invaders in the arms of her mother, was able to affect the judgment.

The two condemned officers were taken that very afternoon from the Posada Veracruzana, where they had been lodged with the other prisoners, to the chapel of the city jail, in the consistorial apartments, where they were confessed that night, García by the priest Campomanes and Alcalde by Fr. Aguilar, guardian of the Convent of San Francisco. Very early the next morning (November 24, 1847), they received Holy Communion, immediately followed by visits from parents and friends. Both officers were serene and resigned; they shaved and dressed strictly in their regimentals; they ate a light breakfast, and Alcalde had a portrait done by the painter Castillo. He asked me to have a certain article of clothing sent to him. I will never forget his sweet and tranquil voice nor his close embrace, bidding an eternal farewell. The military escort then took the condemned men out into the street where they were marched, accompanied by a priest, to the small square of San José and placed a short distance from the wall of the barracks. Alcalde, and only at the insistence of the priest, accepted a blindfold, and fully erect and shouting a cheer for Mexico he, together with García, received the discharge of the North American rifles. In that same place in which the victims fell, a modest column was later erected to their memory. Those bloody corpses, in the eyes of the people, whose reasoning is usually that which comes from the heart, were not the bodies of officers who had paid for violating their word but rather of the firm defenders of national independence who had been put to death by a foreign enemy. And now the very appearance of these two filled the people with sorrow and at the same time inflamed them with rage. Were not those worthy of envy who with their arms in their hands threw themselves into the mountain areas and the back roads, having abandoned the quietness and security of the home to contend with misery and death? Is it not humiliation and opprobrium to have to listen to the foreign accent in which we receive orders and to have to be presented with the spectacle of the raising of the scaffold? From their place of execution the corpses were piously removed, placed in coffins, and taken to the parish church where they were placed on a table covered with black cloth and surrounded by large candles. Meanwhile, the naves of the church resounded with the prayers and the cries of the women. My father had solicited the honor of receiving and holding in his house the corpses until the hour of burial, but Fr. Campomanes said that the house of God came first, over and above those of any of the neighbors. Houses and stores were closed, and the people went into mourning. In the afternoon the march began to the accompaniment of slow music, with the priests wearing black and walking beneath crosses and processional candles. The coffins were carried upon the shoulders of respected people, followed by practically all the people of the area, and were taken from the church to the cemetery, passing by 1st and 2nd Principal Streets, in the second of which Patterson lived. This general and his chief of staff came out on the balcony and uncovered silently and gravely at the passing of the bodies and of the very numerous retinue in mourning, which constituted a mute but unmistakable protest, an act of sympathy and love toward those who had been shot, and a gesture of adherence to the national cause. At the cemetery, when all prayers had been finished and the moment for the lowering into the graves had arrived, someone in the crowd shouted a "viva" for Mexico, which was taken up fervently by all those in attendance before people finally dispersed. Neither this occasion nor any other of the patriotic demonstrations of that day seemed to irritate or surprise any of the invaders.

Memories of the North American Invasion, from Vol. II

Our war with the United States was the double result of inexperience and vanity about our own capacities, on the one hand; and of an ambition unconstrained by concepts of justice and of the abuse of force, on the other.

The rebellion of Texas, more due to the emancipation of the slaves in Mexico than to the fall of the federalist constitution of 1824, would have taken place without the one or the other. It was the result of a plan by the United States, calculated and executed calmly and cold-bloodedly in a manner truly Saxon. It consisted in sending its nationals to colonize lands then belonging to Spain and later to ourselves and in inciting and aiding them to rebel against Mexico, repulsing any counterattack on our part and setting up an independent nation, obtaining in the process the recognition of some nations, and entering finally into the North American confederation as one of its states. Is there calumny or simply happenstance in this? Look at the extensive and illuminating

Translated from *Recuerdos de la Invasión Norteamericana, 1846–1848, Por un Joven de Entonces*, Mexico, D.F.: Imprenta de V. Agüeros, 1902, Vol. II, pp. 540–550.

information presented by General Don Manuel de Mier y Terán, who researched in our archives on the subject of the situation and dangers of Texas and of our northern frontier, long before the rebellion of the colonists; consider the initiatives of our Minister of Relations, Don Lucas Alamán, on April 6, 1830, and, most of all, the note of the North American envoy William Shannon of October 14, 1844, which said about the motion for the annexation of Texas then pending in Washington: "This has been a political measure that has been fostered for a long time and been considered indispensable to the security and well-being [of the United States], and consequently, it has been an objective invariably pursued by all parties, and the acquisition of this territory [of Texas] has been a subject of negotiation by almost all the administrations in the last twenty years."

The rebellion of Texas found Mexico flushed with pride over the brilliant results of its war of independence and believing itself capable of any enterprise. With the presumption and boldness that come with youth and inexperience it sent its ill-equipped and ill-provisioned army across immense deserts to the Sabine River to severely punish the rebels, but in the bewilderment of its first defeat this army was forced to retreat to the Rio Grande, as though signaling in anticipation the entire area that we were going to lose, all the way down to this point. Mexico's later and futile shows and preparations aimed at the recovery of Texas, which took place before and during the act of annexation of that state to the American Union, provided that country with a pretext for bringing war upon us, by virtue of which it took over, in the end, the areas above the Río Grande which remained to us, such as New Mexico and Upper California.

Mexico, if it were to have acted with prevision and wisdom, should have written off Texas in 1835 while fastening into itself and fortifying its new frontiers. It should have recognized as an accepted fact the independence of that colony and, by way of negotiations, should have resolved any differences and settled boundary questions with the United States. It was imprudence and madness not to have done either the one or the other, but one has to agree that such judicious conduct would not have prevented the new territorial losses suffered in 1848. The area between the Rio Grande and Nueces rivers, New Mexico and Upper

California, all these too were indispensable to the security and well-being of the United States, as is demonstrated in its diplomatic correspondence, in various allusions in President Polk's messages to Congress, in Trist's note of September 7, 1847, to the Mexican commissioners, and above all by the armed invasions of New Mexico and Upper California, all carried out when the two nations were presumably in a state of peace. Thus the pretext might have been different but the appropriation of those territories would have been the same.

The war with the United States found us in disadvantageous conditions in all respects. To the physical inferiority of our races must be added the weakness of our social and political organization, the general demoralization, the weariness and poverty resulting from twenty-five years of civil war, and an army insufficient in number, composed of forced conscripts, with armaments which were in a large part castoffs sold to us by England, without means of transportation, without ambulances, and without depots. The federation, which in the enemy country was the bond by which the different states united to form one, was here the dismemberment of the old order to constitute many diverse states. In sum, we changed the monetary unity of the peso to centavos while our neighbor combined its small change to make a stronger monetary unit. One of the more deplorable effects of this political organization, weakened and made even more complicated by our racial heterogeneity, could be seen in the indifference and egotism with which many states—while others such as San Luis Potosí made astounding contributions to the defense effort—entrenched themselves in their own sovereignty, denying the resources of money and manpower to the general government which were needed both to face the foreign invasion and to contain and suppress the Indian uprisings. As for our army, its inferiority and deficiency could be seen from that first campaign on the other side of the Rio Grande, which signaled the beginning of the war in 1846. There a detachment of from three to four thousand men, who, because of a rapid and unexpected movement, called Taylor's attention to their advance, had to stop to cross the river in two launches. They were decimated by the artillery of the enemy while our cannon balls could not reach them, and they had to abandon on the field of battle their wounded to the humanity and mercy of the conqueror, while they retired in complete disorder to Matamoros to regroup and await replacements, only to be defeated again at Monterrey.

For a moment it seemed that the fortune of arms had turned toward us. With the impetus and speed with which in 1829 he reached the beaches of Tampico to repel the Spanish invasion, Santa Anna arrived in the country, established general headquarters in San Luis, enlarged and organized his forces, and advanced with them to encounter Taylor at Angostura. He attacked there and forced the enemy to abandon its forward positions. He captured part of their artillery. He made them think that they had been defeated. But at the ultimate hour, the Mexican cavalry failed in its assignment. It was supposed to have advanced from the direction of Saltillo to Buena Vista. Provisions were exhausted, and the Mexicans had to break camp—again with the abandonment of the wounded. A disastrous retreat was begun toward Aguanueva and San Luis, which turned into an absolute rout.

Taylor had been battered and rendered incapable of launching upon any new operations, but the enemy was rich and powerful and could send army after army upon us. While Taylor was rebuilding along his northern line, other North American divisions invaded and conquered New Mexico and the Californias, and we had already lost at Tampico. The army of Major General Scott disembarked and set its batteries against Veracruz and occupied that ruined and heroic plaza at the end of March 1847. The remains of our only army, abandoning its line of defense against Taylor, set out, tattered and burned by the fires of sun and combat, upon a march of hundreds of leagues to Cerro Gordo where, reinforced by some of the units of the National Guard, it defended and finally lost positions that had been badly chosen. This army was broken up and disbanded but not without having made its victory very costly to the enemy.

The defense of the Valley of Mexico constituted the last and most determined of our efforts. A new army, relatively numerous but composed in large part of new and undisciplined troops, occupied the line of fortifications, designed and constructed by Robles and others of our most skilled engineers. Despite the fact that Scott took a deviant route to avoid the firepower placed at El Peñon [a heavily fortified position] in his approach to the capital, the plan and all the dispositions for the defense seemed to assure us of a triumph, but human will and arrangements are to no avail if the designs of providence are against them. A knowledgeable and valiant general, placed at the head of a detached division assigned the task of falling upon the rearguard of the enemy when it should attack any point in our line, disobeyed, in his zeal to take the offensive, the orders of the commander in chief. He altered and destroyed the total plan for the defense by occupying and fortifying positions on his own and provoking the battle of Padierna. And Santa Anna, who with the troops at his disposal should have helped him in this battle, adding his weight to Valencia's division (now that the two had exchanged roles), remained a simple spectator of the action, thus allowing it to be lost, though he could have been able to win and should have gained the victory, according to the rules of military science. A glorious page among so many disastrous events was written by the National Guard of the Federal District in its defense of the Convent of Churubusco. Not only here, but in Veracruz, New Mexico, California, Chihuahua, and Tabasco we have seen peaceful citizens take up arms to oppose the foreign invasion and to do battle to the point of exhausting all their strength and resources.

After the first armistice, hostilities were renewed with the battle of Molino del Rey, in which the valiant Echeagaray and his Thirtieth Light saw the backs of the enemy and captured their artillery, which was brought back to our line. Again, this military action, so glorious for us despite its loss, should have been a victory if our commander-in-chief had been there and if the cavalry divisions had attacked at the opportune moment. Chapultepec and the battles at the city gates presented scenes of heroic valor on the part of their defenders and were tinted with foreign blood, but they were, nevertheless, lost, leaving Scott the master of the capital and virtually terminating any further resistance on the part of the Republic.

Such were our campaigns from 1846 to 1848, and in them our army and national guard complied with their duties and presented the uncommon spectacle of rallying to do battle again with the invader, practically the day after each defeat—something which is not done by cowards. No country, where the moral sense is not lacking, could view with indifference in its own annals defenses such as those of Monterrey in Nuevo León, Veracruz and Churubusco; battles such as Buena Vista and Molina del Rey; deaths such as those of Vazquez, Azoños, Martínez de Castro, Fronera, Cano, León, Balderas, and Xicotencatl. And as for the commander-in-chief, Santa Anna, his errors and faults notwithstanding, when the fog of political passions and hatreds has cleared away, who will be able to deny his valor, his energetic vigor, his constancy, his fortitude in the face of the repeated strikes of an always adverse fortune, the marvelous energy with which he roused others to the defense and produced materials and provisions out of nothing and improvised and organized armies, raising himself up like Antaeus, strong and courageous after each reverse. What might not the defense of Mexico have been if there had been some years of interior peace, with an army better organized and armed, and under a political system which would have permitted the chief to dispose freely of all the resistant elements in the nation? One word more about the campaign in order to do proper justice to the enemy: his grave and phlegmatic temperament, his lack of hatred in an adventure embarked upon with the simple intention of extending territory, his discipline, vigorous and severe among the corps of the line, which even extended to the volunteers, with the exception of some of the detached forces that were a veritable scourge, and above all, the noble and kind characters of Scott and Taylor lessened to the extent possible the evils of warfare. And the second of those chiefs cited, who commanded the first of the invading armies, was, once the campaign in the Valley [Mexico City and environs] was ended, the most sincere and powerful of the friends of peace.

Not only was this not dishonorable, but it will figure in the diplomatic annals of the Hispanic American countries as having contributed to the result of a negotiation which only the patriotism and intelligence of Peña y Peña and Couto [Mexican president and Mexican peace commissioner] could have resumed on the agreed-upon conditions, when we were completely at the mercy of the conqueror.

CARLOS MARÍA DE BUSTAMANTE

EDITOR'S INTRODUCTION

In *The New Bernal Díaz del Castillo*, the last product of a prolific life, Carlos María de Bustamante writes more as an anguished patriot than as the scholar of the events of his time. Having fought valiantly in the war of independence against Spain, Bustamante was frustrated that as an elderly man he could not take up arms again for his country. He was so distressed by the "North American Invasion" that he died before the war was over. Throughout a vigorous life, he played important roles as journalist, military man, statesman, and historian. A man of ardor, imagination, and passionate patriotism, he was not one given to the coolly dispassionate approach to the writing of history.

Bustamante was born in the state of Oaxaca in 1774. After the establishment of independence, he was elected to the Mexican Congress as deputy from Oaxaca, an office he served in for most of the rest of his life. During the war of independence, he was an officer in the cavalry of Morelos. In his earlier years of public office, he was a strong admirer of the United States and expressed the belief that all nations wanting to progress while at the same time achieving domestic peace and prosperity should emulate the North American republic. However, after watching the diplomatic maneuvers of the United States in Mexico, he became disenchanted with his former model. Joel R. Poinsett, who had attracted so many of the younger Mexican statesmen to his side, increasingly aroused the suspicion of Bustamante. Finally, this first American envoy to Mexico came to be regarded by Bustamante as an insidious enemy to Mexican independence, and the United States came to be considered a nation destined to be "the perpetual rival and enemy of Mexico." In his movement from sympathy for to enmity against the United States, Bustamante was a microcosm of the Mexican nation itself.

His journalistic career began while Mexico was still a colony of Spain. In 1805, with Dr. Jacobo Villaurutia, he founded *El Diario de Mexico*. This was the first newspaper that sought specifically to reflect the life and needs of the capital city and to express itself in a truly Mexican idiom. It provided an outlet for a new literary generation, and before its demise in 1817 more than two hundred poets and prose writers had been given space in its hospitable pages.

Bustamante was the first historian to appear in the era of independence, completing seven historical works in the course of his life. These were: *Gallery of Ancient Mexican Rulers* (1821), a study of the Aztec emperors, *Campaigns of Don Felix María Calleja* (1828) [Calleja was the able Spanish general who sought to put down the independence movement in Mexico.], *Mornings Along the Alameda in Mexico* (1835–1836), an account of Aztec history up to the arrival of the Spaniards at Veracruz, *The Mexican Cabinet During the Second Period of the Administration of President Bustamante* (1842), *Notes for a History of the Government of General Santa Anna* (1845), *History of Emperor Don Augustín de Iturbide* (1846), and finally, *The New Bernal Díaz del Castillo or History of the Anglo-American Invasion of Mexico* (1847).

Not only modern Mexican historians but his own contemporaries recognized his failings as a writer of history. He was variously characterized as emotional, gullible, and capable of serious irregularities in scholarship. According to his contemporary, the august statesman and historian Lucas Alamán, "he debased his considerable gifts through a puerile credulity, allowing himself to be taken in by the last idea he heard, which made him quick to form an opinion, inconsequent in sustaining it, and extravagant in proclaiming it" (*Diccionario Porrua*, 3rd ed., p. 305). However, Bustamante also edited works by now famous writers of the colonial period, such as Gómara and Sahagún. Had he not bestowed his energies on this labor, important Mexican documents might well have moldered into oblivion. In addition to these works, Bustamante wrote numerous editorials, magazine articles, bulletins, and pamphlets. "The man was," according to Carlos Gonzalez Peña, "a stranger to fatigue—he had a mania for writing."

The title that he chose for his last book, *The New Bernal Díaz del Castillo*, reveals a good deal of the author's conception of himself and of his relationship to the events of his times. His self identification with the sturdy chronicler of the conquest of Mexico by the army of Hernan Cortez is consciously ironical. While the original Bernal Díaz del Castillo recounted a series of Spanish conquests over the Aztecs and their allies, the new Bernal Díaz must provide a chronicle of defeats. To further complicate the matter of point of view, the real Bernal Díaz saw his captain as a hero and deeply identified with the conquering Spanish army of which he, Díaz, was a part. But the use here of the persona of Bernal Díaz by Carlos María de Bustamante is doubly ironical, because Bustamante does not identify with the conqueror but with the conquered, the Mexican army and nation. For a Mexican writer and former soldier this is hardly surprising. But the historical analogy goes deeper than the obvious comparison might suggest. Bustamante was among the first of the "Indianists" among Mexican intellectuals. Though, as a *criollo*, he was primarily of Spanish descent, he sought for Mexico a "usable past" by identifying spiritually and emotionally with the great Indian cultures of pre-conquest Mexico, the complex civilizations of the Aztecs and the Mayas. This urge was no doubt intensified by the events of his time in which he took such an active part. He not only fought against the imperial power of Spain to gain independence for Mexico, but he was an officer in the rebel army of José María Morelos, the *mestizo* priest who fought in the name of the mixed bloods and Indians who had been so dispossessed by the Spanish authorities. So to Bustamante, the Spaniards were foreigners in Mexico, hardly less so than the later invading North Americans. It was, therefore, very natural for Bustamante to compare, as he did in the chapter that follows, those Mexicans who aided the American army with the Tlaxcalans, Indians who sided with Cortez against the Aztecs.

Like the tough soldier Bernal Díaz, Carlos María de Bustamante was hardly academic in his approach to writing. Though no doubt he was guilty of inaccuracies—perhaps sometimes willfully so—he was not guilty of the dull prose of the schoolmen. His style has pace and verve. In its onrushing, somewhat breathless course, it may not stop for logical sequences or transitions, but cumulatively the writing has power, and ultimately he has mounted strong and persuasive arguments. A rhetorical device that he uses to give immediacy to his case is to address himself, at various junctures, to a North American audience. He some-times calls upon "American citizens" to admit that his arguments can-not be refuted. At other times he addresses an American whom he calls "Mr. Official," who presumably represents the purveyor of the official American position on events in the Mexican-American War. Another device, which could hardly be deceiving but perhaps is aimed at a show of objectivity, is to claim that he is paraphrasing an article in the newspaper, *El Republicano,* although the choleric stream of writing that follows with its highly personalized argumentation owes nothing but perhaps an initial inspiration to the newspaper article.

In calling up the qualities that he felt that Mexicans must display if they were to sustain themselves in a bitter war in which they had already met such serious reverses, Bustamante cites the example of George Washington during the lowest points in his campaigns. This evocation of the heroism of Washington was far from unusual among the Mexican *criollos,* no matter what their political persuasions. The revolutionary example of the United States was very much alive to them. Incidentally, in the course of his discussion of the American revolution, Bustamante purportedly quotes from an American historian on the subject. He gives no citation, and, since the passage was probably a free-flowing transla-tion into Spanish of an English language original, one can only surmise the source from which he was quoting.

Certain references that Bustamante makes warrant explanation. At the beginning of the chapter he refers to espionage which has taken root within private Mexican society. He probably does not mean espionage in the formal sense but is rather referring to the miasma of suspicions that settled upon the society of Mexico City when it was occupied by the American army. The question, no doubt, in any gathering was how freely one could speak. Who were the collaborators—and who the stout patriots? What lay behind the "masks"? Shortly thereafter he mentions the San Patricio soldiers, who were hanged by order of the American army. The reference here is to a battalion in the Mexican army which consisted of soldiers who had deserted from the American army. As their name might suggest, most of these were Irishmen who, having been treated badly in the States because of strong anti-Catholic and anti-immigrant feelings, succumbed to the lure of Mexican agents who promised them money and lands if they would defect. Later Bustamante refers to General Canales, who invaded Mexico from the frontier with Texan troops among his forces. During the period in which Texas was an independent nation, General Antonio Canales, a Mexican who operated on both sides of the border, nurtured the dream of an independent border republic of the north, which he called the Republic of the Río Grande and which was to include the northern tier of Mexican states. He invited Texas to join. Though Texas declined the offer, many Texans volunteered in the army of the Republic of the Río Grande. Another name which Bustamante mentions in passing is that of Don Alejandro Atocha, who, Bustamante claims, has been sent by the Americans to contact Mexican authorities on the subject of peace. Bustamante deplores this choice of envoy because of Atocha's unsavory reputation. In fact, Colonel A. J. Atocha's principal activity in connection with the war occurred at an earlier date. Though of Spanish birth, Atocha was an American citizen with connections in Washington. He also was a friend of Santa Anna and had been in touch with the general in his Cuban exile. Atocha reported to President Polk that for thirty million dollars Santa Anna was prepared to see that Mexico made large territorial concessions to the United States and a peace favorable to American interests. Accordingly, the Americans gave Santa Anna safe passage from Cuba through the American naval blockade of the Mexican coast, landing him at Veracruz. Once in Mexico, Santa Anna assumed direction of Mexico's resistance to the American invasion. Had Bustamante been more apprised of the part which Atocha played in this maneuver, which so thoroughly duped the Americans, he probably would have been more favorable toward the colonel. As it was, Atocha played no appreciable role in the peace negotiations.

In other matters, too, Bustamante seems not to have been in complete possession of the facts or to have fallen into confusion. For example, in discussing the internal affairs of Texas he indicated quite correctly that the American colonists in Texas had been accepted into the area on condition of becoming Mexican citizens, which in fact they did. Bustamante chastises them for their ingratitude in rebelling against

Mexico, which had offered them so much. However, later Bustamante makes the curious statement that at the time of the rebellion the signers of the Texas declaration of independence from Mexico must have been Americans because the colony had only existed in Texas for ten years and children would not have had the time to be born and grow up in the region. He seems to have forgotten his earlier statement that these people were American by origin but Mexican by citizenship.

When Bustamante takes up the subject of the annexation of Texas by the United States, a subject which necessarily entails a foray into American internal politics, he errs on two accounts. His preoccupation with the Loco Foco Party in the United States almost amounts to an obsession. Yet he clearly has misplaced the blame when he declares that the Loco Focos were the deciding factor in winning Congress and the country to the cause of the annexation of Texas. The Loco Focos represented the radical wing of Jacksonian democracy. As such, they sided with the abolitionists who, in their passion against slavery, strongly opposed bringing Texas into the union on the grounds that this would add to the slave territory. Also, Bustamante maintains that annexation was brought about by the margin of one vote in the United States Senate, giving as his opinion that the deciding vote was cast by Senator Thomas Hart Benton. Actually, annexation was strongly approved by a joint resolution of the House and Senate, with some Whigs, whose party was declaredly against annexation, crossing over to join the Democrats in supporting it.

Bustamante might also be doubted when he moves into the area of colonial American history. At one point he says of the English in North America that they not only used conventional means of warfare against the Indians but they "practiced the infernal device of introducing smallpox among them." Bustamante does not dwell on the fact that European diseases brought to Mexico by the Spaniards ravaged the Indian population to an appalling extent. These diseases, of course, were not purposively introduced by the Spaniards. Certainly, many Spaniards in Mexico and, correspondingly, many English people in North America, were themselves victims of these diseases, although the indigenous people, no doubt, were considerably more susceptible to European diseases because of a lack of immunity.

Bustamante ends his chapter with a discourse on guerrilla warfare, concluding the discussion rather abruptly and on a general note. Yet clearly, especially in the light of preceding arguments, he holds to the position that Mexico should reject peace negotiations and rely on the long-range attrition of guerrilla warfare.

The New Bernal Díaz del Castillo

It is difficult to write with sincerity and impartiality about the great events that have been happening here when, aside from the factions which convulse the citizenry and disturb the inner peace of families, these same families find themselves infiltrated by an espionage that aims its fire from within private society, covering itself with a hypocritical mask, which, when it falls, has already produced the ruin of a family. Such is the position in which Mexicans find themselves today. Their natural enemies are the officers and soldiers of the North American army which dominates them through martial law, but also their enemies are the ungrateful foreigners of other nations whose only desire is the gold from our mines. Enemies too are the horde of citizens who have acted as guides to the American army. As legitimate descendants of the ancient Tlaxcalans, they glory in their immorality and maintain the same hatred as did those who aided in the taking of Mexico City while in the service of Hernan Cortés. Who would have believed that these

Translated from *El Nuevo Bernal Díaz del Castillo o Sea Historia de la Invasión de Los Anglo-Americanos en México*, Mexico, D.F.: *Testimonios Mexicanos*, Secretaría de Educación, 1949, pp. 1–13.

citizens, when they were ordered to hang and to bury the so-called San Patricio soldiers—the North American soldiers having refused to obey such an atrocious order—would carry out the order most willingly to prove their fealty to those whom they had chosen to be their masters? Such is the position in which he, who now aspires to write this history, finds himself. *Nevertheless,* he will do it, because truth prevails over terrorism and imposture. Truth is for all times; it is from God, and not even the Lord himself can make what really happened cease from having happened. One who writes for the public should limit himself to writing about that which is really relevant to his story and not trace the origin of his tale way back, beginning with Leda's two eggs that produced Castor and Pollux. Let them be assumed to be already born. If I speak about the origin of this war, I will do it with the same text as a writer who in number 185 of the *Republicano* writes in the following manner:

The Mexican Republic, impressed by the picture of prosperity in the United States, while at the same time the inhabitants of Mexico desired intensely to consolidate a liberal government, adopted the same form of government as existed in the United States, and by the act of 1824 the federation was established. Later the Republic, desiring to let other nations participate in the blessings which God had bestowed in endowing it with extensive and fertile lands, decided to colonize Texas, and preferred for this enterprise citizens from the United States, because it had more sympathies and friendship for that country. And never thinking that from this generous procedure grave damages would result, Mexico believed that it had taken a sure step toward avoiding the prospect of a people with monarchical habits and customs coming to disturb the establishment of its liberal institutions.

I want you to tell me frankly, American citizens, if up to this point you find anything to throw in the face of Mexico. Let us continue.

Mexico, having conceded these territories, far from asking for revenues, for guarantees, or for any kind of remuneration, granted special liberties to the colonists. It gave them a ten-years' exemption in the payment of contributions and permitted them to sell their products to the other Mexican states. In accordance with the provisions of the constitution of 1824, Coahuila and Texas formed a free and sovereign state which could send, as it indeed did, its deputies to Congress and take part in the direction of the affairs and policies of the country. The colonists accepted these terms and—mark this well—placed no conditions upon them. Rather, they promised to be faithful to the Mexican Republic of which they now formed a part. Nor could they have done anything else, because no one who receives a gift can impose conditions on that which already favors him so generously.

The colonists finally established themselves. They began to distribute the lands, cultivate them, and to make their fortunes—something you cannot deny.

What did Mexico receive in compensation? Nothing, because it did not receive any duties nor collect taxes. On the contrary, from the beginning to this date it has resented two grave wrongs: first, the loss of customs because of the great amount of contraband that has been carried on in the borderlands, and secondly, the eruptions of the barbarous Indians abetted by these same inhabitants of Texas, who carry on a commerce with them in horses and mules that have been stolen from our villages. Indeed, the Texans have celebrated treaties with some tribes instead of warring against them as is owing to a common enemy and one which does not belong to a civilized race. These, too, are undeniable facts which cannot be contradicted.

The fact that Mexico, for whatever reason, changed the constitution of 1824 did not constitute a sufficient justification for the secession of Texas. Since the colonists had received their lands without any conditions attached, it was simply up to them to subject themselves to the will of the majority in the nation to which they belonged, the more so because the great distances that separated them from the center of political affairs protected them from the vexations and molestations that this uprising [the battle of the federalists against the constitutional change] and the other civil wars have produced in other states.

In no way can one cite the example of the separation of Mexico from the rule of Spain to justify that of Texas from Mexico—and for the following reasons:

Mexico did not receive endowments and lands from Spain. The Spaniards conquered its earlier inhabitants, took over their lands, and held those people subject for three hundred years, taking from the land

whatever products they could without giving the inhabitants any guarantees, rights, representation, or education of any kind. The sons of
these same Spaniards and of the Indians, legitimate owners of the land,
were those who raised their voices, proclaiming independence, and
fought for it without the help or intervention of any foreign nations, and
after a bloody war of eleven years, they succeeded in their intent. When
independence was achieved, there were, without doubt, more than
seven million inhabitants.

With nations, as with families, emancipation is a natural outcome,
and one might even say that it is inevitable and necessary for the
formation of human societies. A father has, for example, three children.
These grow up, marry, and separate themselves, finally, from the pater-
nal roof, making up two or three separate families. The same thing
happens with nations. The United States of America, after a certain
time, separated itself from the mother country and has formed through
that eternal law of societies other entities, more or less strong, well or
badly organized, but whose existence has been recognized as fact by the
rest of the world.

Nothing, therefore, would have seemed strange or violent if Texas,
in its due time, had done the same thing. But in the few years since the
formation of this state it has not been able to count on a population of its
own, people born on the native soil to qualify as Texans. Neither has it
had the population nor the necessary elements to make itself independent. Nor has Mexico, even if it might have changed its form of
government, inflicted upon Texas wrongs of any kind—unless one
qualifies as wrongs the giving of lands without receiving any compensation for them.

Mexico, therefore, took the view that its generosity was repaid by an
act of ingratitude, and it could do no less than to consider some of the
inhabitants of Texas (because it is also evident that not all of them took
part in the uprising against Mexico) to be colonists in rebellion who, for
the honor and dignity of the government, must be repressed by force.
Before having done so, and there are documents that prove this, the
government made a gesture of peace, offering the colonists another ten
years' exemption from payment of contributions and agreeing to admit

their products into the markets of Mexico. The Texans refused to listen to anything, and unfortunately the war began. On this subject it is necessary to rectify, even though briefly, certain matters.

The army which General Santa Anna brought to Texas did not exceed ten thousand men, and this can also be proved. One of the first acts of war which he undertook was to lay siege to and take by assault the fort called the Alamo, where he lost six hundred men. Then he advanced through the center and along the coast, conquering the entire country, and at San Jacinto, close to the outer boundaries of Texas, the fortunes of war robbed him of all the fruits of the campaign. The army which remained under the command of General Filisola consisted of more than five thousand men, and with this army he could have destroyed the force which had attacked General Santa Anna and taken him prisoner. You might say: Why didn't he do so? General Filisola, as a foreigner [He was Italian.], did not take it upon himself to perform as he should have and as is provided for in the military code. He retreated to the border. This conduct of General Filisola, who in other respects is a fully qualified and good military officer, has been the subject of criticism which has filled large volumes. The fact is that we cannot regard as reliable the reports that have come from the miserable remnants of his expedition who survived to tell the tale. The war has properly been called a calamity, a blow from on high. Once it burst into flame, the men involved in it lost all reason and feeling and committed acts of cruelty on both sides. But in spite of this, these cruelties, among civilized peoples, are always reprimanded. I must, as a Mexican, vindicate the nation to which I belong of those charges which have been made against it. The excess in the case of Colonel Fanning [sic] and other actions of this order which have been committed have been highly condemned by the press and the nation, and there could not be found among all the citizens of the United States a disgust equal to that which those events have caused in the Mexican Republic. And because they have not been subject to a thorough examination, they have cast their shadow upon the entire nation so that its inhabitants must bear undeservedly the infamy of being called savages and barbarians. I feel, as a Mexican, deep sorrow in my heart that these things should have happened, and I would give half of my life to be assured that they would never, on any occasion, be repeated. I wish for my country valor, energy, decency, patriotism, and constancy—but never cruelty.

During the ten years of war with Texas, the turn of events has resulted in American prisoners, on various occasions, having come under our power. Which of these have been shot or have been ordered to be killed in cold blood? All have been put in fortresses or military compounds, without ever having been mixed in with criminals locked up in our public jails. Finally, they were set free unconditionally, and the same people who came armed to bring an unjust war to our territory and even to communities outside of Texas have been allowed to return to their country without any injury having been done to them. When General Canales invaded the frontier, he took with him some three hundred American citizens whom he had recruited in Texas. With the capitulation of Canales, the armed foreigners who had intruded themselves into our interior wars were not included in the surrender. They deserved nothing more than death. Instead of that, what did General Arista do—the same who later commanded the Mexican armies on the frontier? He treated them all well. He told them that they could stay in Mexican territory or go back to the United States as they wished. In fact, some remained in the country, while others returned to the United States. General Arista used government funds to secure for them passage on a boat, and to those who went unclothed or without shoes he gave ten pesos to dress themselves.

Once when Captain D. Francisco Schiafino was conducting seventy American prisoners from Saltillo to Mexico City, the commanding general ordered him to have the prisoners tied up during the march. The captain, sympathizing with them in their suffering, ordered that they be untied while on the road. The payment that these prisoners gave for the compassion of this commendable captain was to surprise the detachment that was guarding them—during the night at Agua Nueva—to kill two sentinels and a sergeant, and then to flee. They left their protector compromised, and he suffered more than six months of imprisonment.

Among those prisoners there was a rich landowner from Texas named, if I remember correctly, Dimitte, who took some poison that he had hidden in a ring because he was afraid of being shot by Schiafino. Despite the conflict in which he found himself, the captain helped the unfortunate Dimitte with great effectiveness, sparing no efforts to save his life. Dimitte never forgot this kindness, and when he was on his deathbed he sent a letter to Schiafino leaving him thirty thousand pesos. The disinterested young man refused the money and never collected it, preferring the poor and hazardous life of a soldier.

General Santa Anna himself has favored many American prisoners, and a child found among them, whose father it was supposed had been killed in battle, was placed by Santa Anna in the College of Mines, so that now he has received a complete education at the cost of the nation. The name of this child was Hill.

We have had the misfortune that these deeds have not been sufficiently publicized among the citizens of the United States, while at the same time the most insignificant mistakes have been painted with the darkest colors by the American press, which more often than not has been neither just nor impartial.

If one admits that within ten years only children, not by any reckoning an adult population, could have been produced in Texas, who then but citizens of the United States could have drawn up that declaration of independence?

The complaints of Mexico against the United States before the annexation of Texas are the following:

The introduction of troops from the United States army in the course of Mexico's campaign in Texas. A considerable number of cavalry under General Gaines crossed the Sabine. This was protested by our minister in Washington. The public enlistment and military equipping of troops, which has been done on various occasions in the port city of New Orleans, in order to invade Mexico through Texas and other points, despite the fact that the United States maintained diplomatic relations with Mexico and the guarantees of treaties of peace and commerce remained in force. This also has been the subject of altercations between the two governments. Mexico has never had the forthrightness to ask of the United States that it lend its assistance against Texas, but Mexico certainly has had the right to demand of the United States that it maintain absolute neutrality. The above mentioned palpable actions demonstrate that the United States has not done so.

As for the recognition of the independence of Texas by other nations, there is nothing unusual in that. The various powers recognize de facto governments, but that in no way takes away from Mexico the right to recover, if it were possible, the territory which it had lost. The independence of Mexico was equally recognized by the European powers and by the United States itself, but nevertheless Spain did not recognize Mexico until a great deal of time had passed, and it made an attempt in the year 1829 to invade Mexico without opposition from any nation.

Now, if Texas were to be considered strong and capable of backing up its declaration of independence, why did it attach itself to the United States? Why did it seek this method to get the United States to come to its support in Mexico? This is just one more proof that Texas cannot be compared to other nations, including the United States, that have declared their independence and by deed have been able to sustain it and triumph.

As for the annexation, the person who is writing this piece was in the United States when these events were happening and was a witness to the fact that the greater part of the press in the northern states clamored strongly against this step, calling those who belonged to the annexation party thieves and usurpers, and setting forth strong and well-founded reasons, which at this point I will not repeat in order to prevent this exposition from becoming too lengthy. If the wise and honorable Henry Clay had attained the seat of the presidency, would the annexation of Texas have come to pass? Certainly not. The bringing in of Texas was the result of the intrigues and machinations of the Loco Foco party, and that which is done by such a farcical group cannot be considered rational or just.

The question of annexation was much debated in the Senate, and only by one vote (I believe that of Mr. Benton) was the measure passed.

In the Texas Convention [which voted for annexation] the majority present consisted of persons from the Southern states, notably partisan, and the newspapers [presumably of the United States] published their names and inveighed against this intrigue.

Thus matters have arrived at the state in which they are now, because evil parties and evil men, of which there are as many in this country as in the United States, have operated according to their partisan tendencies and have not attended to the well-being and justice of both republics. Can you deny this, American citizens, if you are not blind? Will you not confess that Mexico has suffered more than any other nation? The act of annexation was the equivalent of taking away from Mexico a considerable part of its territory, which had, rightly or wrongly, carried on a dispute with Mexico, but in no way can a nation be construed as friendly which has mixed itself in this affair to the point that Mexico has been deprived of its rights. Did not our minister in Washington protest against the annexation? Did he not declare that it would be a hostile act which would merit a declaration of war? Who, then, provoked the war— Mexico which only defended itself and protested, or the United States which became aggressors and scorned Mexico, taking advantage of its weakness and of its internecine agitations.

The administration of General Herrera, which was in fact one of the best that the country has had and that history will in time do justice to, had arranged the affair in a satisfactory manner to the considerable advantage of both Mexico and the United States, because the administration, composed of illustrious people, looked forward to the future, considering questions not only in terms of politics but from the vantage point of humanity as a whole and in particular of this generation of Mexicans whose fate has been to suffer throughout the last thirty years the lashes and calamities of war. The dignity of the government demanded, in effect, that the [American] naval forces withdraw, which in fact they did. Was it the administration of General Herrera that broke its word? Surely not, and the U.S. commissioner [John Slidell] was not received because the administration had changed. In effect, a cowardly general without honor or patriotism [Mariano Paredes] turned his back to the enemy while at the same time proclaiming a war that he had no intention of waging. Thus, like the villain he was, he destroyed the most legitimate and most popular government that Mexico has had. But I ask: Was this a failure on the part of the nation? Can it be blamed for some of this? And I must answer: Did not the nation manifest in all possible ways its displeasure, to the point of overthrowing this intrusive and evil government? Does not that general pine away in exile, one which he imposed upon himself in order to escape the vengeance of the nation?

Up to this point things could still have been arranged through diplomatic channels, and the rights of Mexico could have been guaranteed by a treaty, but the Loco Foco party was absolutely determined that Mexico should not only suffer the loss of its territory but it should bear the shame and humiliation of having its territory torn from it by force of arms. The sending of troops into Mexican territory doomed all moderation, and Mexico was left with no other recourse but to engage in battle. The territory between the Nueces and Rio Grande rivers neither by fact nor by law could have belonged to Texas. Not by fact because it was not populated by Texans. For ten years there existed only one little ranch in Corpus Christi, inhabited by Mr. Kyney and Mr. Aubry [sic], who had served as double agents, having had dealings with the Texans and with various Mexican generals, using them for the purpose of carrying on contraband trade. Nor did this territory belong to Texas by law because all this coast, through a territorial division recognized by all the nation and by the Texas colonists themselves, has belonged to the state of Tamaulipas. Thus, from the point of view of the Mexican government, the occupying of Corpus Christi by troops of the United States amounted to the same thing as if they had occupied the port of Tampico. In every way it was a violation of all treaties, of friendly relations, and of good faith. I wish now that you would judge these events with a Mexican heart and would ask yourself: Which has been the aggressor country? What would your government have done in the controversy with England over the Maine border if that nation had brought in troops, large or small in number? Without any doubt your government would have declared war and would not have entertained any propositions put forth until the armed force had evacuated the territory.

The war began because there was no other course, and Mexico will always be able to present a serene front before the world and maintain its innocence despite whatever misfortunes might befall it.

Now, in respect to the actions which have already taken place, let me say to you, Mr. Official, that you suffer from some misconceptions.

The number of troops that General Taylor had at Palo Alto and Resaca were without doubt close to four thousand men, not two thousand, and those under General Arista were hardly five thousand. On the first day, our troops were able to spend the night on the field of battle that General Taylor felt obligated to abandon. On the second day, total defeat was the lot of our army, leaving us only the satisfaction that General Arista was honored even by the newspapers of the north, that admitted that he was the last to leave the field of battle.

At Monterrey, on the other hand, the ineptitude, or the wickedness, or the cowardice of a general resulted in the city being surrendered, but if more than two thousand men withdrew, certainly many less than six thousand did.

The Battle of Angostura [Buena Vista] was not in any way won by General Taylor, and, appealing to his own account, one deduces that it was a bloody and hard-fought action in which both armies conducted themselves with daring and valor. General Taylor admits on his part that he had to abandon some of his positions to the Mexican infantry, that O'Brien's artillerymen were completely annihilated by the Mexican cavalry which came up to the very mouths of the cannons. Both General Santa Anna and General Juvera had their horses killed from under them. The number of officers killed and wounded in both armies proves that it was not a defeat but that the Mexican soldiers did not belie the valor that they have always demonstrated.

For lack of provisions and water, General Santa Anna felt that he had to retreat, but if General Taylor was left the victor, why did he not attack and conquer the miserable remains of the army which fell back to San Luis? The Americans should not even speak of the bombardment of Veracruz. The walls of Veracruz are in no way strong or impregnable. It is notorious that the American army at a distance at which it could not be reached by fire from those walls began to hurl large bombs and all classes of projectiles in that direction. More than five hundred innocents, children, women, and old people, perished under the enemy cannonade, and the valiant garrison commanded by the worthy General Morales had to submit to a capitulation, because the entire city would have been ruined and all the innocents sacrificed to no avail. Once the city had surrendered, the fortress had of necessity to do the same thing. Did the fortress assault the squadron? Did the walls assault the army? Neither. So a military action which relied solely on the superiority of missiles should not even be mentioned.

It is necessary that in these matters the truth be spoken, because these events which have just happened now belong to history.

But I would like for a moment to suppose that all those actions not only happened the way you described them, Mr. Official, but that they happened in an even worse manner. What would that matter? Or what could one deduce from that? That the nation should, for its rights and for its dignity, have resisted armed aggressions, and if it has had the misfortune to lose, that has been the decree of fate. There is no dishonor in being conquered, but yes there is—and very much so—in succumbing without making the least effort.

What would have become of Spain if when the armies of Napoleon invaded it it had not put up the least bit of resistance? The French had victory after victory, and the Spaniards ran a thousand times before the enemy armies. When you, the Americans, fought for your independence, you repeatedly ran when attacked by the English troops, but on other occasions you fought with valor and you won.

So that it is not thought that I am speaking purely from memory, I will cite some passages from history. "General Sullivan, dispatched with ten thousand men by General Washington against Lord Cornwallis, took possession of the heights that dominated the church of Birmingham. His left was protected by Brandywine Creek, his artillery well-placed, and his flanks covered by a woods. At four o'clock the English army commenced the attack, and its irresistible impetuosity forced the enemy to flee into the woods. It received reinforcements and took a new position, from which it was repulsed despite a desperate resistance. The rout was complete. The American army fled with precipitation and by various roads, while the Commander-in-Chief, with the only corps that he could maintain, took refuge in Chester." Here is a situation very similar to that of Cerro Gordo. "In the afternoon of that action," continues the historian, "an English detachment sent to Wilmington seized Mr. Mackenlie [sic], the governor of the province of Delaware, took possession of a shallop loaded with the most valuable effects of the inhabitants, with a considerable sum of money, and with all the bills of the public treasury."

After successive triumphs and defeats, the American army had the chance to force the capitulation of General Burgoyne, but in spite of this, what was the situation it found itself in later? General Washington describes it in his letters, saying that he could not count on more than four thousand men, and these without shirts or footwear, without provisions, and without any enthusiasm for combat. As a result of this, he experienced many low points, and more than two hundred of his officers abandoned their commitments and retired to their homes.

Doesn't all this resemble what happened in San Luis after the Battle of Buena Vista?

Later General Sir Williams [sic] Howe took Philadelphia. Congress and other authorities had to flee, and when the [British] command was passed on to General Clinton, he moved up, at will, to New York. The French fleet under Count Estaings [sic], which had come to the aid of the Americans, could not impede Clinton's move, nor did General Washington dare to engage him in open battle.

What would have happened, then, to the Americans if, discouraged by all these reverses, they had abandoned the defense of their cause? The answer is clear. Perhaps they would still be colonists of England. The above narrative will convince you, Mr. Official, that defeats do not matter when a nation is resolved not to succumb before its enemies and when it counts on the rights of justice, and justice is without doubt on our side because the only fault and the origin of this war stem from Mexico's having given to citizens of the United States fertile lands while exempting them from any duties or taxes.

Let us examine now, although lightly, the question of peace and of the future that the war presents for the two republics.

The object of any war is, according to the authorities, nothing more than the search for peace. Mexico, like yourselves, desires peace, but it is not possible for it to treat for peace without discredit to its honor after the events that have happened and particularly because the victory did not come its way. What impression would it make upon foreign nations if Mexico should now open negotiations for peace and bring them to a conclusion? Would not a handful of marines or a band of adventurers think that they had the right to disembark on our coasts and, for the most frivolous of motives, attempt to take over the capital? How in the period ahead can Mexico make its rights respected if they are not supported by physical force? You, Americans, who are the judge, will admit that we have no alternative and that if we acted otherwise we would be in your own eyes no more than a bunch of degraded men, more despicable and insignificant than a horde of savages.

I do not know why you call the Mexicans obstinate and bullheaded people for continuing the war. Without doubt you have forgotten your own history. There is no way in which peace negotiations will be possible unless the Republic of the North withdraws its armies and its fleets.

It is the truth that you are not talking to us about peace, because up until now we have known nothing about your conditions. The one thing that you have done is to commit the error of sending Don Alejandro Atocha as a courier. This step, because of Atocha's notorious past which is also known by the United States, could not appear to Mexico to be anything but a new and unmerited insult.

You speak to us of peace while we are losing Texas, a part of Tamaulipas, Coahuila, Chihuahua, and all of New Mexico. You speak to us of peace and are making us pay fifty or sixty million to cover American war expenses.

And who will pay Mexico the twenty million in customs duties lost during the year, the huge expenses which Mexico has had to make to arm its troops, the damages which its peaceful citizens have suffered as a consequence of the military occupation by foreign forces? Who will pay for the bombardment and destruction of Mexico's cities, the misery of families and of orphans and of the thousands of citizens who have perished since the beginning of this war? And even supposing that Mexico were to resign itself to the losing of all this territory and to paying what has been demanded of it, what would it use for payments? What treasury, what bonds, what time would be sufficient to satisfy this debt? By what principle of justice and legality can Mexico impose new contributions upon a people ruined by civil and foreign wars?

Now you can see that under these hypotheses peace is not possible. It would be better that a conquest be completed, that the cities be reduced to ashes than to enter into conditions that would reduce the Mexican nation to a status worse than what it had when it was a colony of Spain.

The events and future prospects of the present war are prejudicial for Mexico, but nonetheless so are they for the United States. Can there be a comparison between the domestic joys of illuminating the streets of the United States on the one hand and on the other of the immense waste of sacrificing peaceful Germans, Irishmen, and native-born Americans who might otherwise be tranquilly at home, enjoying the harvests of the fertile fields of the North? What peace of mind can the United States enjoy while invading and destroying a nation that far from having offended it has clasped it to its bosom as a brother? Could not the Americans have availed themselves, through peaceful means, of the gold and silver of Mexico? Do you believe that the American nation will not lose, even though it triumphs over us completely, in the poor repute that it will have deserved among the nations of Europe?

Mexico finds itself in this contest absolutely alone. Spain was helped by England, and the Duke of Wellington with a powerful army routed the hosts of Napoleon. The United States had General Lafayette and the fleets and armies of France. The most powerful nations of Europe gathered together to defeat Napoleon. Mexico is alone, but that does not matter, nor do the reverses which it has suffered as long as it maintains its constancy. That is what made the United States triumph in its war of independence, and that is what will make us triumph. I imagine that the American army will triumph over Mexico, but what will happen if it cannot find anybody to make peace with?

It is necessary that you keep these considerations in mind and that you be persuaded that Mexico will prefer ruin before treating for peace while enemy forces still remain on Mexican soil.

The lower classes of Mexico generally believe that you are heretics, barbarians, and bloody-minded types. That is an error like the one that persists in the United States where we are judged as being the same as barbarians. The educated people of the Mexican Republic that know your history and have traveled and lived in the North judge the country with a proper impartiality, respect your human and democratic institutions, appreciate the industrious character of the people, and rightfully admire a nation that in a short time has become powerful, but at the same time these Mexicans have become seriously alarmed about the future fate of Mexico as they remember certain tendencies which are proved by events in that nation's history.

Before the Americans began to advance, the French held Louisiana,

Canada, and parts of the banks of the Mississippi. The French population, one might say, formed a strip that encircled the coastal area where
the American colonies had established themselves.

What has happened to the French race? It has almost totally disappeared and has been supplanted by the English race, invaders by
character and ambitious of possessing more territory than they need.

History records that in addition to the sword, gunfire, and the
dagger, which they used against the Indians, they practiced the infernal
device of introducing smallpox among them.

Did they not send police dogs against the Seminole Indians to
destroy them? And finally uproot them from their Florida lands to
transplant them on the remote banks of the Missouri?

As a strange anomaly in the freest country in the world, slaves are
sold, and the most beautiful women in the world, some of them well
educated and amiable, are looked down upon because they are qua-
droons and are therefore irremediably condemned to dishonor and
prostitution.

Does the United States need Texas? Is it not true that fifteen or
twenty million more inhabitants could fit into the territory of the Union?
Once they have Texas, does not that seem enough? And they still want
three more provinces and California? Does not the press of the United
States daily vociferate that the country should acquire those territories?
They talk to us of peace, and they take California. They talk to us of
peace, and they send expeditions to New Mexico and Chihuahua. They
talk to us of peace, and the troops of General Taylor, according to his
own admission, commit atrocities in the provinces of the north.

Thinking men do not believe the same things as do the lower classes,
but they entertain more serious and well-grounded fears and consider
the possibility of an interminable and profound war between the races, a
war in which Mexico cannot yield without evident danger to its independence. These considerations pose still more obstacles to the peace.

In conclusion, I should like to say a word about the system of
Guerrilla warfare which we have adopted and you have criticized. It is
true that this is a cruel method, because each guerrilla chief, operating
on his own account, can commit inhumane acts, but this is inevitable.
You too took over the properties and cruelly persecuted those who were

labeled as loyalists when Clinton evacuated Philadelphia. These actions were taken against the advice and opinion of General Washington, a man who in all respects can be looked upon as a model. The American people should never have forgotten to imitate his conduct or to follow his sage advice. But returning to the subject of guerrilla warfare, neither is this method new in Mexico, and it is especially appropriate for people situated in the mountains or spread out in country areas. The Russians, after having burnt down their capital, avenged themselves by harrying the Grand Army of the Emperor [Napoleon] throughout the entire course of his retreat. The guerrillas carried on this kind of harassment and not just in that campaign. Hetman Platow, for example, the famous guerrilla fighter, pursued Napoleon all along the emperor's line of retreat, as far as the Rhine. Spain also adopted this system, and the wars of independence in Hispanic America were in essence guerrilla wars.

LUIS GONZAGA CUEVAS

EDITOR'S INTRODUCTION

As Mariano Otero has criticized Mexican society from the perspective of the liberals, so has Luis G. Cuevas from the vantage point of the conservatives. Both writers, contemporaries of the period of the Mexican-American War, have sought to explain Mexico's inability to repel the invasion from the north, and they have sought to do so, not in terms of military equipment or strategy, but in terms of the larger issues of society.

Cuevas was born in Lerma, Mexico, in 1800 and died in Mexico City in 1867. Throughout his life he pursued a career as lawyer, statesman, diplomat, and writer. He served in diplomatic assignments in Prussia, England, and France. He was Minister of Foreign Relations in 1837 and again, in the cabinet of President Herrera, in 1844 and 1845. As Minister of Foreign Relations in the cabinet of President Anastasio Bustamante, he carried on negotiations with the French at the time of the Pastry War of 1838. In July 1845, Cuevas, as Minister of Foreign Relations under Herrera, proposed the resolution that stated that Mexico would declare war against the United States should that nation annex Texas. Nevertheless, Cuevas supported Herrera in his desire to negotiate outstanding issues with the United States. During this period Cuevas, as Foreign Minister, appealed to the governments of England and France for help against the United States, without results. In 1838 and again in 1845, Cuevas submitted memoranda to the Mexican government, denouncing the policies and attitudes of the United States and prophesying war.

Cuevas was one of the three plenipotentiaries who represented Mexico during the negotiations that led to the Treaty of Guadalupe Hidalgo, and he defended the treaty before the Mexican congress. His position was consistently conservative and Catholic. And yet, though he had often been critical of the liberals, he refused to join the monarchist and clerical factions who engineered the placing of Maximilian of Austria on the throne in Mexico. He was firm in his belief that foreign intervention could never be a solution to the internal and international problems of Mexico. The government of Emperor Maximilian tried to win him over by electing him to the "Junta de Notables," but Cuevas refused the appointment.

The Future of Mexico, from which the following passages have been taken, was published in three volumes, the last in 1857. It presents views of Mexican society gained from the perspectives of a lifetime, which encompassed quite distinct periods of Mexican history: the colonial era, the decade of the wars of independence, the Mexican-American War, and the civil war which preceded the imposition of the Empire. Though Cuevas also lived through the period of Maximilian, *The Future of Mexico* does not treat that era. Stately and decorous in style, this work seems characteristic of its period, nineteenth-century *criollo* Mexico, but in its suppressed passion of expression, it is in no way a dull book.

To Cuevas, Mexico had been led away from its better self, that self which had been the result of the conditioning effected by the institutions and culture of Spain, most notably the Spanish Catholic Church. Though Cuevas was not against independence, he wanted an independent Mexico to continue in the best aspects of the model presented to it by the mother culture.

The villain, to Cuevas, was the aggressive and vulgar nation to the north, which threatened the very extinction of Mexico. His most particular vituperation was aimed at the first minister that the United States sent to an independent Mexico, Joel R. Poinsett. This ambassador, as Cuevas saw it, so far exceeded the scope of his proper duties as to intrude himself into the internal affairs of Mexico with the aim of subverting that nation's very soul. The purpose was to remake Mexico into the image of, in fact, a dependency of the United States. Such a Mexico, Cuevas warned, would be helpless in the face of the aggressive designs of the United States. Poinsett's instrument of subversion, according to Cuevas, was the York Rite of the Masonic order, which Poinsett himself helped to establish in Mexico in order to offset the influence of the Scottish Masonic Rite, which was a focal point of conservative and particularly Spanish political influence. The Mexican liberalism, which found its congenial gathering places in the Yorkist lodges, represented to Cuevas an unnatural and foreign implantation into the body and blood of Mexican culture, which, if left unchecked, would sicken Mexico unto death.

The extent to which Poinsett actually played the role insisted upon by Cuevas and other Mexican writers has been a matter of dispute. North American historians have tended to discount the Mexican version, but not completely. Fehrenbach noted that Poinsett finally became "persona non grata" because of his meddling in Mexican affairs. Gene Brack, as noted in the general introduction, to a certain extent supported the Mexican view in agreeing that Poinsett sought to influence the liberals through the milieu of the York lodges. "For to promote liberalism," Brack added, "would be, of course, to promote, indirectly, the American interest in Mexico." In a recent history, *To the Halls of the Montezumas*, Robert W. Johannsen maintains that Poinsett supported liberalism in Mexico out of an earnest conviction that such was in the best interests of that country. Rather than systematically weakening Mexico to prepare it for a North American invasion, as has been claimed by Mexican writers, Poinsett, in Johannsen's view, deplored the Mexican-American War. "Confessing his 'affectionate regard' for the Mexican people, Poinsett," writes Johannsen, "viewed the war with deep regret. . . . They were 'brother Republicans,' more in need of encouragement and assistance than of invasion and conquest. Poinsett feared that the war might strengthen the prejudices against republicanism among upper-class Mexicans and play into the hands of the monarchical faction" (New York and Oxford, 1985, p. 294).

Finding himself in the position of favoring the independence of Mexico from Spain but of deploring the liberals who were the most avid supporters of independence—he particularly hated the anti-clericalism of the *puros*—Cuevas sought a model which could properly represent his ideals in an independent Mexico. He thought he saw his paragon in the dubious figure of Augustín de Iturbide, the *criollo* leader who led the forces of independence against the Spanish army in 1821.

The independence movement in Mexico, however, had two quite

distinct phases. The first was what Cuevas referred to as the "earlier insurrection." This began in 1810 with the famous *grito de Dolores*, when the insurgent priest, Miguel Hidalgo y Costilla, rang the bells in his church in the little town of Dolores in Guanajuato, which summoned a crowd of Indians and mestizos. When he shouted: "Death to bad government!" they answered with the *grito*, the shout: "Death to the Spaniards!" Thus began the first phase of the struggle for independence, the phase which provided the hagiographies for modern, post-revolutionary Mexico. Hidalgo with his insurgent leaders, particularly the brilliant guerrilla chief José María Morelos, another priest, set in motion a revolt that was much more than an independence movement. It was a basic upheaval from below, which took on some of the aspects of a race war, as the long dispossessed Indians and mestizos rose up in fury. As such, it not only stunned the Spaniards but it thoroughly frightened the Mexican upper class, the *criollos*. This was not their idea of a gentlemanly movement for independence. This insurgency, as a formal military movement, was finally put down by the Spanish general Callejas, but, with Hidalgo and Morelos executed, some of the remaining guerrilla chiefs such as Bravo, Guerrero, and Victoria, retreated to the mountains whence they carried on sporadic raids.

With the dreaded "insurrection" finally brought under control, the *criollos* found one of their own to lead the next phase of the independence movement, Augustín de Iturbide. Cuevas was far from being alone among the conservatives in giving his heart to this new leader who had risen from their midst. Many of them thought they saw in him a representative of their own ideals. But Iturbide was, in fact, a shallow and showy man who cast a mold that a number of later Mexican leaders were to fill, most notably his apt protégé Antonio López de Santa Anna. In his growing megalomania, Iturbide finally declared himself Emperor Augustín I. Shortly thereafter, he was banished from Mexico.

Yet the nation does owe a debt to Iturbide. He had the imagination to make an alliance with the guerrilla leader, Vicente Guerrero, having won him over with the plan of the three guarantees, known as the Plan de Iguala. These guarantees were independence, continuation of Roman Catholicism as the state religion, and citizenship and racial equality for all Mexicans. The combined armies, representing a brief coming together of the principal forces in the land, came to be known as the Trigarantine Army. And in the name of the three guarantees this army, led by Iturbide, crushed the Spanish army in the year 1821, referred to by Cuevas as the "glorious" year, and Mexico finally achieved her independence.

The year 1821 represented for Cuevas a magnificent stasis which, if its qualities could have been continued, would have guaranteed for Mexico the kind of society and culture that would establish its authenticity as a true offspring of its majestic progenitor, Spain. It was the year of victory and independence, but a victory by forces quite different from what the *criollos* considered to be the rabble that followed Hidalgo in the earlier insurrection. The Trigarantine Army, led by Iturbide, seemed to promise a continuity of Hispanic values of the sort that Cuevas cherished. So the year 1821 was fixed for him as a vision and an ideal against which other things were to be measured, and to fall lamentably short.

On the basis of this vision, Cuevas posed a mission and possible destiny for Mexico. It was to lead the forces of Latinity in this hemisphere against the threatened domination of the United States, but it could only accomplish this if it could succeed in remaining true to itself and in rebuffing the forces led by Poinsett. And herein lies a judgment with which Latin Americans have exhorted themselves since the nineteenth century. The North Americans might indeed possess superior material wealth and physical force, but in the realm of the arts and of the spirit Latin America was clearly superior. And in this area lay the strength by which Latin America was to ward off the encroachments of a coarser society.

This call was first significantly sounded at the very turn of the century. In 1900, the superb Uruguayan essayist, José Enrique Rodó, published a slender volume entitled *Ariel*. This book became immensely popular throughout Hispanic America and was one of the most influential volumes ever published in that area. Appropriating Shakespeare's characterizations in *The Tempest*, Rodó used the term "Ariel" as a symbol of Hispanic America at its artistic and spiritual apex. Set against Ariel was the monster Caliban, epitomized by the coarse and vulgar but powerful society of the United States. The lines of battle were drawn. For Cuevas, Mexico must succeed in fulfilling its destiny by putting itself in the vanguard of this action.

And yet, in *The Future of Mexico,* Cuevas does not present an optimistic vision. Though there is still a remote possibility of a return to glory, Mexico is well along the way to self decimation and a horrible debasement. The vulturous United States waits and watches.

The Future of Mexico

Our minister and envoy extraordinary to Washington, Don Pablo Obregón, was received by that government, which in turn sent, with the same credentials, Mr. Joel R. Poinsett, who arrived in the Republic in May, at what seemed to be the most opportune time in which to carry out his mission. Thoroughly versed in the political state of the country, he was cognizant of the pleasing perspective which a short period of quiet and a good public administration was able to offer us. He understood, as well, the continued predominance of people of talent and property and of the upper classes generally, and he knew that once order was secured the Republic would make amazing progress. In the full knowledge of all this, he conceived the project, which was favored by contemptible types of Mexicans, of taking control of the popular lodges and organizing them so as to promote civil conflict. Behind the mask of patriotism and beneficence, they would be the better able to foment and inflame the hatred that we were beginning to have for our

Translated from *Porvenir de Mexico*, Mexico, D.F.: Editorial Jus, 1954, pp. 233–237, 418, 419–422, 423–424.

origins, our customs, for the Spaniards, and, although they themselves might take no notice of it, for foreign residents in the country. Poinsett, who had studied well the character of our revolutions, not only in the Republic, where he had lived some years before, but in South America, had no doubt about the evils that would result in Mexico from a war carried on by the lower classes—or more properly by the party that called itself their protector—against the more influential classes. Nevertheless, he adopted all the methods he could conceive of to bring to a boil the passions and hatred that could be excited against the Scottish rite and the Spaniards who supported its policies and aims. If the sentiments of virtue and justice directed governments and were in fact the bases of international policy, the name of Poinsett would not be remembered in Mexico nor in the United States except in terms of actions that should be condemned to the execration of history and posterity. But to the disgrace of the human race, the conduct which he practiced among us is the very thing which has gained for him much praise and has been, at the very least, sanctioned by diplomacy. The only goal of his efforts has been toward the execution of evil projects and purely materialistic designs, whatever may have been the upright principles claimed in his books. Forgetting good faith, loyalty, and real greatness, he has had the impudence to present these designs as the unequivocal testimonial to modern civilization. Our neighbors are the ones who now exceed in the art of corruption and the ones who have not stopped and will never stop bringing about the ruin and disaster of entire peoples in order to add to themselves a span of territory. In this sense it could be said that Poinsett was of more service to the American Union than all of its generals put together in the war of invasion and that he deserves more than any of them a magnificent monument on Capitol Hill.

Whoever might have been the founder of the lodges which are called York, it cannot be disputed that their organization, their influence, and the great success which crowned their anarchical plans are due to Poinsett's maneuvers and the spirit which he infused into those associations. The Scottish Rite lodges, without actively conspiring against the independence movement but still attempting to uphold the respectability of the [colonial] government, maintained themselves through the antipathy which influential Spaniards held for Iturbide. Put off by the insufficiency of the Treaty of Córdoba, they naturally participated in the opposition that existed between Spain and the richest and most envied of her colonies. Everything that favored the war of 1821 worked against their sentiments and opinions, and so much would they have wanted to thwart the glorious events of that year that they preferred the earlier and bloody insurrection for no other reason than that it had been a failure. For this reason, it is easy to explain why the Spaniards and the members of the Scottish Rite saw more merit in Victoria, Bravo, and Guerrero, who had succumbed to the power of the viceregal government, than in Iturbide with all his superiority in war and even in politics. It was, therefore, perfectly just to condemn those two groups as being anti-national. Poinsett, with all the astuteness characteristic of those men who have consecrated their lives to back-room intrigues and in consequence have forgotten all that is honest and just, proposed to set against the Scottish Rite a sect which, by presenting itself in the most popular roles, sought to gain the greatest favor and to be considered the firmest supporter of independence. Having succeeded in this aim, it was easy for it to descend, within a short period, to all the excesses that the minister had previsioned and to go about dragging the country into a situation in which everything was moved in the direction most advantageous to the United States. The systematic hatred for the Spaniards, the depreciation of the country as having been educated according to their values and under the yoke of the colonial government, and the alleged necessity of seeking new means of prosperity different from those that had promoted the union and the mutual relations between the generation which we could call Spanish and the new one which represented the independence—all this kind of thought, adroitly propagated, sought to destroy all that was elevated in the national spirit, depriving it of the possibility of directing itself along the lines proper to itself and indeed depriving it of its very self respect, all of which had contributed in 1821 to give it the force that it needed to constitute itself on a solid basis. Poinsett, if one can judge of his intentions by the evils with which the York lodges have flooded the country, reasoned in the following manner: The members of the Scottish Rite are addicted to the Spaniards, they count many of them among their principal directors, and for that reason, as well as for their opposition to Iturbide, whose fall is attributed generally to this group, it is easy to present them as the most fearful enemy that the country has and the most powerful obstacle toward effectively organizing it. The prevalence of such sentiments should give to the aversion, which the Spaniards and their adherents inspire, a direction that could effectively extinguish all sense of nationality, generalizing the hatred which has been extended toward them so as to make it fall over everything that might represent union, generosity, and principles of order and good government. Poinsett was not deceived in all this, and, knowing full well the ease with which things go from one extreme to the other, he did not doubt that these absurd ideas that were being held about the system would rob the government of all its force. The result would be that a weak and tolerant presidency would make the conflicts among the parties all the more bloody so that no one would triumph decisively and the expulsion of the Spaniards would complete the breaking off of ties between the new society and the older and place the republic in a situation in which it would be forced to seek its security and progress through an incessant change of personnel and institutions. The party of the members of the Scottish Rite could be considered to be the organ of the Spaniards, which, having no thought of revolution nor love for independence, did not even believe that the opportunity for independence existed. The Yorkist party, on the other hand, made such a show of its fear of losing this opportunity and manifested such enthusiasm for liberty without limit that, for these reasons alone, it was reputed to be the most zealous admirer of the United States. One party considered independence to be accomplished when we could hope for more benefits and for more liberty from the mother country. The other wanted to so broaden the concept of independence as to incite an obstinate conflict among ourselves to the extent that we would forget that we were descended from the Spanish race. In this manner the parties were formed, with the Scottish Rite Masons as defenders of the constitutional order and the Yorkists as defenders of independence, both contributing to maintain a spirit which, rather than favoring the one or the other, posed a yet stronger menace to them both by enhancing the violence of the clash that ensued between men who had been partisans of the Bourbons [the

Spanish monarchs] and those who had just put themselves under the orders of the minister of the United States.

. . .

However clever were the policies of Poinsett and astute his intrigues to mix himself in our business, it did not take much to detect the direction which he was taking and the eagerness with which he worked to foment a disorder that could never be reconciled with the respect which was due to our nationhood. It was easy enough to discern that a minister who had acquired in the course of his travels a cultured manner and intimate relations with the most distinguished and estimable people, who was versed in business and had attained the knowledge of how to shine brilliantly in society, could not aspire to friendship and influence with the sort of lost people who had begun to enlist in the Yorkist band without the perverse intent of exciting in this crowd a passion for office and for command, which would render impossible the existence of any sort of government. In the Yorkist lodges, as opposed to the Scottish— and particularly because of a sense of gratitude to Iturbide—there had entered very distinguished men and generals with strong reputations. But Poinsett put little stock in them, since the most turbulent dem- agogues with the most ruinous passions did not figure in society. De- ceiving everyone with the would-be truth that without the masses and the passions of the populace the Scottish Rite Masons could not be resisted, he extended agitation and evil principles throughout the re- public, fomenting a hatred for the Spaniards so as to get them expelled from Mexican territory. Even in the talk that he gave while presenting his credentials to the president there could be noted the poison con- tained in the eulogies that he lavished upon the country for having adopted the federal system to the ample extent to which it is contained in the constitution. At the same time he delivered a severe and hostile judgment upon the Spanish nation for the backwardness in which it had maintained its former colonies. So corrupt, therefore, was the conduct of that minister that he would stop at nothing in his efforts to divide us.

. . .

Although at this time we place no value upon ourselves, Mexico is, nevertheless, called to a destiny which must weigh in the balance of the world. The relations between Europe and the Americas, the emigration

to those areas as well as the combined impact of commercial and
political influences, must of necessity affect the character which Europe
gives to those differing regions, either the steadily increasing preponderance of the people of North America or the counterweight which
those of Spanish race could provide if they succeed in organizing
themselves as they should. In the one case, the Americas will present
the spectacle of great material prosperity with very little culture. They
will go on producing people like those who have come to California,
people who will have no unity, either in religion, language, or customs,
the type who respect the rights of neither people nor nations but only
wish to pit themselves against the strongest force that can be brought
against them. Slavery will be brought into this equation as a principal
element, and Great Britain's program to abolish the slave traffic will
prove insufficient in the face of the incentive to use forced labor in the
less healthy climates of the southern countries. In the second possibility,
there should be a change of aspect, events should take on a more natural
course, with each country prospering in its own territory and all the
Americas gaining through the slow and gradual progress of our race,
which has better inclinations, as well as traits of character better suited
to bringing about notable improvement.

.   .   .

Our country, given a state of peace and public order, with the efforts of a
generation that has had such bitter disillusions, and aided by the inner
conviction of what the country can be, will find itself not far from having
achieved, if it can summon up the will, the progress to which it aspires
and will find that it can put itself into an advantageous position that will
pose a notable contrast to the difficult period of its past political life. If it
can thus restore itself to its rightful place and by example lead the rest of
the Latin American nations, this beautiful continent will see itself free
of a contamination which, no matter how invitingly it presents itself in
its aspects of commercial and maritime growth, cannot satisfy the needs
of culture, of intelligence, and of moral potential—the very qualities
which least recommend themselves to our neighbors. It is not a flatter-
ing illusion to assert that Mexico, with seventy years of peace, will
produce more artists, more savants, and more literary people than the
United States. The traditions of our race, its language and religion, its

love and respect for the hearth and the family, cannot be changed to suit the ways of swarms of adventurers such as infest the United States and all those countries that seek their well-being in spoilage and devastation, that profess no religion and have no other recourse than money, and who give to all their enterprises the character of a conquest. Nor can the civilization of the world advance on the basis of improvements and enjoyments that are purely material, especially when the pressure to gain these things continually incites to the violation of good faith in treaties and to the disowning of all the obligations upon which society rests and of all the respect due to law and to justice.

But above all, before we lose ourselves, we must make again the effort that we so happily made when we invoked religion, union, and independence. From 1810 and for about half a century we have not had a year which could compare to that of 1821, which we remember with glory, forgetting for the moment that we have to get back to the sad business of our civil war. Between the earlier insurrection and the period of independence we saw that year shine forth like the rainbow which announces the calm and proclaims all that we can be as soon as we, animated by generous ideas and by self respect, direct our forces toward everything that can produce unity and strength for our country, setting aside the passions, the special interests, and even the names of the political parties. Now that the generation of the independence is disappearing, it is time to take stock and to recognize what we have become: something that can neither make us happy nor satisfy the men who govern us. With so many years of misfortune and discord, we can say that we have given ourselves over to extraneous ambitions, and we have consumed our abundance in objects that are not relevant to our well-being. If our children could be educated in the love of religion, fatherland, and justice, the European countries and our very neighbors would restore to us their esteem and friendship and would consider us worthy to be at their side. Employment and industry would seek our soil, and all would find here hospitality and abundance. With the reign of order and the consequent protection of guarantees and the recognition of the development of our national character, this country would enjoy that golden age that those who are not Mexicans covet. We would cultivate unity and peace, and, laden with the benefits of divine providence, we would not cease from invoking it and doing homage to it with lively and tender recognition.

This prospect has its horrible reverse side. And since in writing about the present situation I cannot banish melancholy ideas which throng to my mind, in which I picture Mexico as being given over to the fury of interior anarchy and seeming almost to clamor for foreign domination, I will permit myself the liberty of anticipating catastrophe and at the same time of asking that we bear this prospect in mind so that we might yet liberate ourselves from this doom. Maybe these dangers are being exaggerated, but there is no doubt that we are acting in an incomprehensible fashion. While we are repeating to ourselves every day that there is no remedy for our destiny, that the fatal hour is approaching, we act as though the evils which are threatening us either are very remote or have no importance as we pursue our disputes and intestine quarrels. On the other hand, Europe and also the other American countries look at our nation only in terms of the imminent risk that it poses for their independence, and in the United States the phrase is now proverbial: the Mexicans do more for us than we ourselves.

I suppose that our conduct will continue as it has been, and that the political parties will put up with anything rather than unite and prepare a common defense. I also suppose that whatever group can influence the government, can triumph over its enemies in a tenacious, bloody, and endless battle, and which does not concern itself with public disgrace or with the dangers that surround it, will succeed at last, without any principles being established, in leading the public to accept whatever changes it desires in religious matters. This supposition should not come to pass, nor does God wish it to. But it is not a rash one, whatever His sentiments, because the history of Christianity offers us repeated examples of those violent transitions that can be explained without any difficulty by reference to those clashes that occur in countries where a cruel persecution of the church and its ministers has been permitted. If our country ceases to be pious, it will cease to be Catholic, and, having lost the faith in which it has lived, it will have neither morality nor any belief. It has been truly said, alluding to the Catholic countries and to the sublime grandeur of religion, that there is no middle ground between

Catholicism and atheism, and it does not require a long discourse to describe the kind of disharmony that will ensue once the bond of religious sentiments and principles is entirely broken.

The inhabitants of the frontier states, invaded by barbarous Indian tribes, are already despairing of their salvation. When they have lost their cattle and their ranches and fall back to a basic core of population struggling to maintain security, they will think about what political entities they should look to in order to preserve what little of fortune and family they have left. There are no points of similarity, nor can there be, between those Mexicans and the inhabitants of the United States, because, as with us, their moral being is in open contrast with that of the citizens of the United States. They have made and are still making costly and heroic sacrifices in defense of their territory, as they made during the war of the invasion, and there are no words that can adequately praise their suffering and their constancy. But when they cannot count on any aid from the interior of Mexico and do not have a population capable of resisting and must therefore choose between blood-thirsty barbarians with their brutal excesses on the one hand and on the other the slavery that is offered to them as a remedy [absorption by the United States], what will be their choice and what our shame and our responsibility?

And because nothing will be lacking in our shame and in our ignominy and when, destroyed by anarchy, we will no longer believe that we can establish any government that could defend us, we will cry out to our neighbors, and perhaps the only response we will get from them will be: "No, it is not yet convenient for the United States to possess Mexico. First, finish your task of self-destruction, and then we, without being responsible or appearing to be aggressors, will occupy you in the name of progress and liberty. Since the Spanish race has not achieved a society, we will take it to be at the same level as that of the Indian race and exterminate it, as we did in Florida, or we might see if it might be accommodated to another system of slavery by sending it to the least healthy climates to perform the most lowly forms of agriculture. Then we will take possession of the land most envied in the world, and in doing this we will demonstrate that our projects in Texas and California

were beneficent and that the occupation of the entire country has been
an event which should satisfy all the civilized nations."

And thus we will consummate the work we have been engaged in,
and we will lose forever this Mexico, and our houses, our fields, our
temples will receive the people who are the least loyal and least cultured
of all the people in the world, and our name, far from giving rise to
compassion, will come to be confused with the names of the most
debased and degraded of nations. Our fathers, the Spaniards, will
always lament that what was once New Spain no longer belongs to the
sons of their race, and they will infer from this disgrace that we did not
deserve independence and that the war which they undertook to maintain their dominion was legitimate and in the interests of those nations
that have not desired nor do now desire the aggrandizement of the
United States. The European governments will come to realize their
fears, they will confess that we were incorrigible, and they will finally
seek to satisfy the needs of industry and commerce and find an outlet
for their excess population in other nations. There will be no writer or
history that will do us justice, and the power and ambition of the North
American republic, rather than serving to lessen our discredit, will only
further aggravate the charges that have been leveled against us that we
consumed our forces and our resources in actions taken against ourselves. And so, with our society dispersed, with the bonds of religion,
customs, even of family broken, an object of hatred among the nations
of South America for having brought such a dangerous enemy closer,
without being able to live either in the country that gave us birth or in
the foreign territory which despises us, we will become ashamed of
ourselves and obliged to hide our origins and will seek in this degraded
state some title by which to give our sons some sort of identity, sacrificing all and producing a dire change which will serve as a reminder and
an example to other people of the good things which Providence had
destined for us and of the punishment which we have deserved.

MANUEL CRESCENCIO REJÓN

EDITOR'S INTRODUCTION

Manuel Crescencio Rejón was born in the small town of Bolonchen-ticul in the southern state of Yucatán in 1799. However, the active years of his life were spent in Mexico City, where he died in 1849. He was a member of the first Congress after independence, and he was part of the commission that developed the federalist Constitution of 1824. In that same year, along with the eminent statesman and literary man, Quintana Roo, Rejón opposed ratifying any treaty with the United States until the boundaries established by the Adams-Onís Treaty of 1819 were confirmed by the Republic. Rejón's insistence upon the confirmation of this treaty which, among other things, contained a recognition by the United States that Texas was not a part of the Louisiana Purchase but remained Spanish territory, can be taken as an augury of the firm position that he was later to take against ratifying the Treaty of Guadalupe Hidalgo, with its large territorial concessions.

During the administrations of Santa Anna and Herrera and, in the war years, under Mariano Salas, Rejón was Minister of the Interior and of Foreign Affairs. It was as foreign minister that Rejón stood up to Wilson Shannon, the last United States ambassador to Mexico before the commencement of hostilities between the two countries. The two men engaged in an acrimonious correspondence, with Shannon beginning on October 14, 1844, by stating that the United States was negotiating toward the annexation of Texas and that attempts by Mexico to reconquer Texas, whose independence Mexico had not recognized, would not be permitted. The United States, Shannon continued, considered the acquisition of Texas to be "indispensible to [the country's] safety and welfare." Rejón answered by stating that Shannon's note "disclosed the perfidiousness with which Mexico has so long been treated," and he referred bitterly to Shannon's attempt "to base on the security of the United States the right to seize a fertile and vast province belonging to a neighboring nation." The exchange of notes was carried on in this vein until Shannon declared himself unwilling to continue the correspondence. On November 11, 1844, Shannon wrote to John C. Calhoun, American Secretary of State, that "the insolence of [the Mexican] government is beyond indurence [sic]." Shannon continued his note, replete with similar misspellings, and ended by saying: "I think we ought to present to Mexico an *ultimatum*" (reprinted in Price, *Origins of the War With Mexico*, pp. 16–17).

Rejón's mistrust of the United States and his willingness to set himself against that nation showed consistently throughout his career. For example, though he was a liberal and strong federalist, Rejón did not join other liberals in the adulation of Joel R. Poinsett. Instead, he constantly warned against the American minister's "machinations." It was entirely in accord with Rejón's nature and attitudes for him to strongly oppose the ratifying of the Treaty of Guadalupe Hidalgo in the terms that appear in his statements on this subject.

The "Observations on the Treaty of Guadalupe" are parts of a larger volume entitled *Thoughts on Politics*. The "Observations" was originally a position paper sent from Querétaro on April 17, 1848, for the consideration of the Mexican Congress in its discussion of the treaty. It is divided into sixteen short chapters. Rejón strongly objected to both the treaty itself and to the way it had been arrived at.

The first eight chapters of the "Observations" are devoted to a résumé of events leading to the war. Rejón clearly sees the issue of Texas as the focal point of hostilities but understands the wider implications of this local conflict. He notes that American designs on Texas dated back to the Louisiana Purchase of 1803, with some Americans claiming that Texas lay within the Louisiana territory, which the United States had purchased from France. In the early 1830s the United States envoy to Mexico, Anthony Butler, was authorized to sound out the Mexican government on the proposition of selling Texas to the United States. Rejón claims that as a result of Mexico's total rebuff of this proposal, the United States decided to abet the Texans in their revolt against Mexico, sending arms and volunteers in violation of its proclaimed neutrality. The complicity of the United States in this revolt was underscored, according to Rejón, by the hasty U.S. recognition of the independence of Texas. The later annexation of Texas by the United States was, Rejón declares, an act of war. Various moves by the United States are perceived by Rejón as being parts of a concerted plan. In its support for the Texas Revolution, in its pressing for exaggerated claims against Mexico by American citizens, and in its sending armed naval forces along the coast of California, the U.S. government, according to Rejón, hoped to force Mexico into a declaration of war so that it could seize coveted Mexican territory in a way that would seem less odious to the world at large.

Yet, even with the annexation of Texas by the United States, Mexico, though withdrawing its ambassador from Washington, fell short of a declaration of war. The United States, therefore, had to initiate the hostilities in order to accomplish its aims. This step was taken by sending American troops through the area bounded on the north by the Nueces River and on the south by the Rio Grande. The claim to this territory on the part of Texas was strongly disputed by Mexico, which maintained troops in the region. When a clash between these troops and the American forces occurred in this disputed zone, the United States declared war on Mexico, claiming that Mexico had shed American blood on American soil.

Having established, to his satisfaction, America's war guilt, Rejón turns his attention to the Treaty of Guadalupe Hidalgo itself and to the Mexicans who took part in the treaty negotiations. He accuses them of having acted in a clandestine manner and of having violated Mexican law in drafting a treaty without first having consulted Congress, the states, and the people themselves. Why had they not made contact with the growing forces within the United States that were opposed to the war? By working with Polk's opposition in the United States as well as by making use of a third power as arbitrator, the negotiators might have obtained terms more favorable to Mexico. As it was, operating secretly, the Mexican negotiators ended up by making the maximum concessions. What dementia possessed them to agree to yield more than half the national territory for a pittance of consolation money? Mexico should reject the treaty, elect a vigorous president capable of bringing together the great resources of the nation, and should then carry on the struggle until an honorable peace could be obtained.

"Observations on the Treaty of Guadalupe"

OBJECT OF THE FOREGOING REVIEW OF EVENTS

These are, gentlemen, the most important facts to be borne in mind concerning this grave question, facts which I have felt an urgent necessity to record, along with certain obvious commentaries, in order to make palpable the justice of our cause. From this recital we conclude that the conduct of the government of the United States, in the affairs relating to Texas, has been an uninterrupted series of aggressions against us. Having failed in obtaining the objects of its constant attacks, this government has affronted the world by presenting itself as the aggrieved one while, after having violated our territory, it has spilled the blood of our compatriots over it and at the same time has openly declared war on us for not patiently allowing ourselves to be despoiled according to its desires. With all the right on our side, I cannot see by what justification this government comes to us giving us as a condition for the reestablishment of the peace which it itself had shattered the ceding of more than eighty-one thousand square leagues of our terri-

The selections by Manuel Crescencio Rejón were translated from "Observaciones Sobre Los Tratados de Guadalupe," *Pensamiento Político,* Mexico, D.F.: Universidad Nacional Autónoma de Mexico, 1968, pp. 116–122.

tory, the renunciation of our northern frontier from sea to sea, and all for the measly sum of 18,250,000 pesos, when those lands should be worth at least from 450,000,000 to 500,000,000 pesos. The debt which this government claims from us, according to its annual message of '46, amounts to 6,291,604.71 pesos, of which 2,026,139 have been liquidated, which is the beginning of a settlement. That there still is an amount which remains to be paid is more the fault of the administration of the United States than ours. This sum from the 6,000,000 has been reduced to 3,250,000 pesos, which have to be discounted from the 18,250,000 pesos owed to us for half of our territory, and thus we will only see a remnant of 15,000,000, which stands for the price of the purchase they propose to make of our brothers who live in the frontier region. The purport of it all is that the difference between the indicated 18,250,000 pesos and the 500,000,000 which, at the very least, the lands are worth, should be considered applicable to the war expenses that are being charged to us, although this is not being said to us in a definitive manner. President Polk in his message of last December caviled about the nonacquisition of territory, because he said that if we did not accept the indemnity, we could not give satisfaction in any other way, and that this amounted to a proclamation that his republic had declared war on us unjustly. But can we not with a more powerful reason object to the injustice on his side? To agree to an indemnity on his terms would make us appear to be settling for an accounting more severe and censorious than he asks from his own nation, because we would not only be renouncing the expenses we have had and the damages we have suffered, thus implicitly accepting the figments he puts forth for a case, but we would also be paying reparations for all the damages that his country has sustained, which is infinitely worse than the former. I declare that this would degrade the national character. And to accede to the second aspect which this opprobrious treaty demands—would this not amount to covering with slime a nation such as ours, which, in the face of all kinds of provocation, has refused to be provoked into combat and finally offered resistance only in order to defend its territory, something which was not understood by the province [Texas] which was the source of this disastrous war? And so we are not only supposed to remain silent while our unjust neighbors make off with the lands which they had at first selected for themselves, but we must also pay them for coming and taking them and others as well, and finally we are expected to confess that they had a right to all of this. Oh, no! A nation which understands the extent of the sacrifice that is being demanded of it in this way prefers to perish in face of the demand. It will adopt the extremes of heroic resolve before it will consent to such disgrace and such opprobrium.

RATIFICATION OF THE TREATY
WOULD BE THE POLITICAL DEATH OF THE REPUBLIC

Nevertheless, insensible to everything, our national government has entered into those negotiations which are so humiliating to us, thus committing us to grave imputations of perfidy if we should reject the treaty, which we should surely do. This government has demonstrated its misunderstanding of the nature of the institutions by which we live and has thereby brought things to the embarrassing impasse which now confronts us. The result is that we are unable to disapprove a shameful treaty without rendering our country almost defenseless against the disasters of a war which has been so disadvantageous to us because the government has not prepared the country to resist and to continue the war to a successful end. Ultimately, the very nationhood of the republic will be undermined. Now is our last chance to sustain it. Otherwise, it will disappear within ten or fifteen years with the loss of the rest of the national territory, without there being either the means or the sense of national glory with which to resist.

The truth is that in order to blunt the force of this last consideration, to calm the just fears of those who see in these negotiations the funeral of our political existence and a melancholy future for our people in the territory which they have inherited from their fathers, we must teach the necessity of bracing up our courage. The social advantages which would accrue to us by accepting a peace now have been exaggerated, as well as the ease with which we would be able to maintain our remaining territories. It would be necessary, in order to sustain such illusions, to underestimate the spirit of enterprise of the North American people in industrial and commercial pursuits, to misunderstand their history and their tendencies, and also to presuppose in our own spirit less resistance than we have already shown toward the sincere friends of progress. Only through such illusions might one maintain that the treaty would bring a change that would be advantageous to us—as has been claimed.

With the borders of our conquerors brought closer to the heart of our nation, with the whole line of the frontier occupied by them from sea to sea, with their highly developed merchant marine, and with them so versed in the system of colonization by which they attract great numbers of the laboring classes from the old world, what can we, who are so backward in everything, do to arrest them in their rapid conquests, their latest invasions? Thousands of men will come daily to establish themselves under American auspices in the new territories with which we will have obliged them. There they will develop their commerce and stockpile large quantities of merchandise brought from the upper states. They will inundate us with all this, and our own modicum of wealth, already so miserable and depleted, will in the future sink to insignificance and nothingness. We will not accomplish anything by lowering our maritime duties, abolishing our internal customshouses, or suppressing our restrictive laws. The Anglo Americans, now situated so close to our populated provinces, will provide these areas with the marvels of the world, passing them from the frontier zones to our southern states, and having withal the advantage over us of attracting our own merchants as well as our consumers, who will favor these foreigners because of the low prices at which they will be able to buy American goods. This will be the situation because, even if we limit ourselves to imposing only a 20 percent duty on goods brought through our ports, which might well be very difficult for us to do, we will never be able to make our markets competitive with those of the North American importers, who will be able to sell much cheaper because they will have paid very little or no duty on goods which they have slipped through the border. The drawback [reimbursement of customs duties] alone, well known in that republic, is enough to give them an advantage that will finish off our frontier and maritime customs. Meanwhile, we do not even have the resources necessary to maintain our frontier border area.

And what defense would be sufficient, given the fact that we do not have enough troops to guard such an extensive frontier, to prevent fraudulent crossings? Imagine what contentions will arise with the other side, what quarrels and disputes with the brazen smugglers of that republic, what continual claims and demands for indemnity, which will finally amount to such immense sums that they will provide a pretext for the threat of another war, and we will end by yielding, without resistance, the rest of our territory! Why have we so soon forgotten what happened to us in New Mexico, the Californias, and Chihuahua, where large armed bands, sometimes supplied with artillery pieces, continually trespassed into our territory in order to bring in merchandise without paying any duty or submitting to our laws and regulations? Do we think perhaps that the same things will not happen again in those regions because our neighbors have brought their frontiers closer? Gentlemen, what is proposed to us in this fatal treaty amounts to a sentence of death, and I wonder that there could have been Mexicans who would have negotiated it and subscribed to it, thinking all the while that it would be a boon to our unfortunate country. This circumstance alone dismays me and makes me despair of the life of the republic.

Now, as to colonizing, which is another of the most efficient expedients that we ought to pursue in order to gain some stability and strength, how will we be able to oppose the rapid development of the United States, which, due to this type of colonization, has prodigiously expanded its population? This growth, in turn, has fueled the avidity for new lands that consumes that country and the spirit of conquest which animates it. With less than 4 million inhabitants at the time it gained its independence from Great Britain, the United States has increased its population to 20 million in the short space of seventy-four years through that system which it has so well understood and known how to apply to its special circumstances. The rate of increase of our population has been set at 1.8 percent annually, according to the calculations of our National Institute of Geography and Physics, confirmed by the reckonings of Baron von Humboldt. However, despite these projections, we have not even achieved that modest rate of growth, if the recent figures of that same institute are to be credited, because there has not been the doubling of the population over a period of forty years that had been predicted. During twenty-six years of that period, years that have been arbiters of our fate, we could have been able to and should have promoted the immigration of European families in order to establish them in the immense deserts of our northern frontier and thus assure by their presence our possession of that region against the mounting invasions of our ambitious neighbors. But, limited as we have been in our methods of development to what we learned during the colonial regime, we have not wanted to go beyond them and create wide opportunities for those who wanted to speculate in large colonizing enterprises, nor have we understood the advantages of such ventures or given the kind of assiduous and constant attention to them that such important enterprises demand. Far from having followed the example of the United States in interesting people in the large profits to be made in land development, we have turned to other, completely ruinous means to conjure up colossal fortunes, which on the one hand depleted the national store of wealth and on the other diverted capital that could have been used for colonizing. Had it not been for our squandering this money, it would have flowed into those enterprises in which the profit of the individual coincides with the vital interests of the nation. But the time will soon pass when we will be able to arrange things to our own advantage by studying North American legislative actions, the only measures in these parts that are applicable to us and that could reveal to us ways in which to exploit the immense treasures of the frontier region, and to make us feared and respected in the universe.

Once having approved the treaty, however, it will no longer be possible for us to take advantage of those important initiatives that might be indicated to us. It will be difficult enough for us to overcome the resistance, the petty and ruinous ideas that even those men who pass for the most eminent in the party—that party which calls itself the party of the intelligentsia—have placed in opposition to the friends of progress. But how much more difficult will it be for us to overcome the obstacles to our prosperity that face us in the form of the United States, in both its policy and its preponderance of resources, if that country is to take possession of our most precious lands?

The United States has a well-established reputation in the Old World for hospitality as well as a knowledge of how to deal with prospective immigrants, all of which we totally lack. In addition, it has a merchant marine which competes with that of Great Britain and has all kinds of facilities for transporting to the United States the excess population of a populous Europe. What methods can we adopt to divert to our side even a part of this immigration, to overcome the preference that is given to the United States because of the exalted idea of its civilization and wealth which obtains abroad? With the very fertile lands that the United States will be taking from us, with climates milder than any which they have possessed up until now, with brilliant port facilities for maritime commerce such as are offered by that inestimable jewel, Upper California, the United States will cause Europe to empty out, gentlemen, and the European immigrants will amalgamate with the present population of the United States and will take the lead in establishing themselves over us. Our race then, our poor people, will have to become nomadic, searching for hospitality in foreign lands, only to be ejected later to still other places. As almost all of us are descended from Indians, the North American people abominate us, their orators depreciating us even while recognizing the justice of our cause. Since they consider us unworthy of forming with them a single nation or society, they have manifested clearly that in their future conquests they will strip us of our land and thrust us aside. Has their conduct, in fact, been any other in their treatment of the Indian tribes, former owners of the land which now belongs to those same United States?

MANUEL DE LA PEÑA Y PEÑA

EDITOR'S INTRODUCTION

Manuel de la Peña y Peña divided his life between public service and the law, and at critical junctures these two came together. He taught public law at the National University, of whose College of Law he became Rector, and he became president of the Academy of Jurisprudence. He published importantly in the area of law. At various times in his public career he was a Supreme Court magistrate, minister of the Interior, senator, minister of Foreign Relations, president of the Supreme Court, and finally interim president of the Republic. He accepted this last assignment as a "journey to the grave," when Mexico was in its hour of desperation. Its defeated army had evacuated the capital, and the government had fled to the city of Querétaro. Peña y Peña, while still maintaining the title of President of the Supreme Court, agreed to act as Interim President and to oversee the fashioning of a treaty of peace.

On the political spectrum, he represented the conservative wing of the moderate liberals. In 1845, on the eve of the war, Peña y Peña, as Minister of Foreign Relations, warned that differences with the United States should be resolved through negotiations. In the atmosphere of war fever that prevailed at that time, a stance such as his required courage. It was Peña y Peña, who, as foreign minister, wrote to Slidell saying that the Mexican government would not receive him because Slidell insisted upon being received in the full panoply of Envoy Extraordinary and Minister Plenipotentiary. Slidell, in his dispatch to Washington, complained of the "unparalleled bad faith" of the Mexican government.

In his defense of the Treaty of Guadalupe Hidalgo which follows, Peña y Peña cites his early advocacy of peace as part of the moral credentials that he has brought to his bitter task of presiding over treaty negotiations that had to be costly to Mexico. His basic argument was that despite the high-flown and inflammatory statements of those who urged a continuation of the war, such a continuation would bring to Mexico only anarchy, untold suffering, and in all likelihood a greater loss than that which faced Mexico at the time in which he stood before the Mexican Congress to defend the treaty. When he contended that the Mexican people deserved peace after thirty-seven years of warfare, he in effect publicly accused the successive *criollo* governments that had followed the War of Independence of having kept Mexico in a continual state of uproar. His statement that of all the issues that the negotiators of the treaty faced none caused them more anguish than the fate of those Mexicans who, in the ceded territories, faced a future life under an alien government has the ring of sincerity to it. But the contention that he and the other negotiators would have gladly ceded twice as much territory if this act could have secured the liberty of those Mexicans seems at first surprising. After all, the treaty provided that those Mexicans living within the ceded territories could choose as to whether they wanted to maintain their Mexican citizenship or to become American citizens. They were, furthermore, to be allowed complete freedom of movement. The provisions seem to have been quite liberal. However, Peña y Peña may have foreseen that these newly minted Americans, as well as their descendants, were to face several forms of oppression in their new land.

As a skilled lawyer and seasoned public servant, Peña y Peña obviously was well aware of the real and potential opposition he faced in trying to get acceptance of a drastic treaty by a reluctant congress and by the Mexican people at large. The reader of his defense of the treaty senses the great care that Peña y Peña takes to clothe his sentences in the majestic rhetoric of state. Furthermore, he is clearly most anxious to place the negotiations at Guadalupe Hidalgo within the established norms of international diplomacy. Yet withal, the dignity, honor, and sincerity of the man shine clearly through. The text of Peña y Peña's defense of the treaty which follows picks up at the point at which he has finished the preliminary niceties and gets on to the main line of his argument.

"An Address in Support of
the Treaty of Guadalupe Hidalgo"

Delivered to the Mexican Congress on May 7, 1848

Having been convinced for some years that the Republic could not sustain the first of those two extremes [that is, a war with the United States], I made all possible efforts consistent with my loyalty and within the scope of my legal training to bring about a peaceful solution to the differences that had arisen between the two republics. My conviction for peace, once arrived at, was not going to change in 1845, and it never occurred to me that it was incompatible with either the interests or, properly understood, the honor of the nation. I have always been persuaded that all nations, even the most warlike, have at some time or other found themselves in circumstances in which they did not have the power to resist the enemy that had invaded them. They, as do individual men, have periods of vigor and of weakness, and they cannot exempt themselves from the laws of the human condition. A conjunction of circumstances, which need not be gone into in detail but which can be well explained by our interior discord, resulting from a lack of effective

Translated from Alberto María Carreño, *México y Los Estados Unidos de América*, Mexico, D.F.: Editorial Jus, 1962 (Second Edition), pp. 192–194.

public administration, convinced me in my innermost being of the grave difficulties that the country would encounter in attempting to successfully prosecute a war against the United States. Anyone who holds this conviction and yet finds in it an offense to our name and honor does not reason well as a statesman nor, and much the less so, as a man of integrity.

Having been called by the constitution to exercise the office of supreme magistrate at the very time in which our capital was occupied and our army dispersed, I felt that the extent of our misfortune had the more confirmed my ideas about peace. Even though undeserving of holding the reins of government and lacking any title other than that of Chief Justice of the Supreme Court, I could not decline this difficult task to which I have been called without exposing the nation to a horrible anarchy, nor could I fail to conduct myself in this foreign crisis in any manner other than in conformity with the deepest promptings of my conscience. Therefore, the necessity of putting the government in the hands of a person firmly decided upon peace made me believe (if you will permit me the frankness) that Providence had called upon me to continue the work which had begun in 1845 and which could, therefore, end in the advantage and glory of the nation, and which might now, even though costly, still save its honor and secure its independence.

But since representative governments, and more particularly those under the republican form, must abide by public opinion, I decided upon an investigation into public attitudes, and, putting my own opinions aside, I sought in good faith to find out to what extent the states would cooperate in continuing the war should such a continuance be voted upon by a majority in the central government of the republic. I can assure you, gentlemen, that after that examination I can take no other position than that of being in favor of peace.

The cities in the provinces together with their authorities have foreseen, as has the central government, all the evils of a prolonged war, and although disposed to an uprising that could restore brilliance to our arms if there were no other choice in the matter, they will, as long as there are avenues and honorable avenues for peace, condemn the government for its lack of wisdom should it fail to put a prompt end to their sufferings. The people have an incontestable right not to have to suffer more than they are suffering in their present situation. And it would not only be a great injustice but also a great inhumanity to put them through all the horrors of a renewed and bloody battle, especially after the many years of civil war.

I felt satisfied and in a tranquil state of mind in my conviction that a great majority of the people in the nation supported the conduct of the government. Therefore, I acceded to the desires of the American Commission to renew the negotiations which, as the Congress knows, had been suspended due to unfortunate circumstances in September of last year. The interim president, who succeeded me after the first period of my government, named commissioners who had his full confidence, and they took on their responsibilities with all the zeal and loyalty consistent with their well-merited reputations. But he decided not to proceed with anything until the beginning of January. Although faithful to and consistent with the system that I had adopted, he wanted nevertheless to take a further reading of public sentiment to find out what changes might have occurred as the public had become informed about the state of the nation and about the opinions of the press of both nations, which presented so many diverse views of the question at hand. No one can accuse the government of having attacked freedom of thought throughout this period, nor can anyone doubt the sincerity with which it has sought the skills and the support of all good citizens in these negotiations of such transcendent importance. The charges that have been made against the government for not having adopted the extreme measure of continuing the war you may weigh, gentlemen, with all the calm deliberation appropriate in matters that have to do with the most cherished interests of an unfortunate nation, and the judgment of an impartial history will certainly not condemn my intentions because the uprightness which has attended my course has been so evident from the moment of that fatal rupture with the United States.

The instructions handed down by me in my capacity then as Minister of Relations to the delegates commissioned by the Republic, although they sought, as is usual, for more than can practically be expected from such negotiations, never were of a fixed character. The fact that the government was given leeway to modify these instructions according to the successive changes of information that it might receive gave the commissioners freedom to conclude a negotiation, always with the proviso that there not be imputed, either in the text of the treaty or in its spirit, any offense to our honor or any compromise that might bring shame to a civilized people. This government, although very decided in favor of peace and disposed to make the sacrifices demanded by the circumstances, never once thought of subjecting itself to humiliating conditions that would give to the negotiations a character unworthy of their independence. If, as the government so conceived, war had its limits, so too did peace. Even the extreme misfortune of the nation could not excuse the putting aside of consideration and mutual respect between nation and nation, between government and government, for if such things be necessary during the ordinary course of pacific relations, how much the more so in times of adversity? And here I would have you note, gentlemen, that the invitations to discuss peace have come directly from the United States, that it was that country which sent its plenipotentiaries to the [Mexican] Republic to initiate negotiations; and that there has not been a single act on the part of the Mexican government in the course of these sessions that could be characterized as base or weak.

The Ministry of Relations will transmit to the Chambers of Congress all the documents—documents which justify the zeal for the national interest on the part of both the government and of the plenipotentiaries—as well as the articles of the treaty itself, as signed at Guadalupe on the second of February. You will be convinced, as is this government, that the cession of territory was the least that could be agreed upon and that it was not possible to hope that in this matter the United States would modify its demands. As large as are the territories of Texas, Upper California, and New Mexico,* the government of the United States has declared to its Congress that without the cession of these territories it will continue the war under the plan as indicated by the president in his message of the sixth of December of last year. Given the desirability of a peace settlement, the negotiations cannot be condemned for not having lessened the loss of territory, and perhaps they

*The New Mexico territory of the war period comprised the present-day state of New Mexico plus parts of Arizona, Utah, Colorado, and Nevada.

even deserve praise for having seen to it that the first territorial demands were not later increased—especially in view of the facts that the capital was lost and the army, which evacuated it on the thirteenth of September, was disbanded.

If the government could have had any reason to hope that the United States would retreat from claims upon territories for which it had no legitimate right, it would have conducted itself in another manner, perhaps putting off the treaty for a more opportune time. But the solemn and repeated declarations of the American Minister left no room for doubt that there would be no peace without the cession of Mexican territories. The government and its plenipotentiaries, nevertheless, have given prominence to the justness of the nation's cause, and I can declare to you that nothing that should have been done has been omitted. The well-known events of the immediate past amply vindicate the judgment by which the government designated the times for the negotiations to begin and to end.

In achieving the following—in terms of honor and security—the negotiations have accomplished all that could be expected from these types of transactions: the armistice which was celebrated as a result of the treaty and the reestablishment of constitutional order in all its branches; the ample guarantees obtained for Mexicans residing in the ceded territories, whether they retained their Mexican citizenship or became American citizens; the suppression of barbarous tribes that could make incursions across our boundaries; the indemnification of fifteen million dollars and the assumption on the part of the government of the United States of all claims by its citizens against the [Mexican] Republic; the solemn promise to ease, should at any time occasion arise, the calamities of the war and respect the recognized rights of humanity and society; and finally the fixed stipulation that the boundary line established by Article Five will never be changed without the free and expressed consent of both republics, given by their governments in conformance to their respective constitutions.

If the government has had to put up with some things as faits accomplis and has not insisted on obedience to tariff and other public finance laws, when it comes to goods passing through our customs or being introduced into the interior of the Republic, it has done so only because of the recognized principle by which no treaty is considered to be in force until it has been duly ratified. All that has been agreed upon concerning matters of finance or commerce will be easily explained by the above-mentioned principle and the practice generally adopted by all nations under such circumstances.

The treaty, gentlemen, now concluded by our plenipotentiaries in the city of Guadalupe is submitted to the judgment of our national representatives, of public opinion, and also to the assessment that foreign countries will make of it. The end of a war such as the one we have suffered through, with its consequent changes, is of interest to the entire world, merits the scrutiny of philosophers and statesmen, and by its very nature brings about a new period of vital importance for the Republic. The treaties which nations arrive at must, in their various aspects, come to terms with such concepts as justice, humanity, propriety, and honor, but ultimately they will be judged in terms of whether they can be characterized as beneficial or prejudicial. Consequently, opinions will vary considerably, and it is very difficult to weigh the wide range of hardships among which one might choose upon the scales of cold reason and dispassionate calculation. Nevertheless, the Treaty of Guadalupe, however it might be characterized by the present generation or by those that succeed it, will not be blamed for bringing upon the liberty and sovereignty of the nation any taint of the dishonorable or the offensive, nor will it be unworthy of a noble misfortune or of any generous sentiments. The Mexican Republic has dealt with the United States and they with it as independent peoples, and the text and spirit of the negotiations, you may well believe, do not merit the charges that have been made against us during the war.

The truth is that a fertile and beautiful part of our territory is being ceded, a considerable expanse out of which flourishing states could be formed. I have no wish to obscure the truth in such solemn moments as these and much less to deny the pain which I feel at the separation from the national union of the Mexicans of Upper California and New Mexico, and I wish to consign to you in trust a testimony of the concern with which my administration has viewed these people. Be assured, gentlemen, that their future well-being has been the most serious consideration that has faced these negotiations, and if it had been possible, even more territory would have been ceded in exchange for the liberty of the Mexican populations therein. The reflection that should the war have continued their state would only have worsened has brought me the consolation of knowing that the evils they might have suffered will never be the responsibility of my administration. A war always brings with it the most deplorable changes, and a war as unfortunate as ours could not have been exempt from those sacrifices which befall, in such situations, all societies.

But costly as such sacrifices can be, it is nonetheless important that a loss be in conformance with established principles of policy in terms of justice and foresight. And in this sense, our provisions not only do not oppose but are consonant with those that have been carried out with honor and dignity by the most powerful nations of the world. Whoever wishes to characterize the Treaty of Guadalupe as dishonorable because of the amount of territory lost must make the same charges against the principal nations of the world, and yet he will not resolve the question of how to bring to an end a disastrous war. The decorum and honor of governments and nations are upheld by invariable principles of a very different character from those that govern the passions of the populace, often noble but more generally low and mean. To put up a dike before a torrent that devastates everything, to avoid the useless spilling of blood, to return the nation to its normal state so that it can enjoy the benefits of peace and public order—and to do all of this while satisfying the unjust demands of the enemy which has been successful in battle—this requires an act of wisdom that calls upon the joint counsels of Christianity and civilization. The territories ceded by the treaty have not been given up for the sum of fifteen million dollars, but to recover our ports and invaded cities, to put a definite stop to all types of evils and horrors, to console the multitudes of families who have abandoned their homes and trades and are reduced or in the process of being reduced to beggary, to take advantage of the occasion, which Providence has presented us, to bring regularity and order to a people who have not ceased from suffering throughout the long period of thirty-seven years. Let us do the right thing, gentlemen; let us strip off the veil that has prevented us from seeing the reality of things, and let us hope that peace, that precious gift we have not known how to appreciate, will shed upon us all the benefits we have desired and will certainly obtain if we for once are firm in opposing a resistance which drives blindly toward disorder and anarchy.

If the treaty could have been submitted to your deliberation just as it came from the hands of the plenipotentiaries, my satisfaction at seeing the war being brought to a close would not be diminished in the way that it is now being diminished by the modifications the Senate of the United States has introduced and its president has ratified. I would have wished that nothing had been altered in a negotiation with which the government of the United States had been in substantial agreement, not only because I do not consider these modifications to be favorable but also because I would have wished to avoid having them viewed in an exaggerated manner. You will be instructed in detail as to the reasons set forth by the United States Minister to justify these changes, and you will be given full knowledge of the relevant documents to guide you to a more secure and valid judgment. For the moment let me just say that in the opinion of the government it was not in the interest of justice for the senate and government of the United States to introduce these alterations, but that nevertheless our government is persuaded that they are not of such an importance that the treaty should be thrown out on their account. On the contrary, it believes that the treaty should be ratified in the form that it comes to us from that government. It believes this all the more strongly because it does not consider that a new round of negotiations can be hoped for nor that such a development would result in terms more favorable to the Republic.

The nature of this discourse and the sense of security that you will find in the documents that the Minister of Relations will provide to the Houses of Congress—containing all the necessary data—do not permit me to expand further on the subject of the treaty nor to offend your erudition with observations the purport of which you will no doubt discover for yourselves in the course of your examination. But permit me to assure you that it was not a baseless fear nor much the less so was it an unfavorable opinion of the moral and physical force of the Mexican people that obliged me to decide for peace. Nothing less than this: I have lived long enough to witness the heroic efforts that this nation made to sustain an unequal struggle over eleven years and to win at last its independence. In that same civil war I was able to observe what elements of strength this people has when it is directed by valor and energy. In this foreign war, we have just seen, although in few engagements, what have been the valor and constancy of our soldiers when they have been led by honorable and confident officers. And we all have noted that the war would have had a different outcome had there been effective organization in the army and the national guard. I have not believed, nor do I believe, that the Republic is absolutely incapable of carrying on the war or of giving examples that could transmit to posterity a sense of glory. But with the same frankness and good faith I am convinced that the situation in which we find ourselves, with all circumstances considered, loudly calls for peace. The deliberation over the war is not, as some politicians believe, a matter that can be given over to experiments or adventurous sallies. The desire for military glory cannot justify the continuation of present calamities; and especially when it is considered that lacking a national navy and with the ceded territories so distant we cannot prudently expect that a continued war effort would result in favorable negotiations that would salvage our territorial integrity. On the contrary, I believe that our loss would be greater, and the conduct of the government and the congress would not be forgiven for not having prevented yet other and more horrible disasters. In our judgment, nothing should be considered that is not in conformance with the truth, and only reckless passion can characterize this sober realism as being timid or excessively cautious. The resources for a continued resistance cannot be instantly created, nor can it be conceded to the most vigorous administration that it can make the distances of such a vast extension of territory disappear or that it can agglomerate to the coastal and frontier areas all the population of the central region.

The arguments that are now made against the peace are of the same sort that were made in 1845, first against recognizing the independence of Texas and then against negotiating with the United States, as the administration of that time wished to do. Now we lament that there had not prevailed at that time a procedure for preserving the peace. The present disillusion of those men who opposed it at that time can now be of no help to the Republic in its misfortune. Being too late, such an awakening is sterile. But it can give us a lesson that we should never forget. Let us not forget it, gentlemen, and let us make a mighty effort so that our children will not damn our memory.

Contemplate what would be the confusion and anarchy into which we would see our country sink if, with the continuing of this foreign war, all the germs of discord and the fires of passion were to be aroused, as undoubtedly they would be. Already we have seen too much of social disorganization, insecurity among our people, danger along the highways, paralyzation of all the branches of public welfare, and general misery.

FRANCISCO BULNES

EDITOR'S INTRODUCTION

Francisco Bulnes was the enfant terrible of Mexican positivism. He was a skeptic and iconoclast and has even been called a "destroyer." Both his acceptance of the objective viewpoint espoused by positivism and his scientific training inclined him toward rationalistic skepticism. At the same time, the maverick in his nature made him relish coming up with the shocker vis à vis the standard Mexican pieties. He loved polemics, and, no doubt, part of his great success as a teacher could be attributed to his ability to stir up the students with his high-spirited outrageousness.

Carlos González Peña says of Bulnes in *History of Mexican Literature:* "Though much of his work still stands firm, no little part has been rejected as unreliable or even false, both because of its emotional origin and because of his reliance on and presentation of insufficient and incorrectly interpreted information" (Dallas, 1968, p. 347). He was, nonetheless, a man of formidable intellect, and it is quite possible that some of his opinions, thought to be of "emotional origin," may stand as valuable correctives to opposing opinions among Mexican writers that might themselves have been of "emotional origin." At any rate, it is certain that he explored areas of scholarship, particularly North American, that had been neglected by other Mexican writers. His literary style was emphatic and was liberally laced with sarcasm and acerbic humor.

Francisco Bulnes was born in Mexico City in 1847 and died in the capital city, after a long and prolific life, in 1924. Perhaps it was because he was such a resolute *capitalino* that he showed such scant respect for the Mexican provinces. His training was in civil and mining engineering, and his deep avocations were teaching, journalism, and politics. For thirty years he was a deputy and senator in the Mexican congress, where he distinguished himself as a persuasive speaker.

Bulnes's career coincided with the powerful and effective dictatorship of Porfírio Díaz, whose long rule over Mexico, which extended
from 1877 to 1880 and then from 1884 to 1911, has been known as the
Porfiriato. The atmosphere of this reign was congenial to a man like
Bulnes. Díaz was vastly impatient with the anarchy and inefficiency that
had made Mexico a byword among nations. He embraced the scientific
spirit of his times and surrounded himself with efficient technocrats who
came to be known as "los científicos." Foreign investment was not only
tolerated but courted, and Mexico was brought into the modern, industrial age. Political parties and the army were tamed and made to serve the
ruler. In his favoring of the progressive, industrial sector of society, Díaz
neglected the agricultural hinterland, where long-standing—and some
new—injustices festered. But it would take some time before Díaz
would reap the whirlwind caused by this neglect. Meanwhile, Mexico
basked in a prosperity it had not known since colonial times. Firm as was
the rule of the Porfiriato, considerable intellectual freedom was allowed,
as long as there was no direct affront to authority. Intellectuals like
Bulnes and Justo Sierra flourished, and their positivism was in tune with
the scientific spirit of the times. Porfírio Díaz recognized the great
talents of Francisco Bulnes, but he also was aware of the eccentricity and
prickly individualism of that potent intellectual. Díaz did not trust him.
Surely, he could be a deputy or senator—he was both—or he could be
put in charge of some scientific commission—which he was on a
number of occasions—but he could not be trusted with a ministry.
Nevertheless, Bulnes remained a loyal *porfirista* until the end. When the
great revolution finally broke out after the first decade of the twentieth
century, and most of Mexico's intellectuals had rallied to its cause,
Bulnes was defending Díaz and writing articles in *El Universal* attacking
the Revolution.

Both Díaz and Bulnes shared elitist views of humanity and society.
Bulnes, for example, was an unabashed racist and thought that Indians
and mestizos were inferior beings. Ironically, the leader whom he
served and admired was a mestizo in whom the Indian element was pre-
dominant. For Bulnes, even the pure-blooded Spaniard was inferior to
the Saxon, and he was pessimistic about the countries of Latin America.
Among them, only Mexico, Argentina, Uruguay, and Chile might pos-

sibly arrive at a respectable level of national development. "Our real enemies," he wrote, "are not Europe and the United States . . . , they are . . . our tradition, our history, our morbid heritage, our alcoholism, our education which goes against the development of character. If we do not know how to save ourselves, history will write on our tomb the epitaph which the Persians put over the Babylonians whom they had conquered: 'Here lie those who did not deserve this earth, not even as a grave' " (*Selected Pages*, Mexico, D.F., 1968, p. xiii).

Perhaps early travels through both the great ancient civilizations and the progressive modern ones prompted Bulnes to make unfavorable comparisons with the conditions he had known back home. After a trip through the United States, Cuba, Japan, China, Indochina, Egypt, and Italy, Bulnes wrote a book describing his youthful impressions of the world. *Over the Northern Hemisphere, 11,000 Leagues* (1875) owed a conscious debt to Jules Verne. It is a sprightly book, full of irony and humor, as well as of astute insights. It is the book which most reveals the author's personality.

There followed an outpouring of publication from a man whose mind was energetic and tireless. Among the principal works are: *The Future of the Latin American Nations* (1899); *The Great Lies of Our History* (1904); *The True Juarez* (1904); *Juarez and the Revolutions of Ayutla and the Reform* (1905); *The War of Independence Hidalgo Iturbide* (1910); and *The Great Problems of Mexico*, a collection of articles published posthumously in 1927.

The strain of heresy in Bulnes's makeup allowed him to look upon the United States generally and the Mexican-American War in particular from a fresh vantage point. Bulnes differed from other Mexican writers of the nineteenth and early twentieth centuries in his ability and determination to view the Texas Revolution and the Mexican-American War within the context of North American political and social developments of the time, as well as in terms of the thrust of Spanish colonial and Mexican history. He recognized the extent to which the colonization of Texas by Americans was a southern venture, bringing with it the southern institution of slavery. He also understood that the Mexican-American War itself was also, to a considerable extent, a southern venture under a southern president. Observing the situation from this stance, Bulnes suggested some bold alternatives to how Spain, and later independent Mexico, should have devised policies for the borderlands.

Bulnes looked upon the North American heartlands from a sophisticated, geopolitical point of view. He comprehended the urgency by which the power that owned the great Mississippi basin sought an access to the sea. From the same geopolitical standpoint, he understood why the Anglo Texans under Mexico, separated by high deserts from the nearest Mexican centers of commerce, engaged in contraband trade with the United States. They did so, as Bulnes put it, "not in their capacity as colonists and for the hatred of the Mexican Republic but in their simple capacity as men and for the love of their own self interest." The trade was contraband, incidentally, because the Mexican government imposed high and bitterly resented tariffs on trade with the United States.

Bulnes put considerable stress on the militaristic legacy from Spain and its later corruption under the Mexican Republic. In the course of this examination, he takes issue with the numerous Mexican writers who have compared North American Indian policy unfavorably with that of Mexico. A common Mexican view has been that Mexico dreaded the approaching threat of United States expansion at the expense of Mexico because, among other things, North American racism, which had led to the extermination of the Indians in the United States, would then be leveled against Mexicans, who were themselves partly Indian. The Mexican upholders of this view would then make the point that Mexico, in contrast, had preserved its Indian population. Bulnes refutes this cherished position in a devastating manner.

In tracing the development of militarism, Bulnes puts stress on the years 1823 and 1830. In 1823, with Mexico still under Spanish colonial rule, Stephen Austin, with due permission from Spain, took his first group of American families, now sworn to be Spanish citizens, into Texas. The seeds were sown for the Texas Revolution and, by extension, the Mexican-American War. Most Mexican writers have looked upon the Texas Revolution, with considerable justice, as the curtain raiser for the Mexican-American War. By 1830, only five years before the Texas Revolution, praetorianism, that attitude among the military which held that the army did not exist for the welfare of the country but rather for the pursuit of its own ambitions, had, according to Bulnes, thoroughly set in. And it was praetorianism that thoroughly corrupted the body politic of Mexico, according to Bulnes's firm conviction, and which rendered Mexico incapable of defending itself against North American aggression.

In a chapter entitled "The Bellicose Megalomania," Bulnes scoffs at the pretensions of the Mexican army in 1830, shortly before Santa Anna, the arch praetorian, attempted to subdue Texas. Generals boasted publicly that the Mexican army was the best in the world and would soon teach the United States a lesson. Bulnes quotes the French periodical, "Revue de Deux Mondes" of July 1836, in its ridicule of Mexican military bombast, even after the defeat of the Mexican army in Texas. In fact, Bulnes maintains, the Mexican treasury at that time was so empty that soldiers went not only underpaid but often underfed.

When the Mexican army entered Texas in support of Santa Anna's centrist policy, it constantly violated, according to Bulnes, the civil and judiciary procedures contained in the constitution of 1824 and in the state constitution of Coahuila and Texas. Bulnes quotes a letter from Stephen Austin to General Mier y Terán in which Austin says that to the extent that the military presence in Texas is reduced, to that extent peace will return to Texas.

Beyond the ravages of praetorianism, political ineptness contributed to the disasters which Mexico encountered during this period. Bulnes assesses the extent to which the conservatives and the liberals were to blame for these catastrophes. He concluded that they shared equally in the blame. The conservatives, with Lucas Alamán as Secretary of Foreign Relations, exempted Texas from the emancipation proclamation issued by President Guerrero. This, according to Bulnes, was folly because it played into the hands of the American South, which wanted Texas to bolster the strength of the slave-holding states in the South. It was also under the conservatives that the militarization of Texas was undertaken.

In a highly caustic chapter entitled "Alamán's Marvelous Colonists," Bulnes appears to enjoy himself at the expense of Alamán and his colonization scheme by which the Anglo Texan influence was to be

countered by a new style of colonist to be sent north to the deserts of
Texas. These new pioneers were to consist of prisoners from Mexico
City jails and other cast-offs of Mexican society. The total failure of
such a scheme could well be anticipated. Lucas Alamán, Bulnes observed, was a fine historian, but as a statesman highly impractical.

Bulnes now turns his attentions to the liberals, from whom better
might have been expected. However, under the administration of Valentín Gómez Farías, the complete *puro*, the same mistakes were repeated in the areas of militarism, slavery, and tariffs imposed upon the
Texans. In addition, in an interesting discussion of a little-known
subject, Bulnes takes the liberals to task for not alleviating the discrimi-
nations which Texas suffered under its forced linkage with the state of
Coahuila.

Bulnes, no doubt, could be quite harsh in his indictments, for
example, in his treatment of the provincialism of the state governments,
which undermined the federal authority, but he also brings a bracing
freshness and originality to his analysis of how Mexico faced the approaching storm.

The Great Lies of Our History

Our first disgrace was that nobody in Mexico knew, at the opportune time, anything about the social and profoundly economic problem of the United States [slavery] and its necessary political solutions, with which our patriotism and intelligence could have energetically come to grips.

The first effort of Mexican policy, after the country learned of the compromise of 1820 [the Missouri Compromise], should have been to force the southern states to proceed toward the total conquest of Mexico or to make it impossible for them to accomplish the gradual conquest, which was their ambition and design. To forestall the latter, all that was necessary was not to have allowed Texas to be admitted into the [Mexican] Republic as slave territory but to have insisted upon its being completely free.

If Texas had been colonized by a non slave-holding population, a people of the first order of vigor and public spirit, the southern states

Translated from *Las Grandes Mentiras de Nuestra Historia,* Paris and Mexico, D.F.: Librería de la Vda DE C.H. BOURET, 1904, pp. 130–132, 158–160, 182–183, and 341–346.

could not have plotted to convert it into a slave state, because a state with a civilized population and free labor cannot be changed into a population based on slave labor. The South would thus have been thwarted in its policy and would have felt it necessary to pressure the North to join it in a war against Mexico in 1823 to prevent the border region from becoming populated by non-slaveholders of the type who would have prevented the imposition of slavery. Failing in this, the South would then have had to resort to a war of secession, in which case it would have been defeated as it was in 1863. If, by any chance, the South should have been victorious, then there would have been two nations, and Mexico would only have had to fight with the weaker of the two.

In 1823 the United States was in no position to undertake a war with Mexico for the same reasons that I will articulate in asserting that it was in no such position in 1830. The Mexican government should have authorized the colonization of Texas only under the condition that slavery be excluded, which condition would have assured that only northern Americans, not southern, would have established themselves in Texas. These northerners, devoted to free labor and opposed to slavery, would never have permitted themselves, in the case of annexation, to be transformed into a slave-holding population. If the southern states had had as their neighbor a Texas which was settled by northerners who were enemies of slavery, they would have viewed with horror the annexation of Texas to the United States, because that would have meant the addition of one or more free states to the Union, which in turn would have signaled the downfall of southern political and social power. Would prohibiting the concessionaire Austin from bringing colonists into Texas who were slaveholders or imposing on him the obligation of perpetually maintaining his colony as being free of slavery, would such moves have been sufficient to have prevented the storm that arose in Texas? Such a stipulation would have been a great and effective act of prevision. But the *omnipotent ones* are not obliged to have the sort of prevision designed to prevent an evil, because the *omnipotent ones* are invulnerable in the face of evil. In 1823 we considered ourselves to be the *omnipotent ones*, we were the prime military power of the universe, the richest nation, the most illustrious and most virtuous one. Our immediate destiny was to possess a grandeur such as no other nation had ever experienced. To have used prevision would have been to degenerate, to have dishonored ourselves, to have abdicated from a position of infinite power. To have pretended that in 1823 we should have feared the power of the United States and employed a skillful diplomacy to defend our honor and territory would have been like expecting an archmillionaire to stay awake all night wondering how he was going to pay his tailor or feed his children the next day. The *social megalomania* in its most pernicious form, the *bellicose megalomania*, did us great damage in 1823 by impeding us from modifying to any extent our lugubrious destiny.

. . .

The benevolence of the Spanish conquest in its policy of preserving rather than exterminating the Indians—the latter being often thrown in the face of the North Americans—is a confection designed to be swallowed by the ignorant. When one encounters sheep in a territory, one saves them for the shearing. But when, instead of sheep, one encounters wolves and panthers, one exterminates them. The Spaniards saved for the shearing those Indians who were tame, sweet, affable, and submissive, who had been disciplined by the despotism of the Aztecs or by other ferocious chiefs. But as for the barbarous Indians, the Spaniards did the same thing to them as did the North Americans. We have for this, among the statements of other respected authorities, the word of the Baron von Humboldt: "A later, more enlightened legislation hardly served to erase the memory of those barbarous times in which a corporal or sergeant with his patrol would hunt the Indians in the outlying provinces as though they were engaged in a deer hunt" (*Political Essay,* Vol. I, p. 227). The missions did very little and bullets did a lot toward the conquest of the immense territories extending beyond the present states of San Luis Potosí and Zacatecas. After the independence, the Mexicans rid themselves of the barbarous Indians who had been razing the frontier states and had been the first possessors of those territories, and they did this by the process of exterminating them.

The policy of Spain as conqueror was to be absolute mistress of the Gulf of Mexico, for which reason it took control of all of its coasts, but in some places it did not gain mastery over those countries adjacent to those coasts. It would be necessary for the nation or nations that held the richest territory in the world, the valley of the Mississippi, situated between the Allegheny and the Rocky mountains and divided by the second largest navigable river of the globe, to lay claim, forcibly or otherwise, to an outlet to the sea. There has not been, there is not, nor will there be a nation owning a great expanse of fertile territory—and therefore needing for its commerce, at the very least, a good port—which will not attempt to get one, using fair means or foul. It is as legitimate a need for nations as it is for individuals. Civil law favors private property set aside from public highways, thus obliging the property owners to concede passage between property and roadway.

Civilization will not permit that a territory immense in area and riches should remain isolated, unproductive, and impotent in terms of commerce. In such a case, another nation coveting dominion will take over a zone of considerable width stretching the length of the coast. There is no country in the world which, once having taken possession of the valley of the Mississippi, would not have concentrated all its forces toward gaining access to the sea.

· · ·

In 1830 the United States had over us superiority in numbers, superiority in wealth, superiority in organization, superiority in discipline, superiority in will (its soldiers were volunteers), and most of all superiority in the form of government. In the United States the president is the first one in seeing to it that the highest posts in the army are given to the military men who are the most capable and brave. In Mexico the Presidents Bustamante and Santa Anna demanded of their army chiefs that they be first of all followers of Bustamante or Santa Anna, although they might at the same time have been cowardly and inept. In the system of government in Mexico in 1830, any capable general would have been thought to have dishonored himself if, in pursuit of a great military reputation, he allowed the president to give the orders instead of giving him a kick and occupying his place. Correspondingly, the presidents felt the necessity of preventing by all possible means the development of capable generals. In Mexico and in 1830 a general who had triumphed even in a small skirmish would immediately name the price of his feat, and the most desirable would be the presidential seat itself.

The defense of society and of the presidency against anarchy would demand that the top military positions be given only to generals who would not pronounce against the government, but since any general with prestige, whether well or badly acquired, was always a candidate of whatever political party for a *cuartelazo* [barracks revolt], the result was that only incapable generals could be considered really trustworthy in terms of being put in command.

. . .

As has been seen, Alamán was very unfortunate in terms of the measures he undertook with the object of saving Texas for Mexico. In taking power in 1833, the liberal party thought that, guided by its conscience full of liberal principles, it was going to correct the errors that the regressive education of Alamán had brought about in attempting to solve the Texas problem.

But it was not to be so. The administration of Vice President Gómez Farías [Santa Anna was nominally president but busied himself with things other than administration] continued the errors of Alamán and only made the correction of lifting the prohibition against further migration to and settling in Texas by North Americans. But in the questions of slavery, of tariffs, and of military regimes, he maintained, as I have said, with firmness and valor, all the mistakes of Alamán.

The liberal party had the time to remedy the evils, or the root causes thereof, brought about by the conservative party, and it could have saved the situation simply by acting favorably upon the petition submitted by Texas requesting that it be separated from Coahuila and be set up as a state in its own right.

The law of May 7, 1824, demonstrated a marked lack of wisdom on the part of the legislators of that period in assigning Texas to Coahuila as a provisional territory until Texas should measure up to the conditions that would qualify it to be a state, this to be determined by a simple resolution of the federal congress on the basis of an absolute majority of votes. Later, the federal constitution, promulgated that same year, declared that Texas and Coahuila formed a single state and, according to this constitution, for a territory to be converted into a new state it would have to have the approval of the general congress by a vote of three quarters of the members present in both houses, in addition to a three quarters vote in the state legislatures. The constitution of 1824 deprived the Texans of the good position which they had acquired when they were considered to belong only provisionally to Coahuila. A discussion over whether the constitution of 1824 could abrogate the position allotted to the Texans by the law which I have cited was tabled.

Aside from these considerations, the law of May 7, 1824, produced the results that they inevitably would have. When a state receives provisionally into its care a territory, it attempts to exact contributions from it while neglecting it, postponing any action in its favor, forgetting it in terms of any administration or protection, and, at the same time, spending what it has exacted in making territorial improvements of its own. Such is the implacable code of provincialism, which among ourselves constitutes the soul of state sovereignty.

From another viewpoint, nothing seems so disparate as having made Texas dependent upon Coahuila, a small territory in comparison with Texas, without ports, without commercial ties to the interior of the Republic, without fertile lands, almost without population, and without culture. In modern times, the prevision of the federal government prevents at all cost that a colony or enterprise favorable to the government should fall into the rapacious claws of a state treasury. With all the more reason, such a healthy precaution should have been taken in 1830 or 1833.

The states of that period, with some exceptions, were characterized by utter wretchedness, great economic ignorance, and a mystical ardor for rapacity against commerce, industry, mining, and even against agriculture. Generally speaking, the states had the most debased types of governments, similar, as I have said, to the tyrannies of the fifteenth century, to the Assyrian satrapies of pre-Roman times, and the contemporary Kafirs. It was an act of anti-patriotic madness to place genuine North American democrats in the horrible, despotic cage which gives to Coahuila the appearance of a languishing public tuberculosis asylum. Without the patriotic and humanitarian despotisms of the federal government, the states, after having dismembered the Republic in the name of their ferocious provincialism, would have exterminated each other.

The state of Coahuila fulfilled its mission as proven by its provincialism, its misery, and the almost impossibility of its communicating with

Texas across immense deserts ruled by savage hordes. Filisola painted well the provincialism of Coahuila and its lack of attention, consideration, and patriotism for Texas. When there was internal discord in the state of Coahuila, the federal military commander tried to make the dissidents understand the unpatriotic nature of their conduct and the bad influence it would have upon Texan affairs, to which they answered: "We don't care if Texas gets lost, as long as Saltillo [centered in the state of Coahuila] remains the capital of the state."

In the year 1833, that is to say, after nine years of Texas having belonged to the state of Coahuila, that state had not laid out or opened a single road, not even a path, by which to communicate with Texas or to allow the Texans to communicate with it and develop their commerce. In those nine years, the state militia of Coahuila had not engaged in combat a single hostile Indian in Texas. The Texas colonists were left to take care of their own defense or to perish. In this same period of nine years, Coahuila had not stationed a single police officer in Texas, nor opened a single school, nor named a single judge of the primary court of claims, much less a tribunal of the secondary. For one of the Texas colonists to attempt to get a civil judgment against one of his fellows, he had to cross more than a hundred leagues of desert, without water at all, or being inundated, he must battle against savages and must pay an escort to defend him, finally to arrive only to have the Coahuilan judge totally ignore him or decide the case against him, because, as Stuart Henry Foot [Foote] has said: "The *gringos* could not receive justice if this caused any bother to a Coahuilan."

In exchange for this lack of governmental protection, although Coahuila collected taxes from Texas, the one Texan deputy was thrown out of the state legislature, and when the Texans proved that their population had notably increased and that they had the right to a larger representation, Coahuila took four years to deny what had been legally petitioned for. And finally, the legislature of Coahuila in 1832 passed its decree number 183, a tremendously monstrous one. This law peremptorily forbade the colonists, who were *naturalized Mexicans,* to engage in retail commerce because this activity could only be exercised, according to this illegal decree, by those who were native-born Coahuilans. This attempt, beyond law and reason, was the optimum fruit of that provincialism which was so destructive to the nation, of its good name, its wealth, and its integrity.

The liberal party, therefore, shared in all the errors of the conservative party and must take equal responsibility for the situation that existed up to the year 1834 [the year in which the Texas Revolution erupted]. It can therefore be affirmed that this liberal party dishonored itself by its eminently retrogressive conduct in regard to the Texas colonists, in which it demonstrated a complete lack of political, economic, and humanitarian knowledge.

JOSÉ VASCONCELOS

EDITOR'S INTRODUCTION

José Vasconcelos is the example par excellence of the Mexican intellectual as versatile performer. As a scholar and writer he was productive in the fields of philosophy, history, literature, sociology, and autobiography. He was also a man of action, having made important contributions in the fields of education administration, diplomacy, and public service.

José Vasconcelos was born in the state of Oaxaca in 1881. He died in Mexico City in 1959. During one stage of his boyhood, his parents lived close to the Texas border, and the young Vasconcelos went to public school in Eagle Pass, Texas. He was a good student there and was encouraged by his teachers, but he also experienced at that school a dose of racial prejudice, aimed at him by Anglo-Texan students. Perhaps here was the genesis of the anti-Americanism which he felt and expressed consistently throughout his life.

In 1911, the last year of the Porfiriato, Vasconcelos joined with other young thinkers and writers to form the Ateneo de la Juventud (the Athenaeum of the Young). The membership of this study group was to form the intellectual leadership of the new Mexico that was coming into being, shaped by the forces of the Revolution. The founders included, aside from Vasconcelos, Antonio Caso, philosopher, professor, and poet; Alfonso Reyes, humanist and distinguished man of letters; and Martín Luis Guzmán, who with the publication of *The Eagle and the Serpent* was to put himself in the forefront of the novelists of the Mexican Revolution. The Ateneo established itself as a force against the positivism that had reigned during the Porfiriato. Its members espoused the notions of the primacy of idea, spirit, and will to be found in the works of such philosophers as Kant, Schopenhauer, and Bergson.

The ascendancy of Alvaro Obregón to the presidency of Mexico resulted in Vasconcelos being called to public service. From 1920 to

1921, he was rector of the National University of Mexico, but he was called from that post to become the Secretary of Public Education. In this position, which he held from 1921 to 1924, he was remarkably effective. It was he who set up the extensive network of public schools throughout Mexico, a program which was one of the goals of the great revolution of 1910 to 1921. In doing so, Vasconcelos was able to inspire a host of young teachers to go out into remote areas and to set up schools and teach in them. This venture entailed not only considerable hardships and deprivations but also, in a number of instances, definite danger because it meant facing the church-inspired hostility toward a rival school system.

Another important outcome of Vasconcelos's term as Secretary of Public Education was the opportunity he was able to provide to artists who would soon achieve large international reputations. He used public subsidies in support of the rising Mexican painters Diego Rivera, José Clemente Orozco, and David Alfaro Siqueiros and provided them with public wall space on which to paint their powerfully expressive murals. It was through these murals that the painters of the period were able to convey to great numbers of the poorer people of Mexico, many of whom were illiterate, the ideals of the revolution.

Despite his public activities, Vasconcelos maintained a career of writing and publication which went unabated for the remainder of his days. His final bibliography was immense and includes: *The Cosmic Race* (1925); *Treatise on Metaphysics* (1929); *Ethics* (1932); *Esthetics* (1936); *History of Philosophic Thought* (1937); *Brief History of Mexico* (1937); *Hernán Cortés, Creator of a Nationality* (1941); and *Notes for the History of Mexico, from the Conquest to the Revolution* (1942). In four absorbing volumes José Vasconcelos recorded his own stormy life: *A Creole Ulysses* (1935); *The Tempest* (1936); *The Disaster* (1938); and *The Proconsulship* (1939).

In *The Cosmic Race,* a book which has had considerable influence among Mexican Americans, Vasconcelos enunciates a process by which a new spiritual and esthetic era is to come into being to take the place of the former intellectual and political age. The prime agency for this new development is to be the mixed or "cosmic" race of Latin America. In contrast to Bulnes, Vasconcelos saw in the mixture of such primally different strains as the European, the Indian, and the African a dynamic which would bring the results of such a mixture up to another plane of conception and awareness. Meanwhile—and here Vasconcelos maintains his consistent antagonism toward the United States—North America is fated to remain at the grosser level of materialism and utilitarianism.

In 1929, Vasconcelos took one of his characteristic changes in course. He challenged Pascual Ortiz Rubio in a campaign for the presidency of Mexico. Ortiz Rubio had the backing of General Plutarco Elías Calles, former president and still the foremost political power in Mexico. Ortiz Rubio won by a large plurality, and Vasconcelos went into exile in the United States. For Vasconcelos, this experience exacerbated an already growing sense of disillusion with the revolution. He now made a strong turn to the right.

Part of the program of the revolution had been a movement against the political, social, and cultural power of the Roman Catholic Church. Of all the revolutionary presidents, Plutarco Elías Calles had pressed the campaign against the church the hardest. A combined personal hostility to Calles and a resentment toward the measures directed against the church produced in Vasconcelos a pronounced bitterness. He now came to feel that Mexico's religion was the core of her culture. He moved from a sympathy with the indigenous elements in Mexican culture to an intense Hispanicism and finally deprecated totally any contribution that the Indians, as Indians, had made to the culture of Mexico. His colonial hero now became Hernán Cortés, the conqueror of the Indians, and his hero of the period of the independence was that conservative stalwart, Lucas Alamán. To Vasconcelos, those who allowed the Anglo-Saxons into Texas were—to avoid the word "traitors" and to put it charitably—"imbeciles." Alamán had tried to put across measures to restrict and counterbalance the Texas colonists, but the corrupt militarists, of whom, in Vasconcelos's mind, Santa Anna was the epitome, in their greedy power plays would pay no attention to Alamán's statesmanship.

Vasconcelos developed an almost obsessive conviction that all of Mexico's woes stemmed from Poinsett, who, according to Vasconcelos, nurtured the liberals in order to destroy the strength of Mexico, which really lay in the centrist policies of the conservatives. He labeled Mexico's liberals, among whom he included Gómez Farías and even Juárez, as agents of *"poinsettismo."*

His *Short History of Mexico,* from which the following excerpt is taken, is a highly subjective treatment of its subject. Its diatribes include coarsely antisemitic outbursts against American Jews, whom he accuses of fomenting radicalism in Mexico. There are some pungent observations on Monroeism, in the course of which Vasconcelos pronounces the Monroe Doctrine a device by which the United States seeks to maintain a hegemony over Hispanic America. Vasconcelos claims that Poinsett was among those who thwarted Alamán's efforts to cooperate with South American statesmen in setting up pan-Latinist agreements designed to offset the influence of the United States. Vasconcelos considers the Roman and Catholic cultures of southern Europe and Hispanic America to be greatly superior to the shallow and materialistic cultures of the Anglo-American world. In this he echoes his nineteenth-century counterpart, Luis G. Cuevas. As for Mexico's military leaders in the Mexican-American War, Vasconcelos observes that the way to get promotions and preferments in that era was to lose battles, as in the cases of Santa Anna and Arista.

The section of *The Short History of Mexico* which follows, "The Tragedy of California," takes up a subject which a number of Mexican writers have brooded upon, the fate of those Mexicans who were absorbed into the United States as a result of the Treaty of Guadalupe Hidalgo. This section begins with a paean to the people of New Mexico, as Vasconcelos has experienced them. Being from the outer reaches of the old Spanish empire, they have escaped the contagion of Mexico's militarism, factionalism, and corruption. They have stoutly maintained their cultural identity, but, tellingly, Vasconcelos ascribes this in part to the fact that their lands were "not extraordinarily desirable" and thus escaped the cupidity of the incoming Anglo Saxon conquerors.

The case of California presented a very different situation. This was "beautiful land" and most highly desirable. Also, hardly had the ink dried on the Treaty of Guadalupe Hidalgo when gold was discovered in California, an occurrence which must have made for Mexico the loss of that territory all the more bitter. Vasconcelos praises the Mexicans of

California for the robust resistance which they put up in the face of the "brutal advances of a young race with uncontrollable appetites." As against the ineptness and corruption of Mexican militarism as represented by Santa Anna, Vasconcelos poses the heroic resistance of the Californian miner turned bandit, Joaquín Murrieta, the scourge of the Yankee occupiers of California. With the gold rush in full force, Mexican miners and their families, such as Murrieta and his young wife, were pushed off their claims by the "gringos" and were brutalized. Murrieta countered by joining a band of Mexican desperadoes and terrorizing the region.

Vasconcelos laments the fact that the Mexican resistance in California, which deserved epical treatment, has been largely ignored in Mexican letters while, ironically, a considerable literature in English has sprung up in praise of the Mexican resisters. And not only in literature, says Vasconcelos, but also in the cinema. At this point Vasconcelos takes up the motion picture, *The Robin Hood of El Dorado* (Metro Goldwyn Meyer, 1939), in which Warner Baxter played the lead role of Joaquín Murrieta. In his treatment of this film, Vasconcelos anticipates the present interest in the social significance of even "popular" motion pictures.

Vasconcelos makes his discussion of this film serve a dual purpose. On the one hand, he presents the figure of Joaquín Murrieta as the very type of resistance to the North American invasion that should have been throughout Mexico. On the other, he uses the plot line of this motion picture as a microcosm of the Mexican Revolution of his time and its destruction of the most valuable elements in Mexican society. As he gives his summary of the film's plot, Vasconcelos points out along the way the parallels between the fate of the "Spanish" land proprietors in California and the expropriation of the great and traditional haciendas in Mexico during the Revolution. Obviously, Vasconcelos has by this time lost all sympathy with the land reform which was at the heart of the Revolution and was associated with such revolutionary leaders as Pancho Villa and Emiliano Zapata, both of whom Vasconcelos mentions disparagingly. Land taken from the traditional owners ended up, according to Vasconcelos, not in the hands of the Mexican peasantry but in the possession of men like Dwight Morrow, American businessman

and ambassador to Mexico during the Calles regime. Vasconcelos concludes his discussion of the film by saying that the Mexican proprietors
in California, though gallantly facing their doom, were at least able to
practice their religion publicly and in outdoor ceremonies. The last was
a reference to the strictures which the era of Juárez, reinforced by the
Revolution, had put upon the practices of the church, forbidding it to
manifest itself publicly in the form of rituals or processions carried on
outside of the church buildings.

In his praise of the original landowners of California, Vasconcelos
emphasizes that they were of "Spanish" descent, a special "delicate
flower" of a race. In this approach, Vasconcelos's writing takes on a
curious parallel to an episode in North American literature known as
the California idyll. In the early years of the twentieth century, American writers discovered the literary lode of the Hispanic Southwest. To a
reading public seeking an escape from the clanging new industrialism of
the "gilded age," writers such as Helen Hunt Jackson, Gertrude Ather-
ton, Joaquin Miller, Charles Warren Stoddard, and Bret Harte presented romantic tales of gallant "Spanish" caballeros mounted on
beautiful horses, of lovely señoritas complete with black mantillas and
ornamental combs. In the background were the beautiful Spanish mission churches of California.

American readers enjoyed escaping into the pastoral serenities of the
California idyll, and it seemed an innocent, if undemanding, kind of
literature. But later American writers, such as Carey McWilliams in
North From Mexico (Philadelphia, 1949), questioned the innocence of
this romantic genre. The emphasis in this literature was upon the word
"Spanish," and this word was applied to the remnants of the old
traditional families in California. And these landholding aristocrats
were in no way to be confused with the ordinary "Mexicans," the
everyday, half-caste "greasers." The dichotomy that the romantic tradition produced, according to writers like McWilliams, made possible the
simultaneous glorification of the old "Spanish" Californians and the
disparagement of the living representatives of Mexico in California.

José Vasconcelos, too, glorified the old "Spanish" landowning aristocracy in California, and he surrounded them with all the accoutre-
ments of beautiful women with mantilla and comb, fine horses with

decorated saddles, mission vineyards, and baroque churches. But with Vasconcelos the contrast between these people and the ordinary Mexican was not an implied one. It was directly stated. With the loss of the "Spanish" gentry in California, all that was left was the lowly *pocho*, a disparaging term used in Mexico to refer to Mexican Americans. In its Mexican usage the term signifies cultural bastardization and the tendency to imitate North American ways. In "The Tragedy of California," Vasconcelos gets in a final thrust. The habits of the *pocho* are not confined to California; they are now being imitated in Mexico itself.

"The Tragedy of California"

The population of New Mexico, more compactly settled and located on a plain, yielded to the conqueror. And since their lands were not that extraordinarily desirable, there was no real struggle to expropriate them. So the original race remains there, an industrious people who, to the extent that it is possible after a conquest, have preserved not only a certain amount of their property but also a fraction of political power. And it is curious to observe the New Mexican villages and certain barrios of the old cities like Santa Fe. In these we can see what Mexico could have been without the factionalism which has been destroying it since independence. There were not in New Mexico destructive rebellions, nor the expulsion of the Spaniards, nor generals as presidents, and it is there that the Mexicans showed more resistance to foreign penetration, more mettle in the defense of their rights. In more recent years, the waves of Anglo-Saxon immigration have submerged our people, but nevertheless, it is in that region that the Mexican has maintained himself with the greatest dignity.

Translated from "La Tragedia de California," *Breve Historia de México*, Mexico, D.F.: Ediciones Botas, 1944. Fifth Edition.

But where the tragedy reached the proportions of the sublime was in the beautiful land of California. That province was sparsely populated but with a select race of Spanish and Mexican blood. A small landholding aristocracy had jealously developed its Hispanic tradition. Such was this jealousy that even today nobody remembers those sad thirty years in which that territory belonged to our nation, but everyone locates his ancestry and pride in the constructive period [of the Spanish empire] that saw the rise of the missions and the baroque churches, the groves of olive trees, and the haciendas in which the pressing of the grape is still practiced. There were no mercenaries, and perhaps for that reason California was the one territory that defended itself against the Yankee conquest with positive gallantry. For none of the conquerors was the task more difficult than it was for Fremont, the conqueror of Stockton and San Francisco. And all this because in California the ranchers, organized into guerrilla groups, defended their own homes. They were not fighting for any Santa Anna; they fought for their country. And a dangerous guerrilla tactic, invented by the Californians, even became famous. They would allow themselves to be pursued, feigning flight, by the Yankee forces. Then suddenly, when the number of pursuers had diminished, they would turn around with fury and in a sweep eliminate whole bodies of the Yankee troops.

Nobody has sung the military glory of these veritable heroes whose "saga" should be taught in our public schools. And their conduct points up a manifest truth: where government corruption had not yet reached, where Spanish tradition was still maintained, there the resistance was such that it deserved the honor of being celebrated in an epic. A veritable literature exists in English about the conduct of those valiant men with whom the Yankee finally had to come to terms, granting recognition to some of them of their rights to their own lands, even though other lands were incorporated into the new order of things.

Unfortunately, the best of these warriors perished in the fight; so a truce had to be accepted. Also, most unfortunately, in that clash of combat the Spanish/Mexican, who was like a delicate flower of humanity, faced extinction, crushed by the brutal advances of a young race with uncontrollable appetites.

Not only in literature but also in the cinema there has been celebrated the epic of that California which was ours by blood and which, in part, saved our honor in the year forty-seven, so ill-fated for the rest of the nation, not only for what we lost but the more so for the way in which we lost it. There has appeared a motion picture entitled "The Robin Hood of El Dorado," based on the life of Joaquín Murrieta. It tells a story of extraordinary significance. The period is not that of the war of conquest itself but of the time when gold was discovered, and the picture deals with the effects this event had upon the conquest, with the irremediable displacement of the conquered race in favor of the conquering one. With the pretext of the default of mining funds, both the small and the large Mexican mine owners are dispossessed by the use of savage methods. One of these victims is Joaquín Murrieta, a historical person somewhat modified in the screen version, but eminently representative. Murrieta is robbed of his land, and the woman whom he has recently married is violated. A generous Yankee friend offers to support him in his complaints. Instead of justice, Murrieta suffers new outrages. On the way to his brother's property, Murrieta comes across a bandit who has been robbing and murdering in the region for both pleasure and vengeance. Murrieta refuses to make common cause with him. Murrieta seeks a personal vengeance. In a sort of grotto, he encounters one of the men who had attacked his house and violated his woman. Murrieta challenges this man and kills him. The bandit, who had witnessed this scene, is left with the money of the dead Yankee. A short time later, Murrieta is publicly whipped by a group of vigilantes. The bandit revives him and finally makes him the chief of the small band that is terrorizing the countryside. But even with Murrieta, the band goes along without any real program. They are like the Mexican revolutionary leaders who shout phrases in support of this or that cause but do not understand what they are saying nor have the capacity to bring anything to completion except when the accidents of war might bring them a victory. One night Murrieta assaults and begins to rob, not North Americans, but a group of Mexican hacienda owners who have gotten together to devise a method of defending their lands from the Yankee manipulators who are usurping them. Just as in the Mexico of today, the Yankee agents act out their version of the Mexican scenario in which the great wealth of the hacienda owners incites the Mexican lower classes to dispossess them and then to massacre them. After the despoiling of the

haciendas in Mexico, in the manner of Villa or Zapata, Morrow and his
bank arrive to buy up the lands, that is, unless some other foreigner,
who has succeeded in getting some guarantees, does not get there first.
Murrieta and his bandits are equally deceived. After Murrieta takes a
ring away from one of the aristocratic young ladies, all done up in
mantilla and ornamental comb, he recognizes her as the daughter of an
old *patron* and returns the ring to her. The young woman then says to
him that if he does not return the jewelry to all the others, she will not
accept her ring because she does not accept favors. Murrieta hesitates,
and the woman explains to him: "All these hacienda owners are victims
of the new situation in the same way that you are. We are all Mexicans;
so do not attack Mexicans on the pretext that they are rich. Unity will
make us strong." Murrieta understands. The young woman, who has
suffered deception in her personal life and has also been dispossessed
of her lands, joins Murrieta's group and finally convinces him to retire
to Mexico and to buy lands with the money that they have robbed from
stagecoaches. The beautiful dream of returning to Mexico gives a
romantic tone to many of the scenes. But those of us who know what
Mexico was and what Mexico is now sense the deception that lies in
store, while at the same time recognizing the gallantry displayed by the
actor in the film. But who can ignore the fate that befell the Mexican
proprietors in California? The most beautiful part of the film is the
bravura, the passion with which the small group of Mexicans, dispossessed of their country, mount their horses, dance with their long-
legged and narrow waisted women, while in due course one after the
other falls in the fight. When the aristocratic woman, who has come to
be the soul of the group, also falls, one comes to understand the efficacy
of the method used in all conquests, which succeed in destroying the
top leaders, the select individuals. Immediately, the mass submits. In
the general confusion, some few of the conquered race managed to hold
on to some of their possessions, dreamed of being property owners, but
soon enough the best of everything passed on to the new conquerors,
and the defeated nation sank down to the level of the proletariat. Yet the
valiant *Californianos*, with all the verve of their singing and dancing, died
defending their lands inch by inch, and they continued decorating their
saddles Spanish style, and their women wore their laces and shawls, and

they all prayed before the altars where their ancestors had prayed, in the open air, unaffected by any laws that forbade outside worship. At least the Mexicans of California remained free of Juárez. Not only that, the shame of Santa Anna never touched them.

In the defeat of California the pride of being Mexican survives. Honor was there. And it is not so bad to lose, as long as one does not lose in the style of Santa Anna. Years have passed, and as the conquest liquidated the aristocrats in all the area it took over, the survivors are left at a loss. Of all those beautiful people who have given noble characters to the literature of California none are left. There remains only the *pocho.* And it has even come to pass that he has imitators in the interior of our country and in its politics.

LEOPOLDO ZEA

EDITOR'S INTRODUCTION

In "North America in the Hispanic American Consciousness," the modern Mexican philosopher Leopoldo Zea has placed the Mexican-American War within a larger psychological, cultural, and historical framework. In this essay, which appeared in the volume, *Philosophy as Commitment and Other Essays,* 1952, and was written in recognition of the centennial of the war with the United States, Zea treats with two interrelated obsessions which he sees as having occupied the consciousness of Hispanic America since colonial times, the sense of Spain as having provided a drastic heritage responsible for most of Latin America's ills and of the United States as being the beacon light which, if only the Spanish heritage could be disowned, might lead Hispanic America into the modern age of progress and democracy. Zea is very alive to the ambivalence with which the Latin American countries have looked upon the United States. Admiration is mixed with fear and even with disgust. Also, the sense of the Spanish heritage as being an incubus preventing Latin America by its dead weight from being able to measure up to its model, the United States, has given to the Hispanic American countries, according to Zea, a pervading sense of inferiority and fatalism. Added to all this is the uneasy suspicion, fed by some of the Hispanic American writers themselves, that Latin America has further degraded itself by mixing its Spanish blood with that of "inferior" races.

It has been the lot of Mexico to endure, among the Latin American nations, the most pitiless exposure to the United States, the most painful episode of which was the war with that country. And yet, even after invasion and defeat, Mexico seems, in Zea's view, to yearn the more to be like the nation that had conquered her.

After examining these wounds to the Hispanic American psyche,

Zea suggests that therapy may lie in the direction of a more balanced view of Spain, Hispanic America, and the United States. The Iberian heritage has given Latin America some very positive strengths, Zea claims. Also, there are definite aspects of Latin American culture which are superior to what North American society has to offer. Finally, the United States must be seen for what it really is, a mixed society with some strongly negative impulses along with its virtues. These things must be sorted out if Hispanic America is to find any guidance in the United States.

Typical of the time in which this essay was published, the late 1940s, the word *men*, to the exclusion of the word *women*, is used in the description of the activity of people generally.

In the course of exploring the themes of this essay, Zea examines the ideas of several Latin American authors. José Enrique Rodó, Justo Sierra, José Vasconcelos, and Antonio Caso have already been introduced in this volume. Andres Bello (1781–1865), Venezuelan poet, literary critic, philologist, philosopher, historian, and educator, was one of Latin America's great men of letters. He was one of the first to insist upon an authentic Latin American voice in literature. Domingo Faustino Sarmiento (1811–1888) was both a literary man and a president of Argentina, 1868–1874. His best-known work was the massive *Civilization and Barbarism, the Life of Juan Facundo Quiroga*, 1845. In this biography of an Argentine strong man, Sarmiento both displayed his passionate opposition to despotism and at the same time revealed a begrudging admiration for the wild gaucho life of the pampas that produced such a man of action as Facundo Quiroga. Francisco Bilbao (1823–1865) was a Chilean man of letters and a fiery pamphleteer. His outspoken opposition to dictatorial government resulted in his spending much of his life in exile. Clearly, as evidenced by the passage quoted by Zea, Bilbao wrote before the abolition of slavery in the United States.

Leopoldo Zea in his life has lived up to the title of his book, *Philosophy as Commitment*. As a working philosopher and prolific writer, Zea has to his credit an impressive number of publications. His works are divided between professional philosophical studies and writings in which Zea puts his philosophical training to the uses of examining broad issues in Latin American and world culture. Among his most important publications are: *Positivism in Mexico* (1943); *Essays in Philosophy and History* (1947); *Conscience and Possibility in Mexico* (1952); *Philosophy as Commitment* (1953); *The West and the Conscience of Mexico* (1953); *Latin America and the World* (1960); and *Dependence and Liberation in Latin American Culture* (1975).

Zea has been for many years a distinguished professor of philosophy at the National University of Mexico. He has also offered himself to public service. He was a member of the Secretariat on Public Education of UNESCO, and he was the Director General of Cultural Relations in the Secretariat of Foreign Relations in the Mexican government. In this way he has continued in the admirable Latin American tradition of the intellectual as a person of public affairs.

"North America in the
Hispanic American Consciousness"

Perhaps no other example is to be found in all the history of nations to match the manner in which the United States of North America has persisted in the consciousness of Hispanic America. For a long time before achieving its political emancipation, and throughout its history as an independent entity, Hispanic America has always felt the presence of North America: sometimes thought to be the greatest of models and at other times the greatest of deceptions. North America has been for Hispanic America, among other things, the source of all its feelings of inferiority. Perhaps as well, we shall not find any other cases such as that of Hispanic America with its split and divided consciousness. On the one side there is the reality, that which Hispanic America is, by right of its historical destiny; on the other there is that which it wishes to be through the force of conscious decision. Throughout that historical reality always there has surged the driving force of Spain, but in the ideal that Hispanic America has set up, that which it wants to be, there

Translated from "Norteamerica en la Consciencia Hispanoamericana," *La Filosofía Como Compromiso y Otros Ensayos*, Mexico, D.F.: Tezontle, 1952, pp. 55–60, 74–83.

rises the image of North America. In the Hispanic American consciousness a great conflict has been unleashed through which Hispanic America tries to uproot its past, which it considers fatal and the source of all
its incapacities, while at the same time it aspires to be in the south that
which the United States has been in the north. Let us briefly examine
the history of this wound in the consciousness of Hispanic America.

In *Memorial,* an apocryphal statement attributed to the Count of
Aranda with the aim of undermining his position at the court of the king
of Spain, it is claimed that only through a change of policy on the part of
the mother country can the Spanish empire be salvaged. This memorandum already foresees that the United States, which Spain and
France had helped in attaining its independence, will be in the future an
example to the Hispanic American colonies in their aspirations toward
political, social, and economic renewal. Therefore, it will be necessary
that Spain view her colonies as children, not as stepchildren. Only the
community of destinies, the community of similar goals would preserve
the unity of the Spanish empire. This would remain intact as long as its
interests were also the interests of the colonies. The three colonies
liberated by Washington in North America would soon demonstrate
how a community of interests makes for greatness in a country. "That
nation," it was prophesied about the United States, "was born, as one
might say, a pygmy, and it needed the help and support of nothing less
than two countries as powerful as France and Spain in order to gain its
independence, but the day will come when it will be a giant, a veritable
and fearful colossus in that region, and then, forgetting the benefits that
it has received, it will think only of its own interests and aggrandizement." And in addition, speaking of the new political spirit, liberalism,
which animates that nation and will soon attract other countries, the
memorandum goes on to say that "the liberty of conscience, the abundance of fertile lands on which a large population can be established
and developed, as well as the advantages which the recently established
government offers—all these will draw to that country artisans and
farmers from all the nations."

But Spain did not see fit to heed this warning. This was nothing
more than a device to denigrate a noble nation. Its eyes lacked the gift of
prophecy, and they could not see beyond the limited interests of the

heart of empire. Hispanic America continued being a stepchild, or even worse, a natural child, the fruit of an adventure. The "illustrious" elders of the Spain of the eighteenth century continued being as despotic as those of the Spain of Philip II. In regard to its subjects in Hispanic America, no other attitude would do but that which was made known by the viceroy Don Carlos Francisco de Croix to the inhabitants of New Spain [Mexico]. In the name of King Charles III in an edict issued in the year 1767 he said: "For the future, the subjects of the great monarch who occupies the throne of Spain must understand completely that they were born to keep quiet and obey, not to discuss or utter opinions about high matters of state." Such is the Spain which must remain in the consciousness of the Hispanic Americans. In the face of this there is the nation that spoke of liberty of conscience, of "government of the people, by the people, and for the people." Ardently, the Hispanic Americans will try to liberate themselves from the first and make themselves similar to the second. The battle will be the more tragic and desperate to the extent to which Hispanic America feels the Spain of Viceroy de Croix to be deeply rooted within itself. The Hispanic Americans will continue to feel this Spain in their every action, gesture, and attitude and along with these in all the misfortunes that befall them. They recognize full well that being liberated politically will not be enough, that they must uproot Spain from their very entrails. Political emancipation must be followed by another type of emancipation, that which they call "emancipation of the mind." And alongside of what was and of what must come into being stands the model of what is wanted: the United States of North America.

In 1822, Don Diego Portales, that strange dictator who succeeded in imposing upon the recently emancipated Republic of Chile the Spanish order to the letter—but without Spain, said, prophetically, in a letter to his friend José M. Cea:

My Dear Cea:

The newspapers carry the agreeable news of the advance of the revolution throughout the Americas. It also appears confirmed that the United States will recognize the independence of the Latin American countries. Although I have not talked to anybody about this particular situation, I am going to give my opinion. The president of the United States, Mr. Monroe, has said: 'It is recognized that America is for the Americans.' Let us be careful not to get out from under one domination only to fall under another! We should not rest our confidence in those gentlemen who are giving their strong approval to the deeds of our champions of liberation without having helped us in anything. Here is cause for trepidation. Why this great eagerness on the part of the United States to accredit ministers and delegates and to recognize the independence of Latin America without having made any efforts on our behalf? Here you see a curious system, my friend! I believe that all of this obeys a prearranged plan, which is the following: Conquer Latin America, but not by means of arms but through *influence* throughout all spheres. This will happen, maybe not today but tomorrow. It will not do to gratify ourselves with the kind of sweets such as children love to eat without taking account of the poisoning.

What sweets is Portales referring to? To democracy, to liberalism, to the liberty of conscience, in effect to all those ideals that many Hispanic Americans see incarnated in North America and aspire to see realized in Hispanic America. But the Hispanic Americans were not made for these things, that is, not *educated* for them. "Democracy," said Portales in the same letter, "which the visionaries constantly proclaim, is an absurdity in countries such as those in Hispanic America, which are vice-ridden and which totally lack the virtues necessary for the establishment of a true republic." But neither, says Portales, should there be a monarchy. This neither should be the ideal for a Hispanic American government. "A republic," he adds, "is the system which should be adopted: but do you know how I understand this concept for those countries? A strong centralized government whose leaders should be true models of virtue and patriotism and who would thus direct the citizens along the path of order and virtue. When they have gained a sense of morality, then the government will become liberal, free, and full of ideals, a government in which all citizens will take part. That is what I think, and anyone with half a critical sense would think the same."

In other words, what Portales was proposing was a dictatorship in order to reach democracy, despotism in order to arrive at liberty. And so, beginning with that period, the tragic and contradictory dualism has manifested itself, which was to animate the entire history of our countries: a dualism planted only among the Hispanic Americans. Our

liberals do not encounter it in the country which serves them as a
model, the United States. Desperately, they will turn their eyes inward
upon themselves, and they will find in their very guts the cause: Spain,
always Spain. Ah, if they only weren't Spaniards, the sons of Spaniards,
they would not have to educate themselves for liberty! If they were of
the same race that has populated the north, they would be born with
liberty! In the Hispanic American consciousness, the model of the
United States grows in proportion to the extent to which the feeling of
inferiority and fatalism increases. The defeat of Mexico in 1847 only
served to stimulate this feeling as well as the eagerness to be, all the
more, similar to the conquering nation. The recriminations were not so
much levied against the aggressor as against the conquered race. The
war was already lost on the day on which Hispanic America, having
gained its independence, divided itself and then subdivided itself. The
common interest that had united the North American colonies was
lacking. The only unity was provided by the despotic force of imperial
Spain. The consciousness of this division and its causes would also give
a moral victory to those who had denigrated us for reasons which in no
way would be able to square themselves with the ideals which Hispanic
America admired in North America.

                                    .   .   .

As for Mexico, the country that had suffered the North American
impact in the most painful of experiences also reacted in an emulating
manner. To the admiration, which does not abate despite everything, is
added the element of fear. Justo Sierra, many years after that experience, said: "We need colonization, arms that will exploit our riches. We
must pass from the *military* era to the *industrial* era. And we must do it
fast, because the giant that grows at our side and that all the time is
getting closer to us as a result of the industrial and agricultural boom in
the frontier states and the extension of their railroads will tend to absorb
and dissolve us if we are found to be weak." In 1879, some years before
Sierra had stamped these words in his *Political Evolution of the Mexican
People*, he had expressed the same fear in a journal. The immensity of
territory—even immense for us—the lack of communications and the
lack of unity "makes the Mexican nation one of the most weak and

defenseless organisms that lives within the orbit of civilization." Mexico goes on destroying itself while "next to us there lives a marvelous collective animal for whose enormous intestines there is not enough alimentation. It is armed to devour while every day we gain in the aptitude for being devoured." In front of this colossus we are exposed "to being a proof of Darwin's theory, and in the struggle for existence we have all the probabilities against us."

The defeat of '47 was the natural consequence of this internal weakness among the Mexicans, or more amply, the consequence of the weakness of the Hispanic race, the Latin race. To avoid another defeat, it would be necessary for Mexico to be as strong as the United States. Well and good, but how can this be accomplished? Don Telésforo García wrote in the same journal as did Sierra: How are we going to regenerate ourselves, he asked, if we go on multiplying the defects of our race, the defects of the Latin temper, making it overflow instead of putting up a dike against it? We Latins have a dreaming spirit, eminently mystical, from which emanates the absurdity that instead of disciplining the understanding with scientific and strongly severe methods we gratify ourselves with dreams and with fantasy. It is necessary for us to be eminently practical. We must be experimentalists and investigators. We must be *positivists*. All these stern qualities have characterized the great Saxon countries, England and the United States. In these countries, said another of the editors of this same period, "liberty is more secure and law is more guaranteed." Such is what not only Mexico but the greater part of the Hispanic American countries have tried to be. They have attempted to be like their model, the United States. With all the means within their reach they have tried to uproot everything within them that was Hispanic American. Some countries, such as Argentina, almost succeeded in this, but the majority continued in futilely fighting against their own reality. They continued being that which they wanted to avoid, dreamers and idealists, but this against their very reality. Positivism as an educational doctrine took hold in all these countries. But it did not result in practical people, such as the Saxons. Industrialization, the development of natural resources, these things were not done by the hands of these positivists. All of this remained in the hands

of foreigners. All that came forward were oligarchies or new dictator-
ships. The only difference was that now they talked about progress and
science. Hispanic America continued being Hispanic America.

But was or is everything lost? Are we condemned despite all our
efforts to be nothing but that collection of negations which our recent
forebears discerned? Was all our inheritance bad? Was all that is Hispanic bad? Was this so of the Latin heritage? And our racial mixture, the
worst of our defects according to various Hispanic Americans, was this
really such a negative element? To Sarmiento and others, the ill effects
of being descended from the Spaniards were amplified when these
became mixed with inferior races. No, many of these men saw that not
everything was negative. And this by that same faculty, the critical
sense. That is to say that the hard self-criticism to which Hispanic
America submitted itself also revealed that there was something positive. As for Spain, that Spain which many wanted to renounce so
resoundingly, neither was this a pure negation. There was and is in her
much potential that can be tapped. Spain is not only the Inquisition, nor
is all of Spain symbolized by Phillip the Second, Ferdinand the Sev-
enth, or Francisco Franco. There was and there is another Spain, that
which has been called the white Spain, pitted, as are we, against the
black Spain: the Spain of Victoria and Luis Vives, the Spain of Prim and
the Spain which is now in exile or in the jails of the despotic Spain [as a
result of the rule of Francisco Franco].

It was of this Spain, lover of liberty as are the best sons of Hispanic
America, that Andrés Bello spoke when he asked how it was possible
that Hispanic America had gained its independence despite the fact
that the Hispanic Americans were the inheritors from a region apparently full of negations. "Never has a thoroughly debased people," he
said, "a completely crushed people, denuded of all virtuous sentiments,
been able to accomplish the great deeds which marked the campaigns of
the patriots, the heroic acts of abnegation, the sacrifices of every kind by
which various of the Latin American nations won their political emancipation." This spirit of abnegation and sacrifice was inherited from
Spain, and it was this same spirit that triumphed over Spain itself. "One
who observes with philosophic eyes the history of our struggle against
the mother country," Bello added, "will recognize without difficulty

that that which made us prevail over her was preeminently the Iberian element. The native Spanish constancy was pitted against itself in the innate constancy of the sons of Spain." The instinct, if not the conscience, of the fatherland aroused the spirits of the Hispanic Americans so that they performed feats the equal of those accomplished by the Spanish nation at Numancia and Zaragoza. "The captains and the veteran legions of Iberia that were stationed in the Americas were conquered and humiliated by the leaders and improvised armies of that new young Iberia which, while disclaiming the name, maintained the indomitable spirit that had always defended the home and hearth." The one difference in this rebellion was the proclaimed "republican spirit." Spain did not have this. "But in the depths of the Spanish soul could be found the seeds of magnitude, of heroism, of a proud and generous independence. . . . Those qualities served to demonstrate that there was more there than a stupid insensitivity toward slavery." The new ideas, he concludes, will triumph when they are adapted to the Hispanic American reality, "when the borrowed idea, the foreign idea achieves a more intimate penetration into the hard and tenacious Iberian substance."

Francisco Bilbao has asked himself the same question. How is it that in spite of everything we Hispanic Americans have attained political independence and are fighting for freedom of thought? Because we carry these things in the blood, because we yearn for liberty in spite of all. And in continuing, Bilbao goes on to make an assessment of what North America has demonstrated itself to be and what Hispanic America is. "The freedom of thought . . . , the lack of moral absolutism, and the opening of land to the immigrant," he said, "have been the causes of [North American] aggrandizement and glory." In the annals of North American history, that [early period] was the heroic moment. "Everything grew: riches, population, power, and liberty." "Disregarding traditions and old systems and creating a spirit that simply devoured time and space, they succeeded in forming a nation that had its own genius." But, he added, "turning in upon itself and contemplating itself as being so great, it has fallen into the temptation of the titans, believing itself to be the arbitrator of the earth and even the contender for Olympus." This nation, the model of liberty, does not act toward other races and other peoples with the same spirit. "It did not abolish slavery in its states, it did not save the heroic Indian races, nor has it been the champion of universal causes but only of the American interest, the Saxon individualism." And afterwards, he adds, "it hurled itself upon its neighbor to the south." From the North it is necessary that we assimilate that which is positive: "The North has liberty." And in the regions of the South there has been theocratic slavery. Nevertheless, he says, "in spite of that, there were words, there was light in the very entrails of sorrow, and we rolled back the stone that closed the grave, and then we buried in that grave those centuries that had been destined for us." We, as distinct from the United States, "had to organize everything all at once. We had to consecrate the sovereignty of the people in the very midst of a theocratic educational system. . . . We have done away with slavery in all the republics of the South. We the poor, and you the happy and rich have not done it. . . . We have incorporated and are incorporating the primitive races . . . because we believe them to be our blood and our flesh, and you exterminate them jesuitically. We," continues Bilbao, "do not see in the earth, nor in the pleasures of the earth, the final end of man. The Negro, the Indian, the disinherited, the unhappy, the weak find in us the respect that is due to the title and dignity of being human. . . . This," he concludes, "is what the republicans of the America of the South have dared to put into the balance beside the pride, the riches, and the power of the America of the North."

Against "positivism," "saxonization," "North Americanism," and in defense of the personality of Hispanic America there are various voices that have been raised. Such can be found in *Ariel* by José Enrique Rodó. "One imitates," says the Hispanic American thinker, "that which one perceives as being superior or as having greater prestige. This is why the vision of a Hispanic America *delatinized* through its own will, not forced by means of conquest but deliberately sought as an image, as a semblance of the Northern archetype, floats through the dreams of many sincere people among us who are genuinely interested in our future . . . and this vision manifests itself through the constant proposals for innovation and reform. We have our northomania. It is necessary to place limits upon this, limits which both reason and sentiment would enjoin upon us." I understand, Rodó continues, that reform is sought in order that a nation might accommodate itself to new circumstances. "But I do not see the glory or the sense in denaturalizing the character of nations—their personal genius—in order to impose upon them an identification with a foreign model by which they will sacrifice the irreplaceable originality of their own spirit. . . . This is equivalent . . . to trying to incorporate by simple attachment a dead thing into a living organism." And speaking of the North American spirit, he says: "Its prosperity is proportionate to the impossibility of its satisfying an even partial conception of human destiny. . . . An orphan to deep traditions that might guide it, this people has not known how to substitute for the inspiring ideal of the past a high and disinterested conception of the future. This nation lives for the immediate reality of the present, and in this it subordinates all its activity toward the ego fulfillment of personal and collective well being. . . . That civilization can abound in fruitful suggestions or examples; it can inspire admiration, wonderment, respect; but it would be difficult for the traveler when he catches sight on the high seas of the gigantic symbol of that nation, the Statue of Liberty, triumphantly holding its torch over the port of New York, to feel his spirit awaken to the same sort of profound and religious emotion with which the ancient traveler must have been touched when he first saw the luminous lance of gold of the Athena of the Acropolis. . . . Let us hope that the spirit of that titanic social organism, which up till now has only been one of *will and utility*, will also someday be characterized by intelligence, sentiment, and idealism."

As for the mixing of races, something which some Hispanic Americans have come to consider a bad thing after having read certain books written by Saxons, it will come to be seen as the most positive aspect of our reality. Already Justo Sierra has spoken with pride of the *mestizos*. And José Vasconcelos has made of this mixture the pivotal point of his most original thesis, as expressed in *The Cosmic Race*. "Why should they laugh," says Vasconcelos referring to the North Americans, "at our Latin boasting and vanities, those strong builders of empire? They do not have in their mind the Ciceronian blocks of phraseology nor in their blood the contradictory instincts of the mixture of dissimilar races; rather they have committed the sin of destroying those races while we assimilated them, and that gives us new rights and the hope of a mission without precedence in history." Throughout all of Hispanic America, the liberators set about freeing, equally, the Negroes, the Indians, and the Whites. "The Latin amalgamation became something that no one thought of doing on the Saxon continent. There the contrary thesis remained imperative, the admitted or tacit proposition of clearing the earth of Indians, Mongols, and Negroes for the greater glory and advantage of the white." In the ultimate reckoning, universality in culture will be the prize for the sacrifices that Hispanic America has undergone. Not a material triumph, but very much so a spiritual one.

The same attitude, that of assigning positive strengths to the Hispanic American, is assumed by Antonio Caso and others of his generation. His antipositivism is an affirmation of that which had recently appeared to be purely negative. Toward North America he made judgments such as this: There are in the world, he says, "those who make things, but who are without moral grandeur. For that reason the United States has dominated and still dominates. But one must think that, sooner or later, over all the imperialisms there must wave the elevated spirit and high ideals that the Latin American peoples carry in their breast."

Therefore, toward North America the Hispanic American consciousness has come to take two attitudes: one of *admiration* and the other of *rejection*. Contradiction? No, it is that Hispanic America has known how to grasp the two spirits that animate the great country to the north. Two spirits that contest among themselves in the same way that among ourselves the two Spains that we have inherited are pitted against each other. There in the North there exist two North Americas: on the one side there is the North America of Washington, who affirmed the rights of man; of Lincoln, who abolished slavery; of Roosevelt, who extended democracy in a universal sense. On the other there is the North America of territorial ambitions, of "manifest destiny," of racial discrimination, of the imperialisms. In relation to the first, the defects of Hispanic America are made manifest, but toward the second, its qualities. The first symbolizes those liberties that the majority of men in Latin America yearn for, the second the self-centered materialism in which the old Hispanic American despotisms were clothed.

Now, the generation which remembers that fatal centennial [that of the Mexican-American War], conscious of this duality, desires and hopes for the triumph of the first North America, the triumph of Ariel, which is the triumph of liberty, and the defeat of Caliban, the egotistical and despotic materialism. The defeat of the North America of the materialisms will also be the defeat of the Hispanic America of the despotisms, because each finds its major ally in the other. But let us allow the best men of North America to do their part, and we on our part will do ours.

JOSÉ FUENTES MARES

EDITOR'S INTRODUCTION

José Fuentes Mares, modern historian and man of letters, was a northerner, born in the state of Chihuahua in 1919. Though he received a law degree and his doctorate at the National University of Mexico and taught during the years 1944 and 1945 in Mexico City at that institution, he returned to his native Chihuahua, where he became a professor at the College of Law at the University of Chihuahua, later to become the Director of that college. During 1958 and 1959, he was the Rector of the University of Chihuahua. He taught abroad in Spain and in the United States. He died on April 8, 1986.

A prolific writer, Fuentes Mares was primarily a historian, having produced fourteen works in the field of Mexican history, including four studies of the administration of Benito Juárez. In addition, Fuentes Mares was the author of three works in philosophy, a biography of Cortés, two novels, and six plays. He also published his autobiography.

Certainly, on the basis of his writing, Fuentes Mares can be said to be in the spiritual line of descent from Luis G. Cuevas, and, in fact, Fuentes Mares quotes Cuevas in a rather lengthy passage which marks the second time that these lines appear in this volume. Also, both men share a strong admiration for the nineteenth-century conservative statesman Lucas Alamán. But the concern that they share most intensely is their interest in the first minister that the United States sent to an independent Mexico, Joel Roberts Poinsett, and their conviction that he played a pivotal role in subverting the Mexican government in order to soften it up for a North American military conquest.

Given the attention that Poinsett has received in nineteenth-century Mexican letters, one might ask: why another Mexican investigation into the ambassadorship of Joel R. Poinsett? The answer lies in the fact that Fuentes Mares, in writing *Poinsett, the Story of a Great Intrigue,* made use of sources that other Mexican writers did not, principally because they could not, avail themselves of. Fuentes Mares did intensive research at the Pennsylvania Historical Society in Philadelphia, which houses the Poinsett Papers and other Poinsett materials, and at the National Archives in Washington, D.C., where the official papers relating to Poinsett's term as ambassador to Mexico are stored. The result is the revelation of a degree of intimacy Poinsett had with Mexican statesmen that other Mexican writers could only have guessed at. José Fuentes Mares had intended that his book on Poinsett be published in the year of the centennial of the Mexican-American War, thus signaling his conviction of the ambassador's implication in that event, but technical and other complications delayed the date of publication.

The method which Fuentes Mares employs in his biography of Poinsett is to begin with broad themes and then to narrow the focus to the immediate and the human. The Monroe Doctrine of 1824, by which the United States declared that it would not tolerate further extensions of Europe into Latin America, was denounced by Fuentes Mares as a pretext for a North American monopoly on interventions in Hispanic America. The assertion that North Americans were dogmatic and absolutistic about their political system was used as a basis upon which to explain Poinsett's evangelism in promoting North American political concepts and forms in Mexico, where, according to Fuentes Mares, they caused a festering because they were essentially alien to the Mexican reality.

From these broader considerations, Fuentes Mares turns to Poinsett's dealings with specific Mexican leaders. As have most Mexican writers, Fuentes Mares sees the Texas Revolution as the first phase of the Mexican-American War. In this connection, he reveals the correspondence between Poinsett and Lorenzo de Zavala, the brilliant but obsessed Mexican liberal, who allowed his ideological fixations to lead him to make common cause with the Texas revolutionaries against his own country. Correspondence is also revealed that demonstrates the relationship of General Mejía and Vice President Gómez Farías to Zavala in the working out of the Texas affair. In some cases, the samples of correspondence which Fuentes Mares reprints are so brief and out of context that the reader is not necessarily led to the same conclusions that the author is. In fact, on the basis of this correspondence, Fuentes Mares would have us believe that the Mexican plotters, along with Poinsett, were the only significant actors in bringing about the Texas Revolution. Such people as Austin, Houston, Travis, and Crockett would seem to be relegated to the role of extras.

A good deal of the correspondence, however, is relevant and suggestive. For example, we are given a letter which Vicente Guerrero, as president of Mexico, wrote to Poinsett in 1829. It reads in part: "In this delicate position, as in any other, I have the honor of putting myself at your disposition. As it is required of me that all my desires should be directed only toward making myself more worthy of the confidence that the country has placed in me and as I am determined always to maintain her beloved independence and liberty, I will count on your ministering to me the lights of your counsel, as a friend, as a lover of the felicity of nations, and as a worthy representative of that great nation to which you belong" (*Poinsett*, pp. 248–49). Even allowing for the flowery rhetoric characteristic of the Mexico of that period, one must consider this to be an extraordinary letter for a chief of state to be writing to an ambassador representing a foreign nation. The actual extent of Poinsett's influence within the Mexican government and the real nature of his designs have, of course, been a matter of much debate, as Fuentes Mares readily admits. The views of such North American historians as Robert W. Johannsen and Gene M. Brack on this matter have been discussed in the introduction to the Cuevas section of this volume.

There seems little doubt that Poinsett's political, social, and emotional relationship to Mexico and to Hispanic America as a whole (he championed the independence of the South American countries) was a complex one. The southern patrician from Charleston seems to have brought both the generally American and specifically southern aspects of his culture into this relationship. Though the correspondence with Mexican officials may reveal or suggest conniving, it also, in a number of cases, carries along with it a current of genuinely warm feeling. But that there was also a degree of patronage as well as downright racism there can be no doubt. Fuentes Mares says of him that "he sought the indulgence of a healthy nation for a depraved one, of an enlightened people for an ignorant, of a Protestant toward a Catholic nation, of the

Anglo Saxon toward the Spanish" (*Poinsett,* p. 88). In a letter to President Van Buren, Poinsett says of the Mexicans that they have become the more depraved for having interbred with the primitive indigenous races and that they are therefore considerably more vicious and ignorant than were their Spanish ancestors (*Poinsett,* p. 257).

These negative attitudes undoubtedly contributed to Poinsett's having developed the concept that Fuentes Mares calls the theory of "the two sovereignties," whereby the Latin American nations, being weak, were considered to have only relative sovereignty as contrasted to the absolute sovereignty of the European nations and of the United States. Under this theory, the stronger nations could work their will upon the weaker, all, of course, in the name of the greater good. And it was upon this rationalization that the United States, according to Fuentes Mares, sought, through its agent Poinsett, to reduce Mexico to the status of a protectorate. Fuentes Mares, therefore, continually refers to Poinsett as the "proconsul," a term which the Roman Empire used for officers whom it sent out to take charge of the dependencies.

Although Fuentes Mares claims in his prologue that he is not anti-Yankee and that he is managing his themes with historical objectivity, there is, nevertheless, an animus that goes throughout the book which, in fact, gives a definite charge to the writing. *Poinsett, the Story of a Great Intrigue* is anything but a dull book. Its sardonic humor at times reminds one of Francisco Bulnes, as in the cheerfully scornful rebuttal by which Fuentes Mares provides a hypothetical answer, in the absence of a recorded one, by which the Mexican government responds to the list of advantages which would accrue to it if it would only agree to sell Texas to the United States, a list which Poinsett was instructed to present to the Mexican authorities. Such a passage is typical in a book which abounds in lively writing.

Poinsett, the Story of a Great Intrigue

What was really surprising . . . were not the practical consequences of the Monroe Doctrine in terms of the continental diplomacy of the United States, because these were already anticipated, but the absurd repercussions that it had among statesmen in the countries to the south. Among the former colonies of Spain, the doctrine, now transformed into a myth because of the lack of the most elementary critical faculties, came to be seen as the jealous guardian of [Latin American] national rights, threatened by European intrigues. In short, it bestowed upon the diplomacy of North America toward the Hispanic American nations, recently arrived to independence, a philanthropic character. And the absurdity of it all finally became so monstrous that, repeatedly, Hispanic American statesmen expressed gratitude in the name of their people for the protection afforded them by the measures of that doctrine. So much was this the case that it seemed that the expression designed for export

Selections by José Fuentes Mares were translated from *Poinsett, Historia de Una Gran Intriga*, Mexico, D.F.: Libro Mex Editores, 1960 (Third Edition), pp. 75–77, 91, 113, 127–137, 173, 189–191, and 199–205.

that had been slipped into the text of that doctrine, "our brothers from the South," absolutely turned their heads.

They must have been madmen, blind men, or fools not to have understood—or wanted to understand—something which was clear even to those North Americans who had obvious reasons for underplaying the full implications of that miscreated doctrine. And even today, authors determined to demonstrate the excellence and virtues of North American diplomacy toward Latin America do not hesitate to recognize the real character of this message from Monroe. "The Monroe Doctrine," writes Flagg Bemis, "which capped the foundations of American diplomacy in 1823, was not a self-denial ordinance. The last thing that the statesmen who formulated it would have wished to do was to deny to the United States any further expansion into that part of the world where the doctrine said hands-off to Europe, particularly in contiguous regions of the former Spanish Empire in North America, and the island of Cuba."

This was and continues to be the unvarnished truth, but the mentality of Hispanic men, infirm and full of fantasies, led them to a tropical falsification of the problem planted within the Monroe Doctrine, and from what was nothing but a public document aimed at securing the social and political well-being of the Anglo Americans, they made a myth of generous continental protection. When in 1812 the United States witnessed the Napoleonic wars and were confronted in their own backyard with the problem of England, the best of their statesmen, Jefferson, put forth a clear view of what the world situation really was: "We believe no more in Bonaparte's fighting merely for the liberties of the seas, than in Great Britain's fighting for the liberties of mankind. The object of both is the same, to draw to themselves the power, the wealth, and the resources of other nations." It was this clarity that was lacking in our countries. We did not have a Jefferson, either *criollo*, Indian, or mulatto. There was no one to view the philanthropy of the Monroe Doctrine in the same light in which Jefferson viewed the battle of Napoleon for the liberties of the seas or the battle of England for the liberties of mankind.

· · ·

For North American foreign service officers, as for people generally throughout the various layers of American society, the political institutions of the United States were not historical facts, comprising a natural mixture of good and bad principles, appropriate for a certain moment and under determined circumstances, but they represented the absolute good, boundless in their worth. And not only should each North American view his institutions with a blinded pride, but every man, through the very fact of his being one, should participate in the same spiritual attitude, yielding to the dogma of the republican good with the same force with which a Christian places his trust in the resurrection of the body. . . . However unjustifiable, Poinsett's position can only be understood in the light of this political dogma, an attitude shared by the majority of his fellow citizens, and one which proposed not so much to adapt North American institutions to the countries of the south, but rather to adapt the countries of the south to North American institutions. Thus a road was taken whose results were a disaster. Those institutions became denaturalized, and a gestation set in which would bring forth irreparable harm to those countries that lent their portion to such experiments.

. . .

According to Rippy [J. Fred Rippy in *The Rivalry of the United States and Great Britain over Latin America*] . . . , Mr. Ward [British minister to Mexico] had tried to alarm Mexico concerning the security of Texas, and on March 31, 1927, he wrote to Mr. Canning [British foreign minister]: "I do not hesitate to express my conviction that the ultimate aim of Poinsett's mission is to embroil Mexico in a civil war, thus facilitating the acquisition of the provinces which are located north of the Río Grande." In addition, Rippy himself recognizes that Poinsett, seeing himself blocked in the exercise of normal diplomatic functions, turned to extraordinary channels and played an important role in the ministerial crisis that took place between the 23rd and the 26th of September, which led to the fall of Lucas Alamán from the Ministry of Foreign and Interior Affairs. Certain it is that Poinsett, in respect to this affair, rubbed his hands with delight and attributed the fall of Alamán to a personal pique between him and Mr. Ward. The fact was that Alamán fell from the ministry defending the rights of Mexico against North American designs and that his fall was the first of the great triumphs of His Excellency, the Minister of the United States accredited to the government of Mexico.

.   .   .

His Excellency, Mr. Joel Roberts Poinsett, was the key man in the first Republic. Upon his arrival in Mexico in the spring of 1825, he found that part of the underbrush in his path had already been cleared away. Only a few months before, a political constitution had been granted the status of Fundamental Law. This constitution was based on the doctrine of the federal pact and was fundamentally a servile imitation of the North American constitutional system. However sharply the political and social realities of the two peoples might differ, the use of identical molds into which to pour these realities would work powerfully to upgrade those that were inferior, at least so thought the political faction in charge.

The North American statesmen had observed these events with their usual acuteness. That the goal of having the Latin American nations adopt the federal system of government was a matter of importance to the North American leaders is something which cannot be doubted. . . .

In Washington, where there was full cognizance of the Mexican Constitution of 1824, it was foreseen that the new system would be North America's best ally in its future enterprises. It was for this reason that the *Instructions* [which Secretary of State Henry Clay had delivered to Poinsett] recommended that the government of Mexico be congratulated for having taken as its model the Constitution of the United States. Also, the advantages of such a constitution and the manner in which it was to be executed were to be thoroughly explained. Having cleared, almost without effort, the first hurdles, our man could now put his entire energies into the pursuit of more ambitious goals.

When Poinsett arrived in Mexico, the majority of the political leaders were inclined toward the federal system, thus their handiwork, the Constitution of 1824. Led by such leaders as Ramos Arizpe and Zavala, the group undertook to divide the country into *free and sovereign states,* without paying attention to the political realities and historical exigencies that would counsel to the contrary. With his characteristic frankness, Servando Teresa de Mier had protested in Congress the adoption of the federal system, but, lamentably, his was a voice crying out in the desert.

The irrepressible Friar Servando then said that "he would bet his head that none of those gathered there knew what kind of an animal federalism was," and without doubt his position has been supported by succeeding events in the political history of Mexico. And even ourselves, witnesses for over a century and a quarter to a legally established federalism, will testify that in fact centralism continues to survive and that it still dictates to the nation so that Mexico will continue to seek its solutions to internal political problems in the same way as before, always from the center to the periphery. It is not easy to send up history against the current, and it is not necessary to string out, in all its details, that lying foolishness about the principle of the *sovereignty* of the states being implicit in Mexico: here the center continues and will continue to be the supreme dispenser of benefits . . . and of all the rest.

In Mexico, to sum up, federalism lacked a solid base that would sustain it in practice, and, above all, it lacked a national need which would create a demand for it. That the Mexicans—and the Hispanic Americans in general—were far from having a clear conception of what federalism really was in practice had already been demonstrated by the role that the deputies from these countries played in the Spanish Cortes. Furthermore, and as Alamán so opportunely saw it, simply having the example of the Constitution of the United States in no way constituted a proof that the application of the principles of that document would have value in terms of the Mexican reality. In fact, even though the federal system when applied to our neighbors to the north brought them a fulfillment of their political and national needs, this same system, when applied to Mexico, would necessarily have produced the opposite consequences. The federal system, which united North America, would have fatally brought disunity to Mexico. "In drawing up our constitution," says Alamán, "we virtually produced a translation of the Constitution of the United States. But the application would have diverse results from those which obtained in that country.

There the Constitution served to bind together different sections that from the beginning had been separated, and in the joining together a nation was formed. But in Mexico, such a document had the effect of dividing that which had been united and of making separate nations of what was and should be only one." Certainly, succeeding events have validated Alamán's analysis.

Equipped with the best personal armament and everywhere surrounded by a favorable climate, Poinsett could initiate his incursion into our domestic politics. As a starting point, he spurred on the federalists—with their imported ideas and their shoulders still covered with the mantle of constitutional delegate—to strike with escalating force against the traditional centralism. Immediately afterwards, in the realm of religion, he favored the enemies of the Church—the "tolerant ones"—in order to damage the spiritual unity of Mexico. And in the area of social and racial living arrangements, he sought not to annul the discrimination that existed . . . but to aggravate it, deepening hostilities until blood was spilled, and the pain caused was such that there arose hatreds of the sort that would neither ask for nor give any quarter. It was in this manner that he perpetrated the attack against the Spaniards, who had become respected citizens assimilated into the new nation by the Plan of Independence. Rapidly, they were changed into scapegoats for the machinations of His Excellency and his ringleaders.

As a pretext, he put forward, as always, "the shadow of Europe," and particularly the contest with England. A few months after his arrival in October of 1825, Poinsett wrote to his cousin Johnson that there was no opposition to British interests in this hemisphere, but he added that "if Great Britain seeks to divide us or create a European party in Latin America, its minister (referring to Mr. Ward) cannot complain if we avail ourselves of our influence to defeat his aims." And that he did avail himself of his influence, to the limit, is demonstrated by the fact that a year later he could say, again writing to Johnson, that he had dedicated every moment of his time to raising up a powerful American party, accomplishing in Mexico much more than any other citizen of the United States could have done, "but not because of greater talent but because of a greater understanding of the people and the country." Confronted with such testimony from Poinsett's own hand, we cannot deny that Monroe was right in saying that his agent was "the best of them all" when it came to the business of Hispanic America.

But in this regard, it is important to establish with absolute clarity that, despite the declarations of the Charlestonian, the *American Party,* whose efforts run through some of the most lamentable pages of our history, was not created by Poinsett in order to counteract the influence that Mr. Ward had gained or was trying to gain with his *European party,* because in reality things occurred in exactly the opposite way. In October of 1825, only a few days before he had written to Johnson, Poinsett wrote complainingly to Rufus King, minister of the United States to England, that Mr. Ward "had begun to form a European party *in opposition to the one which is considered to have been organized by me,*" and he adds that if Great Britain is seeking to divide the Americas or to destroy the republican principles of government by forming a European party adverse to North American interests, "it cannot complain if we avail ourselves of all the means at our disposal to oppose such aims." Quite apart from the absurdity of charging the Europeans with having played the role of villain in all our farces, the above confession on the part of Mr. Poinsett is sufficient to establish the fact that not England but the United States was the country which first formed allied groups for the purpose of orienting Mexican policy in the direction of its interests. If Mr. Ward set out to form a European party in order to oppose the one that "was considered" to have been organized by Poinsett, it is enough for us to remember that the latter, in the letter to Johnson already cited, confessed to having dedicated every minute of his time toward the creation of an American party. No comment.

But before continuing, it is worthwhile formulating, at this point, a fundamental question: The key to the success which crowned Poinsett's incursion into our domestic politics, did it stem from the *who* of its paladin or the *how* of its organization? Of course the *how* is inexplicable without the *who,* but it is not too much to insist upon the fact that Poinsett's mission, all of it, was founded upon a powerful will toward organization. Among all the viable roads for the attainment of his goals, Poinsett had the talent to choose and the will to pursue the best. The *who* of that incursion, the physical and moral portrait of Joel R. Poinsett, has been the subject of an earlier chapter, but it remains for us to discover the *how* of that incursion. And that cannot be resolved without our embarking upon the foundation and sanctioning of the masonic lodges of the York Rite.

Several years later, when the country confronted one of the most painful crises of its history, Don Luis G. Cuevas, closely tied in to the political negotiations of Mexico at that time, could write in reference to Poinsett's efforts:

He conceived the project, which was favored by contemptible types of Mexicans, of taking control of the popular lodges and organizing them so as to promote civil conflict. Behind the mask of patriotism and beneficence, they would be the better able to foment and inflame the hatred which we were beginning to have for our origins, our customs, for the Spaniards, and, although they themselves might take no notice of it, for foreign residents in the country. Poinsett, who studied well the character of our revolutions, not only in the Republic, where he had lived some years before, but in South America, had no doubt about the evils which would result in Mexico from a war carried on by the lower classes—or more properly by the party which called itself their protector—against the more influential classes. Nevertheless, he adopted all the methods he could conceive of to bring to a boil the passions and hatred which could be incited against the Scottish Rite and the Spaniards who supported its policies and aims. If the sentiments of virtue and justice directed governments and were in fact the bases of international policy, the name of Poinsett would not be remembered in Mexico nor in the United States except in terms of actions which should be condemned to the execration of history and posterity. But to the disgrace of the human race, the conduct which he practiced among us is the very thing which has gained for him much praise and has been, at the very least, sanctioned by diplomacy. The only goal of his efforts has been toward the execution of evil projects and purely materialistic designs, whatever may have been the upright principles claimed in his books. Forgetting good faith, loyalty, and real greatness, he has had the impudence to present these designs as the unequivocal testimonial to modern civilization. Our neighbors are the ones who now exceed in the art of corruption and the ones who have not stopped and will never stop bringing about the ruin and disaster of entire peoples in order to add to themselves a span of territory. In this sense it could be said that Poinsett was of more service to the American Union than all of its generals put together in the war of invasion and that he deserves more than any of them a magnificent monument on Capitol Hill.

We insist upon the fact that it was not the *who* but the *how* of the intrigue that determined the extent of its successes. And even though in the long run these same methods when employed by His Excellency worked against him, the sole fact of his having chosen that road reveals more than anything the subtle intelligence behind his process of choice. Through the narrow door of the secret session, the incursion of Poinsett into the domestic politics of Mexico was initiated. Poinsett showed how the Lodge could be the road toward domination, the broad highway of Empire.

Commonly, in the pages of the Mexican historians, Poinsett has been seen as not guilty of the crimes that have been imputed to him. In all rigor, it must be said that his responsibility lies in his having put into action the machinery that later went to work more or less on its own. His was the responsibility of a chief who only to a certain extent can be held accountable for the excesses of his mercenaries. In this much-debated question, as in many others, Carlos Pereyra strikes the difficult balance: "One does not have to attribute to the North American minister all the evils that befell the country," he writes, "but it would be unjust to deprive him of the glory that belongs to him as the pontiff of the underminers."

. . .

The diplomatic action of England served him as his favorite excuse. Relying on its international prestige, according to Poinsett, England had made several commercial accords with Spain's old colonies that carried over into the new independent governments and brought with them a certain amount of political influence. Immediately after his arrival, the American agent saw as the most pressing and immediate goal of his mission the setting up of a dike in order to contain this influence, with the eventual object of undermining it altogether. With this motive in mind, Poinsett elaborated a picturesque doctrine relating to the sovereignty of nations, as a sort of concomitant theory. According to this concept, one could not place an equal value upon sovereignty when it concerned diplomatic relations with a European power as when such relations were established with an Hispanic American nation, this being the case because the latter was weak and the former powerful. This formulation, of course, was not openly declared; nevertheless, it was the criterion that formed the basis of the concept which we shall provisionally call "the doctrine of the two sovereignties."

The Poinsett doctrine "of the two sovereignties" was characterized by its adjudicating an *absolute* value upon the concept of sovereignty when it related to European nations and only a *relative* one when it applied to the Ibero American nations, the tacit understanding being that these latter had less right to be free because they were not as strong. Poinsett considered that the diplomacy of the United States should differ substantially from one continent to another. As regards Europe, the principle of sovereignty being *absolute,* there must be a barrier against any sort of intrusion. But as to the Hispanic American nations, the situation changes radically, this being so because "if we do not exercise a direct and salutary influence upon the governments of the Latin American states, neither should we permit any European nation to do so." The letter of this text would seem to indicate to us that the American diplomat was disposed to prevent the European governments from exercising any influence upon the Ibero American governments upon the condition that the United States also would abstain from doing so, but later developments in the course of his mission demonstrate to us that his intention was quite other. Taking as his pretext the intervention of Europe—the European specter—he proposed to establish on the part of the United States a virtual protectorate.

. . .

As a sure instrument of domination, His Excellency had sanctioned and installed the Grand Lodge of the new Rite, which the Plenipotentiary himself, in a communication to his government, had simply categorized as a *political party.* This Yorkist party, democratic, popular, American— all names for which it was known—proclaimed a program which, as in all such programs, contained a positive aspect of construction and a negative one of destruction. In the negative aspect of its agenda, the Yorkists inveighed against centralism as a form of political organization, against the religious hegemony of the Church, and especially against the Spaniards who had remained in the country, protected by the provisions of the Plan of Iguala. As for the other face of its program, the positive side, the Yorkists fought for federalism, campaigned for "tolerance," and favored the North Americans—all of which confirms us in the belief that one side or the other of the Yorkist program, the negative or the positive, resulted in being equally destructive for Mexico.

. . .

For the proposed acquisition [the acquiring of Texas], with three possible boundary lines under consideration, [President Andrew] Jackson was ready to pay five million dollars—for the best of the possible arrangements—reducing the price proportionately for minor concessions. With the fundamental object of the new negotiations thus decided upon, Mr. Poinsett was instructed as to the various rationalizations he should put forward in order to win the consent of the Mexican government. These arguments can be reduced to a basic four:

a) The sale of Texas to the United States would be advantageous for Mexico because it would do away with the principal area of disagreement that existed between the two countries as respect to boundary lines.

b) The sale of Texas to the United States would represent a considerable savings for Mexico in terms of the monies needed to pay the numerous garrisons charged with keeping the watch in that far off territory.

c)The sale of Texas to the United States would gain for Mexico sufficient funds to guarantee its economy, and would provide, through the sale of the less, for the conservation and prosperity of the greater.

d) The sale of Texas to the United States would signify for Mexico the additional, but no less important, advantage of placing within a powerful nation—the United States—the numerous tribes of warlike Indians that had been causing constant depredations in Mexican territory.

We do not know what the Mexican reply was to these *rationalizations,* but it does not take a great effort on our part to imagine what it might have been. In the order of the points put forward by the North American government favoring the sale of Texas, Mexico might have answered:

a) That the source of the difficulties in respect to boundaries would not be eradicated by moving the Mexican frontier southward, because

Texas is only the first episode in the policy of expansion toward the Pacific, and, in the eyes of the people and the government of the United States, California was, at the very least, just as important as Texas.

b) That undoubtedly the Mexican treasury would save great sums if it no longer had to maintain troops in Texas, but it would save even more if it ceased to support them in Chihuahua, Sonora, Coahuila, Nuevo Leon, Tamaulipas, etc., etc., surrendering these territories also to the United States. And even more: if the Mexican government decided to sell the whole country to the United States, the saving would be definite.

c) That the sum offered by the United States for the sale of Texas would not be enough to pay up one year's pressing economic demands.

d) That the real danger to the security of Mexico does not come from the destructive marauding of the various tribes of warlike Indians but from the progressive advance of industrious, frugal, and tolerant colonists, lovers of law and order, belonging to that "vigorous white race" which calls forth such bursts of enthusiasm from Mr. Poinsett.

. . .

That in the matter of Texas there existed previous and inviolable agreements between Poinsett, Butler, Zavala, Alpuche, Mejía, and other minor associates is something so clear that there is no room for doubt. In the accord that was reached by the Junta Anficiónica (Junta Representing Both Sides) of New Orleans in its session of September 3, 1835, it was agreed that Sr. Zavala would be the director and chief of the Texas colonists with the charge of calling the attention of the Mexican government to the situation in Texas. Meanwhile, Sr. Mejía, on his part, as chief of the federal army would occupy the port of Tampico in Tamaulipas. Sr. Gómez Farías, in his capacity of Vice President of the Republic, exiled by Santa Anna, would stand by, ready to pursue whatever course was advised by Zavala and Mejía. The *business* of Texas, quite evidently and most intensively, was organized and launched by Mr. Poinsett, Zavala, the government of the United States the most active partners, with participants extending right up to a vice president of Mexico, and up to the last thief in the *American Party*, the party founded by His Excellency, the Minister from the United States.

The plot of this famous *business* becomes so clear, its organization so manifest, that two letters from Zavala to Poinsett [written in 1830], which we found in the archives of the Pennsylvania Historical Society, serve only to clarify some of the details:

I have not wanted to do anything—Zavala writes to Poinsett from Mexico City—until I receive notice from you as to what should be done, especially with respect to the Company with Mr. Butler. As of yet, I have not seen him.

And a month and a half later, still from Mexico City, Don Lorenzo writes again to Poinsett:

It is extremely important that you send immediately [to Texas] people who in my name or yours will take possession of the best sites and arrange for their colonization, making the people who go there understand fully that if they want to remain there they must be on our side.

Don Lorenzo de Zavala then moves to the United States, until 1832, living *honorably* in Brooklyn, New York. Though engaged in pursuing his personal business, he nevertheless finds time to meditate on grave problems of the historical/philosophical type:

We Mexicans and, further, sons of Catholic Spain—he writes to Poinsett on April 30, 1932—are condemned to a series of bloody revolutions. I will be one of the victims, *but on your side and on your account.*

This letter from Zavala convinces us of two things: in the first place that Don Lorenzo was sure that he would go down to posterity as one of the darkest figures in our history, and secondly, that he was completely resolved that the hard adjectives he would necessarily earn because of his acts would not be applied to him without his obtaining proportional economic benefits. Convinced that to be a great rogue required the same exceptional moral conditions that were needed to be a great virtuoso, this exemplary Yucatecan persuades us that, above and beyond, he was, in his line, the greatest of all.

To give an extremely brief account of his life, destiny had already furnished a good deal to Don Lorenzo de Zavala. At the fall, in 1832, of the administration of General Bustamante, Zavala was reinstalled as governor of the State of Mexico, a position he had already discharged in the far off days of El Motín de la Acordada [an episode in the struggle for independence]. Toward the end of 1833 he was sent to France as minister plenipotentiary of Mexico to the government of the Tuileries, and shortly after, when he learned that Don Valentín Gómez Farías had fallen from grace with Santa Anna and consequently from his position of Vice President of the Republic, he resigned his position and went directly to Texas, to fulfill the promise which Butler had communicated to Jackson in 1830. There he joined the Texas insurgents, representing the district of Harrisburg at the Austin Convention, which declared war on Mexico on November 7, 1835. Later he accompanied the Texas delegation that went to Washington to offer unconditionally the annexation of Texas to the United States. He was an important personage in the Texas declaration of independence, which took place on March 3, 1836. He died in Harrisburg on the sixteenth of November of the same year, after having sent to Poinsett one of the most interesting letters of his life.

This letter, dated from Galveston Bay on October 16, 1835, is to be found among the personal correspondence of Mr. Poinsett at the Pennsylvania Historical Society. Considering it to be of great interest, we reproduce it in full:

My Esteemed Friend:

I received through the main post your appreciated letter, which, as you must know, gave me great pleasure, not only because it gave me notice of your good health but because it gave rise to memories, despite the fact that my sensibility is almost paralyzed with all the work, the illnesses, and my forty-eight years.

I received the nomination for Vice President [of Texas] against my wishes and by acclamation. In a few days I realized that I could do nothing among such ignorant and presumptuous people. This poor fellow Burnett [a prominent leader among the Texas rebels] is a most frivolous and presuming man and is the most lacking in understanding of all the people I have known in his state, including Zerecero. It is like those lawyers . . . who know that they are all mixed up and yet try to cover their ignorance through vacuous harangues.

I indicated to them the necessity of organizing a government, of the different divisions needed, of the order that should be followed, the method, the know-how which would be required. Nobody would listen to me, and poor old Burnett believed that getting off letters and notes like an office clerk would do very well.

I got tired of it all, and I retired four months ago—especially after the failure to keep faith with the treaty made with Santa Anna, in which I had no part. Santa Anna fulfilled his part of the agreement, but here they not only did not live up to what had been stipulated but they treated Santa Anna with indignity. I thought at the beginning that Santa Anna should be treated the way he treated us. That was tolerable in the heat of passion. But later it was politic to extract advantages from him.

Do you remember the Caudine Forks [two mountain gorges near Benevento, Italy]? I cannot live in Texas. I have been sick since I arrived here a year and a half ago, and ever since I have been almost moribund and have seen my bed surrounded by my family. It would be better to live in beggary in a healthy country than to die here in one or two years.

I believe that we will see each other later. I will go only to make a visit to you and to Mme. Poinsett. . . .

In my opinion, the imbecile Mexican government will send another expedition against Texas. We will both lose, but our losses will be more easily remedied than those of the Great Mexican Republic.

Goodbye, my friend. I am as I have always been, your most affectionate

LORENZO DE ZAVALA

This interesting document, given by the approaching death of its author the character of a last political testament, breathes a pervasive animosity. It also signals despair and perhaps, as well, repentance. The Spanish in his blood pushes him toward extremes, giving rise to critical rages against his own career. Nonconformist, unadaptable, unrealistic, and adventurous, like a Quijote cherishing contradictory values, the man hurls himself against the new Texan society whose coming into being he so enthusiastically praised before actually living in it. He assails both the Texans and the Mexicans. He is against Burnett and Santa Anna. For him, all of them turn out to be rogues, low-down types, negators of life. Perhaps Washington's reluctance to accept the annexation of Texas caused him to lose his last object of faith, his faith in the United States, which was the only, the last faith that could have accompanied him to the tomb. He died alone, tragically alone, as die all men of his type.

While Zavala lay dying in Harrisburg, Poinsett's destiny burned the more brightly. The strong advocate of the military, fighter against the

royalists in the south of Chile, is now named Secretary of War by the
new President Martin Van Buren, who had won the election of 1836.
North American history refers with praise to his work as secretary, and
it would seem that Poinsett, generally identified with the aims of the Van
Buren administration, manifested his one dissent in the matter of
Texas. While the government, undoubtedly under pressure from the
anti-slavery sentiment of the North, withheld its sanction from annexation, Poinsett recommended it as a matter of immediate urgency. According to Rippy, the agents of the Republic of Texas accredited to
Washington found in him a sincere friend, and the Texas minister to
Washington took note of this in a dispatch dated August 1837:

> In Mr. Poinsett we have a powerful advocate. The southern states and Texas
> will one day know how zealously he supported the measure [annexation], and if
> I mention the distinguished name of this gentleman it is because the archives of
> the Legation can yield, sufficiently enough, testimony to his valiant efforts in
> behalf of our goals.

A man of convictions, he knew how to maintain his aims throughout
the years, and many years later, in 1843, we still find him pursuing the
goal of the annexation of Texas to the United States as the best measure
to satisfy the interests of both parties.

Joel Roberts [Poinsett] laid the juridical and political foundation for
this argument in an article published in 1846 in *De Bow's Commercial
Review of the South and West,* a New Orleans periodical. Poinsett maintains that by virtue of the [Mexican] Constitution of 1824, under whose
provisions the Texans made their agreement with Mexico, the Texans
had an indisputable right to change the basis of their political pact and
to separate themselves from Mexico in order to annex themselves to the
United States, any arguments against this original and fundamental
right notwithstanding. In addition, this right was sanctioned in the text
of the constitution.

Poinsett was not right in this case, but neither was it necessary that
he be. Zavala had spoken of the "dikes of paper" filled to the top by the
"impetuous torrents of Niagara," and the restrictions which Alamán
fostered from Mexico City could so be described, as well as Poinsett's
allegations designed to twist the judgments of history.

In response to the restrictive measures that the Bustamante administration adopted to prevent any further colonization of Texas from the United States, Mejía provoked the uprising of the colonists and forced the surrender of the garrison under General Terán. "I remind you of your promise, I await your orders, and after we have talked, I will do what you want me to do." So wrote Mejía to Poinsett from Washington on February 26, 1830. Certainly they spoke later, and Mejía did what his "dear friend and master" ordered him to do. The *business* of Texas was consummated.

CARLOS BOSCH GARCÍA

EDITOR'S INTRODUCTION

Carlos Bosch García was one of that distinguished group of Spanish emigres who fled oppression in their native country to contribute richly to the intellectual life of Latin America. He became, in 1944, a naturalized citizen of Mexico. The cosmopolitan aspect of his training, reflected in his writing, is indicated by the academies that he attended: La Universidad Autonóma de Barcelona, in Spain; Oxford University, in England; and in Mexico: La Escuela Nacional de Antropología e Historia, El Colegio de Mexico, and La Universidad Nacional Autónoma de Mexico. He holds a doctorate in history and has taught at the Instituto de Investigaciones Históricas at the Universidad Nacional Autónoma de Mexico since 1975. He has taught widely in universities throughout the United States.

The titles in his extensive list of publications reflect his strong interest in the diplomatic history of Mexico, and particularly as this history deals with Mexico's relations with the United States. These books include: *Diplomatic Problems of Mexico Since the Independence* (1947); *History of the Relations Between Mexico and the United States* (1961); *Basis of the Foreign Policy of the United States* (1975); and *Latin America, a Global Interpretation of the Dispersion in the Nineteenth Century* (1978). In recent years he has been occupied in the publication of *Documents in the Relations of Mexico with the United States* for the Instituto de Investigaciones Históricas, Volume IV of which was published in 1985.

As Bosch García considers the events that have occurred in the interrelations of Mexico and the United States, he discerns process, patterns of behavior. In *The History of the Relations of Mexico with the United States*, he sees that the Indian wars, which accompanied the movement west in the United States, accustomed that nation to model its behavior on the "situation of fact." The Indians were an obstruction to the "transcontinentalism" of the United States. Faced with that fact, the nation acted to remove the obstruction, forcibly. Because the United States government faced that situation many times, the response became a conditioned reflex. One reacted to a "situation of fact" with force. Juridical considerations did not act as constraints. When the westward-moving impulse of the United States resulted in that country's having to confront the boundary line of Mexico, there resulted another "situation of fact," and the United States, in Bosch García's interpretation, reacted according to its historic conditioning.

In *The Basis of the Foreign Policy of the United States,* Bosch García, displaying a keen sense of the geopolitical, looks at United States–Mexico relations from a global perspective. He sees the treaty that ended the Mexican-American War as an event that had worldwide repercussions. Important though it might be in itself, the treaty was the more significant because it established precedents that set in motion a march of events that would establish the United States as a world power. With original insight, Bosch García links the Mexican-American War with the later Spanish-American War, where the United States used techniques it had learned in Mexico to considerable advantage. The war with Mexico closed for the United States what Bosch García calls the "terrestrial frontier." The United States had satisfied its urge to extend from sea to sea, but the basic impulse was still alive. What had been the "terrestrial frontier" becomes with the Spanish-American War the "maritime frontier." Bosch García sees a repetition of patterns. Before, there were Texans rebelling against Mexico while being abetted by the United States, with the result of a general war in which the United States gained considerable territory and extended its continental frontier. Later, there were Cubans rebelling against Spain while being abetted by the United States, with the result being a war between the United States and Spain in which Cuba gained its independence, as did Texas, but remained under the hegemony of the United States. But as a result of the Spanish-American War, the United States gained territories that changed its very nature: Puerto Rico, which made the United States a Caribbean power, leading to its intervention in Central America to make way for the construction of the Panama Canal; the Philippine

Islands and Guam, which opened the way for the United States becoming a power in the Orient. Thus the Treaty of Guadalupe Hidalgo led the way to the Treaty of Paris, which ended the Spanish-American War, and the "terrestrial frontier" became the "maritime frontier." In *The Basis of the Foreign Policy of the United States,* Carlos Bosch García has endowed the plains of Mexico with powerful shock waves whose force would reshape the world.

History of the Relations Between Mexico and the United States

On the first of March, with the intention of breaking the impasse which had lasted for more than a month, the minister [John Slidell] considered the possibility of an ultimatum to force an immediate answer from the Mexican government [to the American offer of economic aid in exchange for territorial concessions], threatening to leave the country if he were not answered within a period of fifteen days. The moment was judged to be favorable because it was rumored that certain groups were planning to bring over a monarch. Therefore, the republicans (liberals) would be forced to look to the United States for assistance.

After many rumors and with the period of ultimatum fast coming to an end, the Mexican government, on March 12, 1846, delivered a negative answer. The government refused to give its *placet* (vote of assent) to Slidell. The warships putting on an American show of force in the harbor of Veracruz were considered to be incompatible with the

These selections by Carlos Bosch García were translated from *La Historia de Las Relaciones Entre Mexico y Los Estados Unidos, 1819–1848*, Mexico, D.F.: Escuela Nacional de Ciencias Políticas, 1961, pp. 107–108, 111–112, and 275–278.

announced aim of (Slidell's) mission, and the presence of the squadron along the coasts of Mexico was interpreted as confirmation that the United States planned to extend its territory at the expense of Mexico. Those intentions were for Mexico a *casus belli*, and there seemed to be no reason for proceeding with such futile negotiations. Slidell's problem consisted in the fact that Black [John Black, American consul in Mexico City] had not indicated that the Mexican government would reestablish relations [broken off because of the annexation of Texas] only if there were a prior discussion on the problem of Texas, which in Mexico was the principal cause of the rupture. Yet a minister had been sent [from the United States] who, in being received, would signify that Mexico was ignoring the cause of offense and was consenting to the existence of friendly relations, which in fact did not exist. The only acceptable alternative for Mexico was the sending of an *ad hoc* minister of war. In the latter case, Mexico would simply have to defend herself because the United States would be the invader and would be the responsible party.

.   .   .

Internationally, the Mexican position assumed a special significance as the problem of Mexico became one of general interest to the small nations, who had to ask themselves what their position would be before the great powers. North America would achieve its aggrandizement at the expense of Mexican territory, a situation which would threaten the equilibrium and peace of the world. Mexico would suffer from not having accepted terms of peace which would have compromised its own future.

.   .   .

With the ascent of General Paredes to power in March of 1846, Slidell's hopes, in view of the arrival of a new government, were revived— only to be dashed again. At this point Slidell gave up all efforts at reaching an understanding. He had tried all possibilities, including the economic inducement, without results. Now he resolved to advise his government to resort to the use of force.

In May of 1846, the North American Congress decided upon a declaration of war against Mexico while at the same time maintaining that peace was its ultimate objective and that this was so desired by the nation that it stood ready to sign a treaty of peace as soon as Mexico offered "reasonable" conditions in terms of the pending problems.

In this way, diplomatic activities came to a halt. Mexico internationalized her problem by sending forth a pathetic plea to the rest of the world: What will be the future of those weak nations which find themselves living beside the great powers?

The North American armies moved forward and penetrated into the north and center of Mexican territory. In February of 1847, Mexico signified that it would negotiate if its rights were respected, among them being the national integrity and independence. The war continued. In April the representative arrived [from the United States] who had the power to end the war with proposals considered to be acceptable.

The United States at this point did not anticipate any major difficulties: New Mexico (the Southwest), Lower and Upper California for fifteen million dollars; then, New Mexico and Lower and Upper California for twenty million dollars; then, Lower and Upper California plus the right of transit through the Isthmus of Tehuantepec for twenty million, and, finally and as a minimum cession, New Mexico and Upper California for twenty-five million dollars. Those were the alternatives.

The Mexicans had only to choose, and in order to give time to close the agreement a truce could be ordered. Nicholas Trist's instructions were the finale of the situation perceived as fact. Nobody had spoken before about New Mexico or the Californias—except in the project put forward by Butler.

Scott's disobedience in not forwarding on to the Mexican government Trist's letter with its peace proposals can be interpreted as a device to guarantee with all military might the situation as fact: the invasion of Mexico pursued to the point that would force the signing of the American proposals. This would appear to be confirmed when, with the transmitting of the Mexican proposal in which the discussion of the peace issue was centered around the point of disagreement, that is, the annexation of Texas, the withdrawal of Trist was ordered on October 6, 1847, at a time in which Scott had taken the capital and had held it since the month of September. The situation on that occasion can be explained by the fact that (Trist's) first instructions had been drawn up at a time before the taking of the city of Veracruz and the fall of San Juan de Ulúa (a fortress off the coast of the state of Veracruz), in other words, under different circumstances. That is to say: a situation of fact produced by the invasion of the capital had supervened, and there were recriminations against the prolonged duration of the armistice (November 27, 1847), which had stalled amid discussions that were leading nowhere.

Trist felt driven to continue the discussions and finalize the treaty, even though he had to proceed without the approval of his government. Under the presidency of General Pedro Anaya (November 22, 1847), Trist began the negotiations, but hardly had he gotten them underway when he received the order to return home—which he promptly disobeyed, being convinced that he was serving his nation's peace aims now that the new boundaries being shaped amounted to the acquisition of approximately half of Mexico's territory. He continued following his original instructions, along general lines, but he adapted himself to the situation as fact, as he had foreseen it would be, in order to make it possible for the treaty to be signed. He took into account Mexico's requests, the goals of the United States, and his knowledge of former treaties that the United States had signed, which served him as precedents. He succeeded, furthermore, in reducing the payments to five million dollars less than his government had previously stipulated.

The treaty was signed, and Trist left for the United States on February 12, 1848. The ratifications were exchanged in Querétaro on May 30 of the same year. There remains the question of how it was that, in view of the final order to Trist to withdraw and his subsequent disobedience, the United States ratified the terms of the treaty. Is this another case of a situation of fact, which the United States preferred to act upon rather than to prolong the war?

To synthesize, the experience the United States had acquired and applied in its expansion across areas that had been inhabited by the Indians was now projected in terms of the territory of Mexico, so the United States turned away from juridical considerations in favor of practical means, whose efficacy was supported by the nation's history. Having learned from the mistake of attempting a settlement on juridical grounds with Spain, the United States was determined to make use of

the methods learned in the course of its historical development in which
there was a recurrence of situations of fact, and before the compulsive
force of such a situation, Mexico had no redress. Discussions about
boundaries, incidents provoked in the adjacent zones, demands, offers
of money, and, as the final resort, war—these were the instruments that
forced Mexico into the situation of fact, which was the end result of the
United States' implementing in 1848 the plan it had established at the
beginning, when it opted for the thesis of transcontinentalism, which
was the subject of dispute with Onís in 1803 and 1819. [Luís de Onís
was the Spanish minister with whom the United States negotiated an
early treaty, which it later regretted because of limits placed upon its
expansion westward.]

The Basis of the Foreign Policy
of the United States

The manner in which the North American colonists understood and treated the various Indian peoples, including relationships formed in their daily lives as colonists, established a tradition which became the type that determined their later treatment of foreigners, as well as their ways of dealing with each other. In his relationship with the Indian, the American colonist was exclusionary, and because this attitude was not only maintained over a long period of time but entailed increasing danger, it forged his very character and discipline. But as a starting point there was the puritan and religious configuration, which gave rise to the basic traits of competence and economic self-sufficiency, virtues which all members of the new nation aspired to.

As a result, these people brought to bear a sense of the practical in their confrontations with nature and with life. From this sense of the practical and of the economic came the very coloration of their being, and from it also surged the force by which they met the hard test and

These selections by Carlos Bosch García were translated from *La Base De La Política Exterior Estadounidense,* Mexico, D.F.: Universidad Nacional Autónoma de Mexico, 1969, pp. 12–16, 40–41, 53–54, 82–83, 90–91, 98–99, and 159–160.

accomplished their extraordinary expansion within a relatively short period of time—from the Atlantic to the Pacific, in the course of which they occupied the territories along the eastern coast and vaulted over the mountains to the basin of the Mississippi. Then followed the Louisiana Purchase, the acquisition of the Floridas, and the crossing of the plains of Utah, and finally the collision with the Mexican frontier, resulting in the annexation of Texas, New Mexico, and California, repopulating all those areas.

But from the beginning of this expansionist movement, one idea shone clear, the crossing of the continent. And it was this concept that was discussed with Onís in order to establish the first frontier with the Latin world. If this frontier fixed limitations upon the lands occupied by the Latins in America, it also offered them the security of a prime demarcation, a line which was agreed upon by both powers, Spain and the United States, and which also served as a point of departure for future discussions. This line was of great importance because, while signaling the boundary between the United States and Mexico, it at the same time divided the Spanish-speaking from the English-speaking world, thus constituting the great cultural demarcation upon the American continent.

But while the United States carried on its important internal traffic in people, merchandise, and animals, it felt at the same time the lure of competition with the powers traditionally interested in the American continent, such as in its northern regions where, descending from Canada through the great rivers, there came down cargoes of furs and of gold.

The insatiable thirst for lands and the idea of Manifest Destiny had at the beginning, as a subconscious goal, the avoiding of areas where the European powers had already established themselves upon the northern continent. But in time, the process of colonization began to mold itself to fit the necessities of circumstance, and it developed a repetitive formula: provoke a situation of fact and from there begin discussions which could provide a variety of solutions.

Sometimes a peaceful occupation of territory was managed, such as when colonists took over an area, presented a de facto colonization, which then had to be regularized (Florida). On other occasions territory was acquired by an international treaty of sale (Louisiana). Then there were acquisitions which arose out of resolutions of independence declared by colonists who had injected themselves into foreign lands. After independence there was recourse to annexation (Texas). Finally, outright territorial expansion, which sought the sanction of international peace treaties (New Mexico, California, and, somewhat later, the Philippines and Puerto Rico).

Characteristically, the heritage of the colonial period was a preoccupation with land, the possession of which signified the "imperium." This was vividly demonstrated by the signing of the Adams-Onís Treaty which, while it rendered impossible the dreams of grandeur of the Empire of Iturbide [self-styled Emperor of Mexico] by which he projected converting the Gulf of Mexico into the "bosom of Mexico," put into the hands of the United States the possibility of realizing its concept of transcontinentalism. [Note: By the Adams-Onís Treaty, the United States took possession of Florida from Spain.]

The steps were numbered and methodical. Florida and Louisiana were the first. They opened the road by 1819, which led to the second, Texas. The third would be the result of the war of 1847.

In this way, the idea of transcontinentalism was firmly planted into the idea of Manifest Destiny, which at the same time subsumed a variety of concepts of strategy, communications, commerce, and politics. For the United States, the discussions with Mexico about boundaries were simply a problem of procedure, but the real purport of these discussions bore heavily upon Mexico and were resented by her. In the first place, in posing the problem of the land and of the push southward for new lands, one cannot accept the notion that this drive was due to a real necessity for *habitat* on the part of the North American population. The problem had to do with the desire to increase the power of the United States and with goals that were speculative and financial. The North American agricultural population was still a scattered one, and in order to establish themselves in Texas, American farmers passed through many miles of empty territory. The real necessities for population and speculation, which began in about 1820, reached a crisis stage in Texas in the following ten years, and then the pushing forward of these things would be done in earnest.

. . .

[Anthony] Butler and [Andrew] Jackson were those who first conceived the definitive boundary between our two nations, outstripping in their idea the march of events. This formulation dated as far back as 1835, during the time in which events were happening in Texas which led to its refusal to tender further obedience to the government of Mexico. The new conception of the boundary line was made to extend from sea to sea, across the continent, but in such a way as to conform with what had been foreseen as the needs of a modern United States in the Pacific, which called for the use of the port at San Francisco for the fishing industry. Thus the line was to follow the 37th parallel, instead of the 42nd, across the land. There was talk of a million dollars extra in compensation for the additional lands which would be encompassed. What was projected at that time turned out to be what was, in fact, the basis of the final settlement of the war of 1847 and of the future relations of the United States with the Orient. From that time forward, there were to be only small modifications in the contours of that line.

Those two moments, that of Butler and of Guadalupe Hidalgo, were the definitive ones in terms of the dividing line between the two nations, and if Butler had done nothing else, his projection would have been enough to qualify him as a key person in the history of the relations between Mexico and the United States, a projection made ten years in advance of the facts, the events of 1847, which closed that great chapter in the expansion of North America, in its period of the "terrestrial empire."

. . .

The preoccupation with the "terrestrial empire," as we have seen, resulted in the concept of a transcontinental nation, and the argumentation and battle with Mexico corresponded with the need to establish a frontier that would be adequate to this concept in its territorial dimensions, the working out of which took place over a long period of time. This preoccupation explains the manner in which many authors, writing from the Mexican point of view, have interpreted that cycle of events as the putting into practice of a policy established well beforehand. The first two writers to project this version were J. M. Bocanegra and, a few years later, Crescencio Rejón. Both established a juridical foundation for the defense of the national sovereignty faced with the aggression which resulted from the putting into effect of American policy, and this legal construct has remained as one of the basic principles of Mexican foreign policy.

Nevertheless, this phase of North American policy, without putting aside the basic concepts of the land and of transcontinentalism, was also tied into the establishment of a maritime frontier, a conception which came into view with increasing clarity until it became an essential factor in the shifting of the grounds of the debate. The first notice which called attention to this new theme appeared in the instructions given to Poinsett on March 26, 1925, in which there was reference to the security or lack of security of the island of Cuba and of the problems that would arise there if it were to fall into hands other than those of the Spaniards. It is a curious fact that this theme did not really take shape until the discussion over the terrestrial frontier was well terminated, and at this point, when the discussions with Mexico were brought to an end by a conclusive war, the new theme came forward as a concept associated with that frontier. In fact, the discussions about the island of Cuba projected the methods and techniques perfected in the course of the procedures that were generated in the dealings with Mexico.

· · ·

With the advent of a type of continental reasoning [which saw the United States as having a more legitimate interest in Cuba than did the European powers of England and France], there followed, in increasing number, concepts of a strategic-political nature, which were to contribute a maritime extension to the concept of transcontinentalism. First, there was the judgment that the acquisition of the island would not prejudice existing international relations. The possible transference of the island of Cuba to the United States was seen as legitimate because the island was situated "on our doorstep," intercepting the Gulf of Mexico, a body which was surrounded by five American states and into which the Mississippi River flowed, that great river transport which divided the North American continent in half. Finally, the island was proclaimed to be the guardian of coast-to-coast transit, which, by

means of the Isthmus of Panama, was linked to California. With the use
of this argument, the island was definitely tied into the theme of the
maritime frontier and took on a fundamental meaning and importance
in the history of the United States. This reasoning, which gathered an
increasing momentum, can be seen as the inevitable result of the
readjustments made necessary by the Treaty of Guadalupe Hidalgo.

·   ·   ·

By the protests that Spain made because of the intervention of North
American citizens in Cuba, it could be seen that neutrality was being
interpreted in the same way in which it had been interpreted with
respect to Mexico, and that the United States continued using the same
frontier techniques. . . . From then on, the United States measured the
steps which should be taken, and Spain followed them with what
counter measures it could think of, always belatedly, though logically
from its point of view, but without being able to reap the benefits of what
it could have obtained had it acted in time. At this point, the United
States was sure of itself and resolved to put an end to the question. To
satisfy the need for a direct reason for intervention, there was the *Maine*
on a friendly visit to the port of Havana, resulting in the incident of its
sinking on February 15, 1898. [Note: The sinking of the U.S. battleship
Maine, proclaimed by the United States to have been engineered by
Spain, provided a pretext for the declaration of war.]

·   ·   ·

The Spanish-American War was fundamental for the international life
of the United States. In social and economic terms, it can be considered
as important as the Civil War. What was actually gained, in concrete
terms, was not of great importance. But the war was decisive in terms of
the projection and direction which the United States would shortly
take. The international policy of North America, which had moved
along a north/south axis with a relatively small amount of penetration, if
compared with its later east/west expansion, and which had directed
itself with greater intensity toward the east, now set about opening up an
important line of contact westward, taking a generally horizontal line of
direction around the globe. Thus was put into motion an encircling
policy. The prime line of contact would be with the Far East and

secondly with Europe, two arms stretching outward and meeting in the
Orient in a major expenditure of force.

. . .

The famous historian S. F. Bemis asserts that the Spanish-American
War established the supremacy of the United States in the Isthmus of
Panama and that, in the period between the Treaty of Paris and 1914,
the United States consolidated its position in Central America, constructed the canal in that area, and thereby assured access from one
coast to the other.

All of this is certainly the case, but we believe that the consequences
of the war have been more profound than Bemis has indicated. Basically, the United States was again putting into operation the concepts of
Manifest Destiny and of the Monroe Doctrine, but transformed so as to
be adequate to a new age with quite different resources.

This Manifest Destiny contains within itself the concept of the
maritime frontier in the Caribbean, but it was not until it extended itself
to include the Pacific route to the Philippines that it reached its full
evolution, converting the United States into the principal power of the
second half of the nineteenth century by impelling it to launch a bridge
across the Pacific to the Orient, by which it was able to establish its
proper relations with the Far East where it had formerly taken up the
rear in the procession of nations.

. . .

Thus it was that the Atlantic, the Caribbean, and the Pacific were
brought together to function as the true strategic frontier of the United
States and to form its security zone. These projections complemented
each other through the one point that remained open, the island of
Cuba. The signing of the Treaty of Paris on December 10, 1898 [the
treaty with Spain that ended the Spanish-American War], confirmed
the consolidation of this entire frontier from the international point of
view. . . .

Cuba was the central point of the treaty, and to it was joined the
question of the island of Puerto Rico. But at the same time the situation
in the Pacific was completed by giving the United States an opening to
the south through the cession by Spain of Guam and the Philippines.

There was only lacking the ultimate passage, and that was accomplished through the construction of the Panama Canal, resulting from the creation of the Republic of Panama and the Canal Zone.

The idea of Manifest Destiny established a wide vision of the American frontier which encompassed three bodies of water of vital importance to the world and put the United States into definite contact, through a line extending horizontally around the globe, with the Far East at one extreme and Europe at the other, creating the American strategic system, which confronts it in the twentieth century with very delicate problems both in Europe and in Asia, but which we must recognize as the necessary results of its having extended itself horizontally in its effort to embrace the globe.

JOSEFINA ZORAIDA VÁZQUEZ

EDITOR'S INTRODUCTION

As a historian, Josefina Zoraida Vázquez has shown a particular interest in the pressures and counterpressures that have marked the relationships of Mexico with the United States, beginning with the colonial periods of both nations. Several of her books have reflected this interest. Among her most important publications are: *Nationalism and Education in Mexico* (1970); *Mexicans and North Americans on the War of 47* (1977); *The History of Historiography* with Lorenzo Meyer (1978); and *Mexico Faced with the United States, an Historical Essay, 1776–1980* (1982). The fact that Josefina Vázquez received her doctorate in history from Harvard University has undoubtedly been an important element in providing her with a dual perspective. Certainly, her knowledge of the history of the United States is rich and deep, to which she adds a most thorough knowledge of the history of her own nation. As a result, she can trace parallel developments in the history of both countries with equal adeptness on each side of the equation.

In Mexico, she has taught both at the Universidad Nacional Autónoma de Mexico and at the Colegio de Mexico, Mexico's prestigious center for graduate studies. She has also taught extensively in the United States. While at the Universidad Nacional she was active in the Centro de Estudios Angloamericanos and was the editor of its publication *Anglia.*

Her book *Mexicans and North Americans on the War of 47,* much of whose introductory essay is printed here, is an example of her versatility in joint exploration of the histories of Mexico and the United States. Her studies of the causes of the Mexican-American War and of the course which the war followed go back to the histories of the mother countries and of the respective colonial periods. By examining the war in such an extensive context, Josefina Vázquez goes quite beyond the often rather surface judgments that have been made about this conflict, and in the course of this informed reflection she challenges much of the conventional wisdom that has gathered around this period.

She begins her essay by deploring the lack of attention the war has received, both popularly and in the writing of history, despite its immense importance to both nations, and she ventures some reasons for this neglect. Certainly, when one considers the outpouring of writing occasioned, on the North American side, by the Civil War and, on the Mexican side, by the intervention of the French which put Maximilian on the throne of Mexico, and by Benito Juárez and La Reforma, one must admit that writing on the Mexican-American War seems rather thin in comparison. But, as this book seeks to establish, it has been steady, and, as Josefina Vázquez points out, it has received a new impetus in recent years.

Certainly one of the contributions that Josefina Vázquez has made in her comparative studies is to introduce to Mexican readers aspects of North American history about which many of them are not familiar, the history of the United States not being a field of study that gets a great deal of attention in the educational curricula of Mexico. Such readers are told, for example, that the North American Puritan fathers felt that it was their mission to establish the City of God on earth, and not on any earth, but specifically in the North American wilderness. From this revelation of an aspect of early North American psychology, she goes on to explain that this mindset was one of the elements that was later to lead to North American expansionism and ultimately to the Mexican-American War.

While Josefina Vázquez is thus making a contribution to the knowledge of the Mexican reader, she is at the same time giving the North American reader a new perspective on the history of the United States, coming at it from quite a different stance. From her long view, the circumstances which were to lead to war between the two nations were already well underway when John Quincy Adams, as a secretary of state, sat down with the Spanish minister Luis de Onís, in 1819, to make a treaty.

Her knowledge of the westward movement in the United States is detailed and goes beyond the usual generalities. At one point she is summarizing the various impulses that went into the movement and mentions such lesser-known phenomena as the various exotic communal arrangements that were set up to create "more perfect societies," and finally she lists among the exalted aims that led to westering, and perhaps with a sly touch of humor, the effort "to preserve polygamy," a reference, of course, to the Mormons.

Josefina Vázquez is attuned to cultural differences between the two societies and sees them as playing a definite role in the misconceptions that paved the road to war. For example, the great northern reaches of Mexican territory were largely uninhabited. Why then, thought the North Americans, won't Mexico sell this empty land to us? They're bound to lose it anyway. To this hard-lined, pragmatic point of view, such Mexican presidents as Herrera and Paredes answered, knowing full-well that Mexico could not, in the long run, defend these territories, that we cannot possibly sell this land. No Mexican can sell this land. It is part of the "national patrimony."

Certainly, Josefina Vázquez is not only in possession of the full range of facts, she also comprehends the nuances that emanated from two societies on a collision course toward the "inevitable war."

Mexicans and North Americans
on the War of 47

The war between Mexico and the United States is, without any doubt, a fundamental event in the history of the two countries. The conquered nation lost in that war a half of its territory, laying bare in the process the lack of national cohesion brought about by political pursuits that were at cross purposes and doomed to failure. The inability to meet the invasion with any degree of effectiveness conveyed a dramatic lesson which was to leave a profound mark upon the Mexican people, resulting in a more practical attitude, even in the lists of ideological warfare, which would continue for two more decades.

The United States emerged from the contest transformed into a continental nation. The great extensions of territory would permit an industrial and commercial expansion almost without parallel. But this same territory was to accelerate the regional conflict of which it was a harbinger. With the exception of Texas there was no slavery in the Mexican territories, and it was obvious that with the admitting of

Translated from *Mexicanos y Norteamericanos ante la Guerra del 47*, Mexico, D.F.: Secretaría de Educación Pública, 1972, pp. 9–23, and 41–44.

California as a free state in 1850 the crisis was inevitable. The drive across the continent and the discovery of gold in California postponed the conflict, but in doing so, only made it the more bloody.

The dimensions of the battles which followed the war of 47, in Mexico the Reform and the French Intervention, in the United States the Civil War, distracted attention, with the result that by comparison, despite its importance, the war of 47 was reduced to a minor status. This public downgrading does not serve as an adequate explanation for the limited attention which the event has received in the historiographies of the two nations. Doubtless, there exists the psychological element of failure among the Mexicans and of guilt among the North Americans. But the fact is evident: Mexican historiography is yet to produce the definitive "history" of the war, and North American historiography, which has so exhaustively studied the North American past, has, in great measure, put aside the "war with Mexico." Admittedly, the historians of the neighboring country have studied the episode to a somewhat greater degree and have at least produced a work which continues to be a classic because of its exhaustive study of documentary sources. *The War With Mexico* by Justin Smith, published in 1919, is, nevertheless, an antiquated and completely partisan work. It is not that we believe in the possibility of writing history with total objectivity, but certainly there is a profound difference between a determination to justify an event and the effort to understand the past. Smith exonerates his country of all culpability, laying all the blame on Mexico, whose fatuousness and inability to comprehend its own weakness led it to provoke a war which would bring it to disaster. Striking the note of social Darwinism, Smith presents the United States as having no other recourse than to conquer the weak. The task was not difficult because the United States was the more fit. The exhaustive labor in consulting primary sources allowed Smith to utilize these in support of his thesis, through a process of selection that was generally careful though at times heavy-handed.

But all of this does not obviate the question: What is it that has made it so difficult to understand the history of this war? To the complexities which make it difficult to determine the real causes of any event are added in this case and on the North American side a puritan morality which has tended to avoid blame, or at least to throw it on special people or groups—the southern slaveholders, Polk, Mexico, the Democrat expansionists—all in an effort to avoid a sense of guilt. Secondly, there is the emergence of a phenomenon which is so difficult to classify, "Manifest Destiny." There is no doubt that this conception played a major role in overseeing the general plan by which, with a shove here and a shove there—by Polk, by the slaveholders, by the Texans, and by the Mexicans—a war was brought into being. In any event, the most difficult problem with this war, as with any war, is the problem of origins. Perhaps we need a Thucydides, who would probably take the question back to the basic nature of humanity, but we believe that the difficulty in gauging the war lies in the very clarity of its origins. Perhaps with this event, more than with others, one can observe that in the face of an obvious situation people seem bent on making it obscure.

Mexican historiography has obliterated, in an almost systematic manner, the period between 1821 and 1854. Why this is so can only be surmised. A principal reason would seem to be the complexity of the period together with its lack of luster. It is a period that we all consider to be a dark one and one which, until very recently, no one has wanted to stand vigil over.

THE INEVITABLE WAR

The very conditions of colonization, with the Puritans' belief that destiny decreed the constructing of the city of God on earth and their experiences of building their version of it in the wilderness, were the elements that went into making the North American colony a new society, with all the dynamism that comes from throwing off the limitations imposed by a traditional order.

Those who colonized North America were obliged to emigrate because of religious persecution (particularly true of the leaders) or of the consequences of the economic transformation in England by which the rise of textile manufacturing led to a process through which farmers were displaced from their lands in order to make room for the raising of cattle. This whole mass of displaced people saw in the New World an alternative for survival, and they took the risk of selling themselves as indentured servants in order to pay their passage. The life which they had to confront was hard, both for masters and servants. It had to be built upon the same basic beginnings. The conscious intention of these men was to reproduce the society which they had left behind, but the American experience was leaving its mark on everything. The most extraordinary part of the venture was the availability of immense tracts of land, which in the eyes of those arriving Europeans became a veritable promise of a better life. Those same indentured servants, who in Europe would never have dreamed of being landowners, received, as payment for their term of servitude, a piece of land, and, since it was cheap, they could acquire more with a bit of work. Thus from the beginning there arose the lure of the lands farther off, toward the west, which always seemed richer than those they had already cultivated. Once they had struggled with the wilderness, it became easier to go off into the unknown, and since the immigrants kept coming, it was easy to sell off the land already possessed and to set off in search of yet better lands.

This scheme of things set the pattern for North American expansion, but independence and the industrial revolution brought new forces into play. The English textile industry with its demand for cotton stimulated the ambition to own "all the cotton lands of America of the North," which resulted in the colonization of Louisiana and Texas. The War of Independence and the discovery of the formula for "a perfect government" brought forth an apparition, a vision that would justify expansionism: "to extend the area of freedom," to extend its institutions to those unfortunate ones who have not known them and to those prisoners who remain in the clutches of tyrannical governments. Not everybody noticed the irony which was implied in much of this—such as in the case of Texas—whereby the area of freedom was extended by extending the area of slavery.

Physiocratic thought resulted in statesmen like Jefferson supporting the acquisition of new lands because they would assure the well-being of the nation, despite his fear that the growth of the country would put in jeopardy the liberty guaranteed by the Constitution. And if all this were not sufficient, the various forms of utopian or reformist thought, which proliferated during the first half of the nineteenth century, also served to stimulate the drive westward: to outdistance slavery, to set up more perfect societies, or even, as in the case of the Mormons, to preserve polygamy.

All of these elements combined to make of North America a dynamic society that nourished the ambition to dominate the lands to the west, to the north, to the south. The merchants, obsessive in their search for new markets, discovered first Santa Fe and later San Francisco, which was to provide a base for the opening up of the incredible Asiatic trade. In this same mode, statesmen like Jefferson, John Quincy Adams, and Jackson went on to lay the foundations for what was to become a spontaneous expansionism. Jefferson, for example, not only bought Louisiana but, after receiving Humboldt at the White House and obtaining from him a copy of the map of New Spain, sent forth the Lewis and Clark Expedition on its trek westward. This quest apparently reactivated the fears that the Spaniards had expressed ever since the founding of the new nation. During the presidency of Monroe, his Secretary of State, John Quincy Adams, a nationalist who wanted everything, south, north, west, managed to threaten the Floridas and Texas in such a way as to convince Spain to sign the Adams-Onís Treaty of 1819, by which the Floridas were obtained in exchange for the establishment of a boundary for Louisiana—which the North Americans had maintained included Texas—plus five million dollars. The North Americans also succeeded in getting the Spaniards to concede a northern limit of 42 degrees, which gave the North Americans a basis for claiming Oregon. Adams was convinced that all of North America was the "natural dominion" of the United States. All the Spanish possessions to the south and the British to the north would fall, little by little, under the control of the United States, and it is evident that this was the thinking behind the Monroe Doctrine of 1823.

The independence of the former Spanish colonies seemed to facilitate the task. Those who were discontented with the renunciation by the United States of Texas in the Adams-Onís Treaty saw those lands being opened up to colonization, and some people legally and others illegally began to enter upon those coveted lands. The North Americans kept up this continuous expansion, and the United States government followed their footsteps. Its first ministers in Mexico had instructions to buy Texas, a pursuit which greatly offended the Mexicans but which for the North Americans was a normal method of obtaining lands. (Hadn't they been doing this from the beginning? They had bought lands from the trading companies, from the Indians, from the French, and from the Spanish.)

Being unable to carry out Jackson's wishes in this matter of Texas, Anthony Butler then converted the individual claims of North American citizens, for damages suffered during the upheavals, into an instrument of diplomatic pressure against the Mexican government. So effective was this device that ultimately the claims were cited by Polk as being among he reasons for the declaration of war.

Meanwhile, in Texas the North American population had so surpassed the Mexican that everyone surmised what the immediate future would be. The dependency upon Coahuila, about which the Texans had complained so much, had in fact facilitated the colonization, because in Saltillo [capital of Coahuila] the concessions were easier to get since there did not exist there the consciousness of danger [of a pending Texas revolt] that existed in the capital of the republic.

Texas entered the decade of the 1830s with the certainty that independence was not far off. Stephen Austin made a final effort toward the establishment of Texas as a separate state, independent of Coahuila, but in reality he recognized the impossibility of accomplishing this. The atmosphere had turned antifederalist. An effort to straighten things out, which had not worked well in the republic, led the Mexicans toward a new formula of government, centralism. So now the Texans at least had the pretext they were looking for. The republic succeeded in vanquishing federalism in the state of Zacatecas, and it looked as though it would have the same success in Texas. On the second of March 1836, the Texan Declaration of Independence was signed and, with the fiasco at San Jacinto, it would swiftly acquire validity. Hundreds of North Americans crossed the Louisiana border to fight for the independence of Texas. The rebels received arms and support, but Jackson did not dare to go as far as extending official recognition.

The claims continued being used to pressure the neighboring republic, but in the face of the law, which Mexico, in its weakness, learned to wield as a defense, the United States had to accept arbitration. After long and vacillating deliberations, an agreement upon just claims was reached, and Mexico began to pay.

In the meantime, trade with Santa Fe had familiarized North Americans with regions west of Texas, and eyes began to be fixed upon California. Despite all the efforts of Mexico to prevent a repetition of the history of Texas, California was filling up with Americans. A North American squadron appeared along the coasts of the Pacific. The Mormons settled in Utah, and thousands of North Americans established themselves in Oregon. Expansionism was popular and spontaneous, but it cannot be denied that its impulses were coordinated, informally, from Washington. This can be demonstrated in the attitude of Commodore Jones, who in October 1842, believing that war had been declared, took the port of Monterrey. Something such as this could only have happened as a result of secret instructions given in case hostilities were opened. Diplomatic apologies were given, and the matter ended there.

In the decade of the 1840s, expansionism became a veritable fever, which began to rationalize its urges. Some felt it was their obligation to extend democracy; others saw it as a fulfillment of the biblical mandate: "Increase and multiply and fill up the earth and subjugate it and be master over it." The militants clamored for Oregon (*Fifty-four forty or fight!* was their slogan) and Texas. Many thought about ways to acquire the Californias, too. The climate of this passion for lands was ready to become a genuine movement, which only needed a name. In 1845 John L. Sullivan coined the fortunate phrase: "Manifest Destiny," which expressed that vague conglomerate of ideas and sentiments that were used to justify North American ambitions and which he, himself, articulated into a veritable doctrine. Any neighboring people could establish self-government simply by contract, could solicit admission [to the Union], and if it were considered to be qualified, it would be admitted. Some people, such as the Mexicans, would, of course, have to be educated for some time to live in freedom, before being admitted. A decision so important could not be made hastily, and of course nobody should be forced to enter the system.

The popularity of the movement varied in the different regions of the country. The commercial East, interested in land speculation and in the establishments along the Pacific, and the frontiersmen were the most enthusiastic supporters of Manifest Destiny. In the North and in the East, where the abolitionists had entrenched themselves, there was considerable opposition to expansion because of the fear that it could serve to extend the "peculiar institution." The South never lacked enthusiastic expansionists, but since their leaders had become convinced that the new lands would favor the North and that, outside of Texas, they would not be slave territory, these leaders resisted the expansionist spirit. Despite the reservations which the South had toward this movement, one of the most popular interpretations of the war between Mexico and the United States accused the southern slaveholders of having provoked it in order to increase the number of slaveholding states. In much of northern and southern antiexpansionism there could be detected a strong tint of racism. There was fear that in having to absorb Mexicans, mongrel races, North American democracy would be brought to its ruin. "We cannot hope that a people who over many years have refused to obey their own laws will tranquilly submit to ours. If we take this semi-barbaric people under our jurisdiction, thousands of unlooked for evils will be the consequence." So said a member of the House of Representatives, while a senator affirmed that the Mexicans were "free men of a race superior to the Africans." But another stated: "We never dreamed of incorporating into our Union any but the Caucasian race—the free white race." But when the southerners were expansionists, their exalted form of expansionism made them into optimists and, although admitting a certain superiority for themselves, they expressed confidence in the long-term effects of education [upon the Mexicans] or that an avalanche of [European] immigration would assure the predominance of the Whites. The expansionists tried to keep the theme of slavery outside of the discussion, fearing that it would throw a shadow upon the panorama. The antislavery forces, having become convinced during the war that the acquisition of new territories was inevitable, proposed the Wilmot Proviso:

Upon the condition that, and as the expressed and fundamental condition upon the acquisition of any territory from the Republic of Mexico by the United

States, by virtue of any treaty that might be negotiated . . . neither slavery nor involuntary servitude shall ever exist in that territory.

But those who have scruples are always the minority of the population. The popularity of the [expansionist] movement was such that the new type of politician who appeared in the decade of the 1830s and was symbolized by Jackson, responsive to popular causes and attempting to interpret the popular will, found it very difficult to stay on the sidelines of the movement and not try to capitalize on it. President Tyler, to increase his popularity, openly supported the annexation of Texas, and during the election of 1844 the Democratic candidate, James K. Polk, based his campaign on the themes of Oregon and Texas, which were the ones that excited the expansionists. At that time, the minimum that they were asking for was for the boundary to be set at Alaska and that all of California be taken. There were even those who talked of going all the way down to Patagonia. For such people, it was providential destiny that the institutions of North America be extended throughout all the hemisphere.

In the first attempt, the annexation [of Texas] was rejected by the North American Congress, and to avoid a second failure it was suggested that the measure be put before a joint session of Congress where it could be passed by a simple majority. Said and done, on March 1, 1845, the resolution was passed that provided for the addition (as it was called thereafter) of the new state. On March 6, Juan Nepomuceno Almonte, the Mexican minister in Washington, asked for his passport by way of protest. The British diplomats, meanwhile, had convinced the administration of Herrera that there was no other way to avoid total disaster than to recognize the independence of Texas on the condition that it not join itself to any other country. On the fourth of June, the president of Texas, Anson Jones, submitted to the Texas people the treaty proposed by Mexico, but by now it was too late. The Texas unionist party succeeded on June 21st, also by a joint resolution, in getting approval of annexation to the United States.

Polk was now the president, and with an expansionist in the White House, it was easy to guess what was going to happen. A minimum of decorum prevented Polk from attacking his neighbors straightaway. He tried to negotiate with Mexico over California and with Great Britain over Oregon. An opportune moment and a compromise of 49° instead of the hoped for 54° 40′ solved the problem of Oregon without conflict, and the treaty was signed in June 1846.

The negotiations with Mexico failed. The administration of General Herrera could in no way receive Slidell, who was carrying a proposal for purchase. The seizure of power by Paredes Arrillaga made a pacific arrangement all the more difficult. But behind it all lay the problem that there existed two different conceptions. The North Americans considered that the Mexican properties were only nominal because the lands were uninhabited. With the need that the Mexicans had for money, it seemed incomprehensible to the North Americans that they would not sell those empty lands, lands that they were bound to lose anyway. The governments of Herrera and Paredes understood perfectly well the impossibility of defending those areas, but they could not sell that which as Mexicans they considered to be the "national patrimony." In addition, the many insults and the offensive propositions which the North Americans had put forward had given popularity to the notion that it was now necessary to make answer to the North Americans with a show of arms.

Polk was ready for anything. The North American consul had precise instructions to repeat the pattern of the Texas episode, the method advocated by the defenders of Manifest Destiny. [Admiral] Stockton was in Texas trying to make the Texans provoke a war with Mexico so that the United States would find it necessary to intervene in order to protect its new state. President Jones botched the effort. This failure made Polk impatient, and he decided to order General Taylor, on January 13, 1846, to occupy the area between the Nueces and Rio Grande rivers, land which Texas claimed. As soon as news reached Washington that an incident had occurred on April 25th between troops of the two countries, Polk sent a message to Congress asking for a declaration of war (11 May 1846). Polk claimed that Mexico had committed a series of offenses against and had caused injuries to North American citizens and their properties and that not content with this, Mexico "has finally invaded our territory and spilled the blood of our citizens on our own soil." Despite the opposition to some of the falsehoods contained in Polk's allegations—such as his claim as to where the boundary was—Congress voted a declaration of war by a vote of 40 to 2 in the Senate and 174 to 14 in the House. During the months which followed, the Whig party voiced its opposition to the war and its conviction that Polk was embarked upon a war of conquest. But even after the Whigs became, by the election of 1846, the majority party, they took no action to prove their opposition. When it came time to vote, they always approved more men and more money for the war. [Frederick] Merk has clearly demonstrated the dilemma of the Whig party and the fear that they felt for the adjective "treasonous," which had buried the Federalists as a result of their opposition to the War of 1812 against the British.

Considerably after Matamoros was occupied by American troops (May 18, 1846) and Taylor had begun his penetration into the country, the Mexican government felt obligated to make a declaration of war, July 7, 1846. Article One of the congressional decree summarized Mexico's reasons: "The government, acting in defense of the nation, will repel the aggression which the United States of America has initiated and sustained against the Mexican Republic, having invaded it and committed hostile acts in various of the departments of its territory."

There was an element of the defensive in the tone of the declaration, which bespoke the fear that the several Mexican governments had felt toward a war about which they had done whatever possible to avoid. Nobody doubts that a great part of public opinion, at least that part which had an articulate voice, had been demanding war. But in spite of the popularity of the war, the country was unable to organize the defense, and the lack of war materials was such that it could not make real use of the dynamic leadership which Santa Anna undoubtedly had to offer, after his return from exile (September 14, 1846). The North Americans, who blockaded our coast, allowed free passage to the restless Santa Anna, sure that they would be able to buy his cooperation, a supposition in which they were apparently mistaken.

THE OBSTACLES TOWARD
THE COMPREHENDING OF AN ENTIRE EPOCH

Something that all those who take it upon themselves to describe the Mexican insist upon is that for him there is a characteristic impediment toward regarding his past as really past. The [Mexican] historian himself cannot avoid this tendency and tries to change the past, falsifying what actually occurred. After four-and-a-half centuries, he does not accept the Conquest, and at the distance of a century-and-a-half he is incapable of coming to an agreement on the manner in which independence was arrived at. If this is the case with events in which the participants were "in house," it is comprehensible that we are incapable of assimilating the war of 47. The event was traumatic and still is, because we accept the loss of territory, the inevitability of the clash and its results, but we can only lament the ease with which the war was won and the total impotence in the face of the North American offensive. We do not understand all of this because we have not forced ourselves to come to an understanding. The historians have undertaken to set forth the various parties of the period and to accuse various of the sets of contenders of failure. Gómez Farías or Paredes Arrillaga, Santa Anna—the favorite villain—the army, or the church are the guilty ones. For ourselves, the case seems to be completely different, and in order to comprehend it we will make use of a comparison with the history of the United States—though such comparisons have been used to obstruct a comprehension of our early years.

The United States began its revolution for independence by rising up against the British effort, as a result of the Seven Years War, to organize its empire recently acquired at the cost of France. The general methods used by the British, which were also applied to the three colonies [the north, middle, and southern groups of states in North America] which up until then had enjoyed autonomy, provoked a powerful reaction which led to independence (1776–1783). The colonies found themselves confronted with an England which, though victorious [in its European wars], was also bankrupt and in the middle of a struggle between political factions (1760–1770), which the colonies no doubt took full advantage of. England remained isolated. France was easy to conquer, being burdened by its alliance with Spain. The northern countries, seeing that the battle was being prolonged, formed the League of Armed Neutrality. Thus the international scene favored the North Americans. The simplistic manner in which we view the history of our neighboring country tells us that since the North Americans had experience in government, a group of exceptional citizens was able to

find a magic formula, resulting from their own experience, which led
them to a happy conclusion. There is an element of truth here, but in
order to arrive at the Constitution of 1789 the North Americans had to
undergo years of chaos and, when they finally achieved a political
organization, thanks to the French Revolution and events which resulted from it, the United States was left alone until 1812, at which
time, due to international affronts, it felt forced to declare war upon
England. Notwithstanding the fact that it was distracted by its real
enemy, Napoleon, England managed, with a small army, to launch a
military drive against the United States which resulted in an occupation
of the capital. But England was essentially concentrating upon its
European interests and not upon the American territories. The politics
of those years in the United States were also partisan and factional. The
difference with our situation was that the country continued its way west
and, open to steady immigration, it absorbed dynamic elements into its
society.

Mexico came to its independence in 1821 after a long battle which
had to a considerable extent weakened its socioeconomic structure.
Furthermore, the economic debilitation had begun in 1804 when people of exceptional talents began, in an uninterrupted stream, to return to
the Peninsula. The country, then, entered upon independence in a state
of bankruptcy. It is in no way certain that there were no people with
political experience, because the first congresses were enriched by the
experiences which the delegates had had at the Cortes [congress of
Spain], many of them figures of importance in that institution, such as
Ramos Arizpe. Nor can it be said that the choice of federalism was a
mistake. As Nettie Lee Benson has said to the point of satiety, federalism, once rooted into our tradition, saved the integrity of the country,
avoiding a repetition of the case of Central America. What turned out to
be most surprising, in view of the experiences of our own times, was the
extent to which federalism functioned effectively.

The difference with the United States was that Mexico faced a Spain
sustained by the Holy Alliance, which neither England nor the Holy
See dared openly defy, recognizing its independence. Mexico was, until
the following decade, bereft of protection and exposed in such a way
that English, French, and North American ambitions warred on its

territory ceaselessly. It was not left for a minute to put into practice the clear body of ideas developed by some of its men. Instead, shortly after its emancipation, Mexico had to face three international problems: the independence of Texas (international to the extent to which the United States was a participant, though not in an official capacity), the Pastry War [a short war with France], and the war with the United States. The lack of money and the low level of national sentiment, due to the briefness of its experience as a nation, completed the picture. The hoped for support from England never arrived. Its statesmen sought to prevent a war which the Mexicans, who expressed an opinion, desired. But Paredes Arrillaga, who had seized power so that the Mexican government would present a firmer front to the United States, changed his opinion in taking over the responsibility for the situation.

BIBLIOGRAPHY

Alamán, Lucas. *Historia de Mejico.* Vol. 5. Mexico, D. F.: Editorial Jus, 1942.

Altamirano, Ignacio M. *Historia y Política de Mexico.* Mexico, D. F.: Empresas Editoriales, 1958.

Bancroft, Hubert Howe. *History of Mexico V, 1824–1861.* San Francisco: The History Company, 1887.

———. *History of the North Mexican States and Texas.* Vol. 2. San Francisco: The History Company, 1889.

Bemis, Samuel Flagg. *A Diplomatic History of the United States.* New York: H. Holt and Company, 1950.

———. *The Latin American Policy of the United States.* New York: Harcourt Brace and Company, 1943.

Bosch García, Carlos. "Dos Diplomacias y un Problema," *Historia Mexicana,* vol. 2, no. 1 (Julio-Septiembre de 1952), pp. 46–65.

———. *Historia de las Relaciones entre Mexico y Los Estados Unidos, 1819–1848.* Mexico, D. F.: Escuela Nacional de Ciencias Políticas, 1961.

———. *La Base de la Política Exterior Estadounidense.* Mexico, D. F.: Universidad Nacional Autónoma de Mexico, 1969.

Brack, Gene M. *Mexico Views Manifest Destiny.* Albuquerque: University of New Mexico Press, 1975.

Bulnes, Francisco. *Las Grandes Mentiras de Nuestra Historia*. Paris y Mexico: Libreria de las Vda de CH. BOURET, 1904.

———. *Páginas Escogidas*. Ed. Martin Quirarte. Mexico, D. F.: Universidad Nacional Autónoma de Mexico, 1968.

Bustamante, Carlos María de. *El Nuevo Bernal Díaz Del Castillo*. Mexico, D. F.: Secretaria de Educación Publica, 1949.

Carreño, Alberto M. *Jefes del Ejercito Mexicano en 1847*. Mexico, D F.: Imprenta y Fotolipia de la Secretaría de Fomento, 1914.

Carreño, Alberto María. *La Diplomacia Extraordinaria entre Mexico y Estados Unidos, 1789–1947 (The Special Diplomacy Between Mexico and the United States)*. 2 vols. Mexico, D. F.: Editorial Jus, 1951.

———. *Mexico y Los Estados Unidos de America*. Mexico, D. F.: Editorial Jus, 1962.

———. *Nuestros Vecinos del Norte*. (Colección Obras Diversas, vol. 4). Mexico, D. F.: Ediciones Victoria, 1937.

Caso, Antonio. *El Problema de Mexico y la Ideología Nacional*. Mexico, D. F.: Libro-Mex Editores, S de RL, 1955.

Castañeda, Carlos E., trans. and ed. *The Mexican Side of the Texas Revolution*. Dallas: P. L. Turner, 1928.

Chaney, Jr., Homer Campbell. "The Mexican–United States War as Seen by Mexican Intellectuals, 1846–1956." Doctoral dissertation in history, Stanford University, 1959.

Cosío Villegas, Daniel. *American Extremes*. Trans. Americo Paredes. Austin: University of Texas Press, 1964.

———. "Donde Está el Villano?" *Historia Mexicana*, vol. 1, no. 3 (Enero a Marzo de 1952), pp. 429–48.

Cosío Villegas, Daniel, Ignacio Bernal, Alejandra Moreno Toscano, Luis Gonzáles, Eduardo Blanquel, Lorenzo Meyer. *Historia Mínima de Mexico*. Mexico, D. F.: El Colegio de Mexico, 1973.

Cuevas, Luis G. *Porvenir de Mexico*. Mexico, D. F.: Editorial Jus, 1954.

DeVoto, Bernard. *The Year of Decision 1846*. Boston: Little Brown & Co., 1943.

Fehrenbach, T. R. *Fire and Blood: A History of Mexico*. New York: Macmillan Publishing Co., Inc., 1973.

Fuentes Mares, José. *Santa Anna: Aurora y Ocaso de un Comediante*. Mexico, D. F.: Editorial Jus, 1956.

———. *Poinsett, Historia de una Gran Intriga*. Mexico, D. F.: Libro Mex Editores, 1960.

Garrison, George P. *Texas: A Contest of Civilizations*. New York: Houghton, Mifflin Co., 1903.

González, Luis. "El Paréntesis de Santa Anna." In *Historia Mínima de Mexico.* Ed. Daniel Cosío Villegas, et al. Mexico, D. F.: El Colegio de Mexico, 1973.

González Peña, Carlos. *History of Mexican Literature.* Trans. Gusta Barfield Nance and Florence Johnson Dunstan. University Press in Dallas, Southern Methodist University, 1968.

Hale, Charles A. *Mexican Liberalism in the Age of Mora.* New York: Random House-Knopf, 1968.

Heroles, Jesus Reyes. *Mariano Otero Obras.* 2 vols. Mexico, D. F.: Editorial Porrua, 1967.

Howren, Alleine. "Causes and Origin of the Decree of April 6, 1830." *The Southwest Historical Quarterly,* vol. 16.

Johannsen, Robert W. *To the Halls of the Montezumas: The Mexican War in the American Imagination.* New York: Oxford University Press, 1985.

Jones, Anson. *Memoranda and Official Correspondence Relating to the Republic of Texas, Its History and Annexation.* New York: D. Appleton & Co., 1859.

McWilliams, Carey. *North From Mexico.* Philadelphia: J. B. Lippencott Company, 1949.

Merk, Frederick. *Manifest Destiny and Mission in American History.* New York: Alfred A. Knopf, 1963.

――――. *The Monroe Doctrine and American Expansion, 1843–1849.* New York: Alfred A. Knopf, 1966.

Muñoz, Rafael F. *Antonio López de Santa Anna.* Mexico, D. F.: Editorial "Mexico Nuevo," 1937.

Otero, Mariano. "Consideraciones Sobre la Situación Política y Social de la Republica Mexicana en el Año 1847 (Diciembre de 1847), *Obras,* vol. 1. Ed. Jesus Reyes Heroles. Mexico, D. F., Editorial Porrua, S. A., 1967.

Paz, Octavio. *The Labyrinth of Solitude: Life and Thought in Mexico.* Trans. Lysander Kemp. New York: Grove Press, 1961.

Price, George W. *Origins of the War With Mexico: The Polk-Stockton Intrigue.* Austin: University of Texas Press, 1967.

Ramírez, José Fernando. *Mexico During the War with the United States.* Ed. Walter V. Scholes. Trans. Elliott B. Scherr. Columbia, Missouri: The University of Missouri Studies, vol. 23, no. 1, 1950.

Reeves, Jesse S. *American Diplomacy Under Tyler and Polk.* Baltimore: Johns Hopkins Press, 1907.

Rejón, Manuel Crescencio. *Pensamiento Político.* Mexico, D. F.: Universidad Nacional Autónoma de Mexico, 1968.

Rippy, J. Fred. *Rivalry of the United States and Great Britain Over Latin America.* New York: Octogon Press, 1964.

Rives, George Lockhart. *The United States and Mexico, 1821–1845.* 2 vols. New York: Charles Scribner's Sons, 1913.

Roa Bárcena, José María. *Biografía de D. José Joaquín Pesado.* Mexico, D. F.: Imprenta de Ignacio de Escalante, 1878.

———. *Recuerdos de la Invasión Norte-Americana,* 1846–1848, Por un Joven de Entonces. 2 vols. Mexico, D. F.: Imprenta -e V. Agueras, 1902.

Rodó, José Henrique. *Ariel.* Cambridge University Press, 1967.

Rosaldo y Hernandez, Renato. "D. José María Roa Bárcena, Vida y Obras." Doctoral dissertation in literature. University of Illinois, Urbana, 1942.

Sanchez, José María. Viaje a Tejas. Collección de Documentos Históricos Mexicanos 3. Mexico, D. F.: Libros Latinos, 1939.

Santa Anna, Antonio López de. *Las Guerras de Mexico con Tejas y los Estados Unidos, Documentos para la História de Mexico.* Mexico, D. F.: Documentos Ineditos O Muy Raros Para La História de Mexico, Publicados por Genaro Garcia, Tomo 29, Mexico, D. F.: Libreria de VDA DE CH. BOURET, 1910.

Sierra, Justo. *Evolución Política del Pueblo Mexicano.* Mexico, D. F.: Fondo de Cultura Económica, 1910.

———. *The Political Evolution of the Mexican People.* Trans. Charles Ramsdell. Austin: University of Texas Press, 1969.

Smith, Justin H. *The War With Mexico.* 2 vols. New York: The Macmillan Company, 1919.

Tamayo, Jorge L. "Lo Que Perdimos y Lo Que Nos Queda," *Cuadernos Americanos,* vol. 40, no. 4 (Julio a Agosto, 1948), pp. 31–53.

Tornel, José María. "Tejas y Los Estados-Unidos de America en sus Relaciones con la Republica Mexicana." Translated and reprinted in Carlos Castañeda, *The Mexican Side of the Texas Revolution.* Dallas: P. L. Turner, 1928.

Valades, José C. *Santa Anna y La Guerra de Texas.* Mexico, D. F.: Imprenta Mundial, 1936.

Vasconcelos, José. *Breve Historia de Mexico.* Mexico, D. F.: Editaciones Botas, 1944.

———. *The Cosmic Race/La Raza Cósmica.* Ed. Didier T. Jaen. Los Angeles: Centro de Publicaciones, Department of Chicano Studies, California State University, Los Angeles, 1979.

———. "Visiones Californianas." In *Obras Completas.* Vol. 1. Mexico, D. F.: Sep-Setentas 19, Secretaría de Educación Pública, 1972.

Vázquez, Josefina Zoraida. *Mexicanos y Norteamericanos ante la Guerra del 47.* Mexico, D. F.: Sep-Setentas 19, Secretaría de Educación Pública, 1972.

Zea, Leopoldo. *La Filosofía Como Compromiso y Otros Ensayos.* Mexico, D. F.: Tezontle, Fondo de Cultura Económica, 1952.

Zorilla, Luis G. *Historia de las Relaciones Entre Mexico y Los Estados Unidos, 1800–1958.* Mexico, D. F.: Editorial Porrua, S.A., 1965.

INDEX

ABOUT THE EDITOR

Cecil Robinson has found the borderlands between Mexico and the United States a natural habitat. He first became acquainted with the region as a student at Columbia University, where he took a masters degree in American history with a minor in Latin American history and completed a doctoral program with a major in American literature and a minor in Latin American literature. From there, he set up his own interdisciplinary and regional studies programs before such things made their formal appearances in university curricula.

During thirty years of teaching at the University of Arizona, Tucson, he explored, both in his teaching and in his writing, the interaction of North American and Latin American cultures. Also he spent extensive periods of time living, studying, and teaching in Mexico, Chile, and Brazil.

In *Mexico and the Hispanic Southwest in American Literature*, published by the University of Arizona Press in 1977, he examined the ways in which American writers have reacted to Mexico and its culture. Conversely, in *The View from Chapultepec: Mexican Writers on the Mexican American War*, he presents the Mexican writer, from the mid-nineteenth century to our own times, speaking out upon that great trauma in the Mexican experience by which Mexico lost more than half of its territory to the United States.

At present the author is working on a series of essays based upon the culture of the borderlands that will be included in a collection entitled *No Short Journeys*.